Francis Plowden

A Short History of the British Empire

From May 1792, to the Close of the Year 1793

Francis Plowden

A Short History of the British Empire
From May 1792, to the Close of the Year 1793

ISBN/EAN: 9783337168964

Printed in Europe, USA, Canada, Australia, Japan

Cover: Foto ©ninafisch / pixelio.de

More available books at **www.hansebooks.com**

A

SHORT HISTORY

OF THE

BRITISH EMPIRE,

FROM MAY 1792

TO THE

CLOSE OF THE YEAR 1793.

By FRANCIS PLOWDEN, LL.D.

AUTHOR OF THE NATIVE RIGHTS OF BRITISH SUBJECTS,
JURA ANGLORUM, ETC.

Ne quid falsi dicere audeat, ne quid veri non audeat.   CICERO.

PHILADELPHIA:

PRINTED FOR MATHEW CAREY,
NO. 118, MARKET-STREET.

AUGUST 4, 1794.

INTRODUCTORY CHAPTER.

THE History which I have undertaken the arduous task of writing, is interesting to the Public, in proportion as the events of it involve the internal peace, energy, and welfare of this Country. The general good of the State is the common point to which all ministers, of all times, and in all circumstances, have always pretended to direct their different systems of measures; but there has been, within these last twenty months, such a variety of events, such contrariety of judgment, such singularity of public measures, that the mind is nearly overset in tracing the origin, or in calculating the consequences of them. No just conception can be formed, no fair opinion can be adopted, no profitable inference can be drawn from any, even of the leading facts, if taken singly, and considered upon the naked grounds of their insulated merits. The whole train of operations must be collected into one view, and each link of the chain examined with scrupulous, but unbiassed severity. The plot of the piece is not so new, as the winding up of the catastrophe threatens to be alarming. The general utility, then of tracing events to their causes, of viewing them in their immediate effects, and following them through their remote operations, becomes, in the present period, interesting to the country beyond measure or precedent.

It has been reserved for the punishment of the present generation, to undergo the fatal experiment of reducing the theory of modern philosophy * into practice. The baneful emanations from

---

* By this term, I mean the aggregate of the doctrines of Rousseau, Voltaire, Diderot, &c. who, improving upon their *freethinking* predecessors, have devoted their lives to seducing mankind into the

B

Pandora's box were but faint prefages of its direful effects. Since the fatal eruption from this philofophical receptacle of modern doctrines, the political fyftem of Europe feems to have undergone a general change. The old and true principles are derided, denied, and abandoned: new and falfe maxims are adopted and fupported. Folly, fear, and malice operate varioufly upon the multitude, and, in the general alarm and confufion, the voice of truth is nearly ftifled.

France had long been the feat of modern philofophy; and unfortunately for that country, and for the world at large, its theories had convinced but few, of the dreadful evils which its practice and fuccefs have caufed all to lament. The deftructive infection was beginning to fpread abroad, before the full effects of the grand experiment had been completely known at home. In the delufion of its vifionary fuccefs, fome infatuated zealots were found daring enough to attack the very exiftence of the Britifh Conftitution, though fortunately they were not fufficiently aftute to difguife their defign. Their publications produced various effects in an unfettled ftate of the public mind. To fome, they reprefented the Conftitution as a fyftem of abfurdity and inconfiftency; to others, of defpotifm and tyranny; in fome they created contempt, in others hatred; in moft they raifed doubts, in all alarms. It is difficult to determine, whether the progrefs of the evil were more forwarded by the illjudged exertions of individuals to oppofe it, or by the impunity with which, for a time, it was permitted to fpread.

In the early feafon of this political ferment, I applied my retired thoughts to an impartial inveftigation of the origin, nature, and effects of our Conftitution, and in the cool ftudy of her lineaments, form, and features, I traced in her a fimplicity congenial with nature, a ftructure calculated to furvive the ravages of time, and a harmony productive of every human blefling.

My admiration begat a love for the Conftitution; and when

mockery of Chriftian Revelation, and the adoption of a fyftem of Atheifm and Licentioufnefs.

I beheld her fo rudely affailed by Mr. Paine, I could not refift the impulfe of raifing even my feeble hand in her defence. I entered the lifts clad with no other than the fimple defenfive armour of civil freedom; for fuch only is to be found in the arfenal of the Britifh Conftitution. Yet I beheld with aftonifhment and with alarm my fellow-combatants rufh forth againft the enemy, encumbered with foreign arms and weapons, which for the laft happy century had been difufed by Britons. I dreaded the return of their unruly courfers and fcythed chariots amongft their own ranks. And henceforth I pledge to my countrymen my moft determined efforts to exterminate for ever the fatal ufe of thefe anti-conftitutional weapons of deftruction.

When I lately publifhed the book which I entitled *Jura Anglorum*, I did it with the immediate and direct view of reprefenting the Conftitution in its genuine colours. I deemed no other defence of it neceffary againft a man who would ridicule it by denying its very exiftence. In that work I have fully committed myfelf to my country upon the true principles of its Conftitution, and have thereby contracted a duty to maintain and vindicate them to my lateft breath.

Mr. Burke in the year 1770 moft judicioufly obferved,*
" That in the filent lapfe of events, as material alterations have
" been infenfibly brought about in the policy and character of go-
" vernments and nations, as thofe which have been marked by
" the tumult of public revolutions." That there has lately been brought about a material alteration in the policy and character of this government and this nation, the moft obftinate blindnefs alone will not difcover. *Nec tam pertinaces fore arbitror, ut clariffimum folem fanis atque patentibus oculis videre fe negent.* What the ultimate effects of fuch alteration may be, I will not even hazard a conjecture. I know too well that the tafk of denouncing future evils is often dangerous, generally fruitlefs, and always invidious. But as far as the alteration has hitherto been operative, every man muft fooner or later fee the events which

---

* Caufe of the prefent Difcontents: viz. in 1770.

it has produced; for every man by being somehow affected must feel their consequences, and it therefore behoves every man to form a right judgment upon them. To this end have I undertaken to submit to the dispassionate review of my countrymen, the system and detail of measures carried on during the last twenty months, as the most important period of our national existence. In taking up our history from the month of May, 1792, I shall chiefly rest upon such events as may affect in their consequences the fate of the Constitution of the Country, more than the actual administration of its Government: and as this period comprises the time from the publication of my *Jura Anglorum*, which was a mere exposition of the actual state of the Constitution when its very existence was called in question; so it throws upon me the necessity of examining into the causes of every apperance of deviation in practice from the theory of those principles, which I there laid down as its true basis.

I have always conceived the British Constitution to be founded upon a democratic basis, the free will and consent of the people*: that the monarchy and aristocracy, the other two component parts of that Constitution, are emanations and creatures of that original source of human power: nd from this base alone can I view a monarchy or an aristocracy either take root, or acquire vigour and permanency. The democratic part of the Constitution, which voluntarily for the most wise and salutary purposes, shared its power with the monarchy and aristocracy, will ever feel an interest in preserving that which it so providently conferred. Hence that admirable equipoise of the three powers, which upholds the stupendous structure; but its origin, foundation, and security rest in the free choice and consent of a free people. To weaken but in idea this foundation, would

---

* Not so Mr. Burke: who says, that the democratic and aristocratic parts of our Constitution are founded upon the Crown *as their essential basis*: from the Crown do they originate, and by the energy of that main spring alone must they be set in action. Vid. Appeal, p. 46.

endanger, if not overthrow, the moſt puiſſant ariſtocracy, and ſhake, if not unprop, the firmeſt throne that ever ſuſtained a monarch. But thus ſecured, it may bid defiance to the rudeſt aſſaults of open violence, as well as to the inſidious attacks of diſguiſed malice or miſguided zeal. The people of England are too ſenſible of the bleſſings of their Conſtitution, madly to ex- poſe themſelves to the unmeaſurable evils of a pure democracy; but they will alſo preſerve themſelves from ſimple ariſtocracy, and from unbalanced monarchy. In the compoſition of the three, they alone reſt their ſecurity: the experience of ages juſtifies the happy mixture; and to perpetuate the equilibrium to the lateſt poſterity, it requires but that degree of vigilance in its guardians, which is neceſſary to detect the deſigns of thoſe who daringly invade, or thoſe who may from ignorance or malice miſrepreſent the Conſtitution.

Mr. Paine in attempting to debauch the people into the mania of a *pure democracy* directed all his efforts towards convincing them, that becauſe they exerciſed not the whole, they therefore poſſeſſed no ſhare whatever in the powers of our Conſtitution. I then ſtood forward to repel this daring attack, merely by ſtating to the people the rights and powers which they had retained to themſelves, and thoſe which they had delegated to the other two component parts of the legiſlature. I then ſaid, that * " the object of this delegation of power was, to render the diſſolution of government as difficult as poſſible; and the perfection of its execution was that ſtupendous equipoiſe of power, that renders it almoſt morally impoſſible that one branch of the legiſlature ſhould outbalance another."

Having ſtood forward to repel the attacks of thoſe who denied the exiſtence of a Conſtitution in this country, I cannot feel myſelf free to retire from the challenge of others, who appear to have miſunderſtood or wilfully to have traduced it. My alarms for the public ſafety become too ſerious, when I perceive dogmas

* Jura Ang. p. 154.

propagated and countenanced by those to whom the public looks up with confidence, which go to deprive our Constitution of its fundamental vigour and peculiar perfection.

In developing the principles of the Constitution of England, any observation upon, or even reference to the actual administration of the Government might have seemed irrelevant to the subject. But in the application of those principles to the system of measures actually pursued within the last twenty months, it becomes indispensably necessary to speak of the advisers as well as the actors of the various scenes. I know the full extent of my duty to the King, of attachment to the Constitution, and love to my Country. I mean never to lose sight of any of these considerations in the task I have undertaken; and I now once for all assure the individuals whom I shall have occasion to mention in the following sheets, that I intend no personal adulation nor censure; but merely to use the common right of every Englishman, to discuss and examine public acts, public writings, and public speeches.

It is a political aphorism, that to a reflecting people there can be no other partiality for any particular ministers, than a conviction of their earnestness and ability to follow up and support the genuine principles and spirit of the Constitution. The people of England are an indulgent and a patient judge. Prodigal of their confidence, they are tardily roused at the abuse of it. In their generosity, they seldom give to the score of malice what the most indulgent candour can refer to error of judgment. But there is a moment of misfortune and suffering, in which simplicity itself cannot be misled. Recovered from the shock of a quick transition from prosperity and ease to dismay and wretchedness, they inquire upon reflection, as Memmius did of old, " But who are these men that have placed themselves at the helm * ? " I have a firm reliance upon the cool and deliberate verdict of

---

* At qui sunt ii qui rempublicam occupavere? Homines sceleratissimi, immani avaritia, nocentissimi, iidemque superbissimi. Sal. de Bel Jug.

Englishmen; and when matter of fact is plainly told, the decision of their judgment will, I am confident, receive effect.

Such is the alteration of the public mind since I wrote my late work, that, if I had it now in hand, I should doubt of the safety of publishing those passages in it, which I (perhaps weakly) then judged to be the most emphatically constitutional of the whole. I should probably have dropped my present pursuit: but it is sometimes wise to borrow instruction from our opponent: *fas est & ab hoste doceri.* I shall therefore avail myself of Mr. Burke's justification for hazarding the attempt †. "It is
" an undertaking of some degree of delicacy to examine into the
" cause of public disorders. If a man happens not to succeed
" in such an inquiry, he will be thought weak and visionary:
" if he touches the true grievance, there is danger that he may
" come near to persons of weight and consequence, who will
" rather be exasperated at the discovery of their errors, than
" thankful for the occasion of correcting them. If he should be
" obliged to blame the favourites of the people, he will be con-
" sidered as the tool of power; if he censures those in power, he
" will be looked upon as an instrument of faction. But in all
" exertions of duty something is to be hazarded. In cases of tu-
" mult and disorder, our law has invested every man, in some
" sort, with the authority of a magistrate. When the affairs of
" the nation are distracted, private people are by the spirit of that
" law justified in stepping a little out of their ordinary sphere.
" They enjoy a privilege of somewhat more dignity and effect,
" than that of idle lamentation over the calamities of their coun-
" try. They may look into them narrowly; they may reason
" upon them liberally; and if they should be so fortunate as to
" discover the true source of the mischief, and to suggest any pro-
" bable method of removing it, though they may displease the
" rulers of the day, they are certainly of service to the cause of
" Government." It is a common assertion, that the truth of

† Vid. Mr. Burke's Thoughts on the Causes of the Discontents in the Year 1770, pages 1 and 2.

history, is only the portion of a succeeding, and therefore of a disinterested generation. Such history may be a faithful portrait of form, feature, and character; it may keep memory alive; it may stimulate ambition; but it cannot regulate, correct, nor improve the conduct or principles of the actors in scenes long since closed. In regions of despotism, where flattery or servility are the preservatives of existence, *truth* may not be found in the mouth of the over-awed annalist; but in the free Constitution of Great Britain, I trust *truth* may yet be spoken, *truth* may yet be published, *truth* may yet be operative.

Before I enter upon the narrative of events which have distinguished the period of my intended history, I feel it a duty to notice the rise, progress, and effects of certain opinions, sentiments, or prejudices, which appear to have paved the road for the whole train of evils which now afflict our suffering country.

The year 1789 was remarkable for the most astonishing of all revolutions, that of France. The general impression of horror, under which it is now viewed by all ranks of people, creates an impossibility to speak of it with that temperate precision which the circumstances of its first year's existence might have warranted. It will be foreign from my purpose to enter into its origin or progress. Suffice it to say, that whether the nature or the abuses of the ancient Government contributed more to the revolution, it was principally planned, and has been uniformly supported and carried on by men of the most consummate abandonment, profligacy, and impiety. It was, however, rather singular, that Mr. Burke, who in his public and private capacity had been the avowed and steady friend of the Revolution of America, should stand forth as the first and most implacable enemy to that of France. His Reflections on the Revolution of France, though written with more than his usual brilliancy and eloquence, brought forth Paine's *Rights of Man* as an answer, and kindled that political flame of controversy which has been productive of the evils we all now sorely lament, and of which no mortal hath yet foreseen the end.

From Mr. Burke's character and rank in life, from the influence of his opinions upon his fellow-subjects, it does not seem unreasonable to have expected from him sentiments at least consistent with the most manifest and general leading points of our Constitution. To account for any deviation in his books from this obvious tract of duty I shall not attempt. If the plea of ignorance can serve him, he may rest his defence upon it, and I shall content myself with having endeavoured to expose and counteract the effects of his delusive eloquence upon a very great part of this nation; to the effects of which I attribute the whole series of misfortunes which we now bewail.

In the enchantments of rich imagery Mr. Burke bewilders his loyal reader, and under the warmest professions of his own attachment to Government he beguiles the unguarded and unsuspecting into principles the most destructive of the British Constitution. Thomas Paine on the other hand, taking every advantage of Mr. Burke's denial of the first principles of civil government, secured the confidence of the multitude by persuading them into the easy belief of the true origin of civil power; he had the address to make proselytes of them to undeniable truths, in order to seduce them into the most mischievous of errors.

As Mr. Burke's Reflections upon the Revolution of France appeared in the year 1790, it will be but candid, in making any observations upon them, to confine (if possible) our ideas to the previous circumstances of that revolution which could alone have given ground for what he has advanced upon it. Few persons, I believe, at this hour think or feel upon that singular event as they may have thought or felt at the period of Mr. Burke's first publication. Without any pretensions to a more prophetic or intuitive endowment than my neighbours, I profess from the first revolutionary symptom in France to have been decidedly of opinion, that it would end in confusion, destruction and horror. I still profess what I then admitted, that the nature of the French Government was intrinsically bad, that the abufes of it were become intolerable, and that the political and moral fyftem of the whole kingdom called loudly for a general reform. Such circumftances muft fupply the fteady, peaceful, and inactive, as well as the fpeculative, turbulent, and feditious, with ftrong arguments, juft motives, and plaufible reafons;— weapons, in the hands of the profligate and impious fatally deftructive, as in the hands of the virtuous they would have enfured peace and bleffings to the country in the caufe of which they were employed. Thefe fentiments I publicly declared within fome months after the publication of Mr. Burke's Reflections:* " That the general abandonment of all revealed religion by the " higheft ranks and armies of France, had, more than any other " caufe, been productive of the prefent revolution; that it had " been planned, carried on, and fupported by the moft avowed " atheifts and deifts of that kingdom; and had been uniformly " difrelifhed and oppofed by all thofe who were actuated by any " impulfe of religion or morality. The fuppreffion of every re- " ligious inftitution, the degradation of the clergy, and the fanc- " tification of the afhes of Roufſeau and Voltaire, were the in- " famous proofs of thefe melancholy truths." -When I make this avowal of my own fentiments upon the early ftages of the French Revolution, I would not even hint an imputation to others, that their differing in opinion from me upon the fubject involved either folly or criminality.

I conceive many of my countrymen to be fo enraptured with the charms of liberty, that they nobly fympathize with every fellow-creature in the real or imaginary enjoyment of it. What wonder then, if many of them, at the dawning of the French Revolution, rejoiced at the ftruggle of a powerful nation to throw off the yoke of defpotifm which had galled them for centuries? In fact, had the effort been made by men of refpectability; had the members of the Conftituent Affembly been true to their truft, in following the inftructions *(cahiers)* of their electors; had they not been feduced by the fallacy and impiety

---

* Cafe ftated by the author, page 15, publifhed 1791.

of levelling philosophers, and philosophizing levellers, France probably would enjoy at this hour a Government and Constitution nearly resembling our own, which would have commanded the admiration and respect of the universe. The latter scenes of this bloody tragedy have unfortunately confirmed my judgment, and I believe changed those of most others, who differed from me upon the subject of the French Revolution.

Much elucidation upon this subject will arise out of the reflections upon the spirit and conduct of this country in the reign of Elizabeth towards those who struggled against the absolute, though legal and long constituted Governments of Spain and France. So far from its being then reputed criminal to commend a republican form of government, or to sympathize with those who were struggling to enlarge and secure their liberties, even by force, against their lawful Sovereign, that the public and private efforts of this nation were mainly conducive to the final establishing of the Republic of Holland, and to the procuring of an honourable capitulation to the valiant defenders of La Rochelle. Nay, some not unuseful observations may be drawn from the conduct of the counter-revolutionary Mr. Burke, in the late contest of our American colonies to throw off the mild government of their parent country. In his hard-laboured attempt to justify his sentiments and conduct upon that great struggle of the colonists to establish a free and independent republic, he even boasts *, that, as " *they had taken up arms from one motive only, that is, our attempting to tax them without their consent; he certainly never could and never did wish the colonists to be subdued by arms.*" It was surely less criminal in an Englishman to sympathize with a foreign nation struggling against the despotism of an arbitrary monarchy, and to exult in the success of their arms against other foreign powers confederated to keep them in their ancient slavery, than to justify the rebellion of his fellow-subjects against the best of sovereigns, and to wish success to their arms against the mildest of governments.

* Appeal, 38, 39.

In reflecting upon the Revolution of France (as far as it had proceeded in 1790) Mr. Burke has taken occasion to deliver a political code of doctrine upon our own Constitution, which has operated a very general (I wish I could add innoxious) effect upon this country. And, as he observes himself*, " men some-
" times make a point of honour not to be disabused, and had
" rather commit a hundred errors than confess one," so has he in his subsequent works followed up, confirmed, and defended these doctrines, which it remains for me to prove, have brought such mischief and evils upon the empire of Great Britain.

Mr. Burke tells us, that in writing his Reflections † " he
" proposed to convey to a foreign people not his own ideas, but
" the prevalent opinions and sentiments of a nation renowned
" for wisdom, and celebrated in all ages for a well understood
" and well regulated love of freedom: this was the avowed pur-
" pose of the far greater part of his work." And he adds, ‡
" It is clear, he is not disavowed by the nation whose sentiments
" he had undertaken to describe. His representation is authen-
" ticated by the verdict of his country." This is not the first verdict obtained by dint of eloquence. Mr. Burke has certainly reason to boast of his success upon this score; but he generously waves the glory. " Had his work, says he, been re-
" cognized as a pattern for dexterous argument and powerful
" eloquence, yet if it tended to establish maxims, or to inspire
" sentiments, adverse to the wise and free Constitution of this
" kingdom, he would only have cause to lament, that it possessed
" qualities fitted to perpetuate the memory of his offence; ob-
" livion would be the only means of his escaping the reproaches
" of posterity." That Mr. Burke did actually deliver in his Reflections the opinions and sentiments of the people of England, I must ever deny. That the sentiments and opinions, which he there displays, were afterwards adopted by the majo-

* Letter to a Member of the National Assembly.
† Appeal, p. 3.
‡ P. 4.

rity of the people of England, I reluctantly admit; for, in admitting it, I behold the lamentable revival of a spirit and of principles for more than a century estranged from Britain.

Mr. Burke himself has said, that nothing " ought to be more " weighed, than the nature of books recommended by public " authority. So recommended, they form the character of the " age." By this test I mean fairly and boldly to try his own works. He has lately spoken unequivocally and repeatedly upon the nature of our Constitution; I also have lately committed my sentiments to the public upon the same subject*. I profess *my principles to be the antipodes to his. I must therefore believe, as I do not mean wilfully to abandon my cause and my reputation, that principles fundamentally at variance with those of my book are fundamentally false.* Upon their falsity or truth I am fairly at issue with Mr. Burke: the public will judge upon the subject; for if I am correct, the difference of opinion, sanctioned as it is, interests them not lightly †. In such case, I might say, ‡ *Non nunc agitur de vectigalibus, non de sociorum injuriis: libertas & anima nostra in dubio est.*

* Letter to a Member, p. 30.
† Vid. Appeal, p. 29.
‡ Cato's speech apud Sal. Bel. Catal.

The Doctrines and Principles of the BRITISH CONSTITUTION, *as maintained and supported by*

Mr. BURKE AND The AUTHOR.

Mr. Burke	The Author
The doctrine, that the sovereignty whether exercised by one or many, did not only originate from the people, but that in the people the same sovereignty constantly and unalienably resides, tends in my opinion to the utter subversion not only of all government in all modes, and to all stable securities to rational freedom, but to all the rules and principles of morality itself. *Appeal,* 56, 57.	The true and real basis of civil or political power or sovereignty which exists in each state, is the original agreement, compact, or contract of the society or community, which forms that state, to depute and delegate the rights, which were in them individually in the state of nature, to those whose duty it should become to rule, protect, and preserve the community; for in them *the sovereignty of power* to alter, change, amend, and improve the constitution and government of the community indefeasibly resides. The Acts of 4. and 6 Ann make it treasonable, not to think, but to express a thought to the contrary. *Jura,* 63. 157.

It would be presumption to superadd many observations to the words of the statute. " If any person shall, by writing or " printing, maintain or affirm that the Kings and Queens of this " realm, with and by the authority of Parliament, are not able " to make laws and statutes of sufficient validity to limit the " Crown, and the descent, inheritance, and government thereof, " every such person shall be guilty of high treason." And i have said in Jur. Ang. p. 164, " In the present constitution of

" our Government, there can be no Act of the People which is
" not an Act of Parliament, nor any Act of the Parliament
" which is not an Act of the People.

All things in this his (Dr. Price's) fulminating bull are not of so innoxious a tendency. His doctrines affect our Constitution in its vital parts. He tells the Revolution Society in this political Sermon, that his Majesty is almost the only lawful King in the world, because the only one who owes his crown to the choice of his people. This doctrine, as applied to the Prince now on the throne, either is nonsense, and therefore neither true nor false, or it affirms a most unfounded, dangerous, illegal, and unconstitutional position.

Reflections, p. 16, 17.

That our Sovereign owes his crown and station to the free assent of the people, which is the efficient cause of every free Constitution, I take to be true, found, and genuine Revolution doctrine, and as such was it expressly delivered by Mr. Locke immediately after the Revolution had taken effect. " These which remain, I hope, are sufficient to establish the throne of our great restorer, our present King William, to make good his title in the consent of the people; which being the only one of all lawful Governments, he has more fully and clearly than any prince in Christendom." And Bracton, after enumerating the duties of our King, says, " for this end was he created and *elected*.

Jura, 167. 316.

No one, who knows Mr. Burke, will believe him ignorant that the principles of the British Constitution are almost the only free principles of any Monarchy in the world. No one, who knows him not, can suppose, that he wilfully traduces the obvious meaning of Dr. Price, in order to impose upon the nation. All agree, that Bracton in the 13th, and Mr. Locke in the 17th century, neither affirmed unfounded, dangerous, illegal, nor unconstitutional positions, in advancing what Dr. Price has repeated, and Mr. Burke denied.

His Majesty's heirs and successors, each in his time and order, will come to the Crown with the same contempt of *their choice*, with which his Majesty has succeeded to that he wears. Whatever may be the success of evasion in explaining away the gross error of fact, which supposes, that his Majesty (tho' he holds it in concurrence with the wishes) owes his Crown to the choice of his people; yet nothing can evade their full explicit declaration concerning the principle of a right in the people to choose, which right is directly maintained and tenaciously adhered to.	It is very certain that by far the greatest part of the people of England do now believe and maintain, that both his present Majesty and the late King William became entitled to the sovereignty of this Country upon those principles, which from the days of King William have been called *Revolution* principles; not that they were formed, given, or even established by the Revolution; but that the *Revolution* was effected by them. No Sovereign, in fact, from King Egbert to his present Majesty, has ever owed his Crown to any other, than these identical principles.
Reflections, 20.	*Jura*, 167.

His Majesty can be little pleased with Mr. Burke, for insulting any part of his subjects with the assurance that he holds his crown in *contempt* of any of those, whose consent, as Mr. Locke says, can alone make good his title to it, and without whose consent his government would not be lawful. What can be so unconstitutional as to attempt to deprive the Crown of its only true and solid basis? On what other ground will he secure the throne, but on the choice and consent of a free people?

It is far from impossible to reconcile, if we do not suffer ourselves to be entangled in the	As for all the other rights, liberties, and privileges, which are commonly said to have been

mazes of metaphysical sophistry, the use both of a first rule and an occasional deviation: the sacredness of an hereditary principle of Government, with a power of change in its application in cases of extremity, if we take the measure of them at the Revolution, the change is to be confined to the peccant part only, to the part which produced the necessary deviation; and even then, it is to be effected without a decomposition of the whole civil and political mass, for the purpose of originating a new civil order out of the first elements of society.

Reflections, 29.

acquired, secured, or confirmed unto us at that period, by the Bill of Rights, or otherwise; it appears evident, that nothing more was in fact gained by the people at the Revolution, than an express acknowledgment or recognition by the Sovereign, that the people were entitled to, and might for ever enjoy, those rights, to which without any such acknowledgment, or recognition, they had an indefeasible title; not co-eval and co-equal with, but prior to the Sovereign's title to the Crown: for the rights of the people preceded the original compact upon which society was formed, and the rights of the Sovereign were granted by the people for their preservation.

Jura, 169.

If this doctrine of Mr. Burke can be at all understood, it implies the grossest absurdity and most palpable contradiction. A *necessary* deviation from a rule imports an impossibility to observe: the actual deviation then becomes an act of necessity: *that* precludes free will, without which neither election nor consent can even be conceived. And Mr. Locke, who knew something of reasoning and something of the true Whig principles as well as Mr. Burke, compliments this very King William upon his making good his title to the throne, not by the necessary deviation from the old rule of succession, but by his being preferred to it without any other right than that of the consent of the people: the only title to any lawful government. Swinish indeed muft be the multitude, that can digeft fuch hufks of argument upon neceffity. No, they will ever believe that William the Stadtholder was feated on the throne of England by the free choice and confent of their anceftors, as his Majefty is, and his fucceffors will be, by the like free choice and confent of the nation.

It is indeed difficult, perhaps impoffible, to give limits to the mere abftract competence of the fupreme power, fuch as was exercifed by Parliament at that time: but the limits of a moral competence, fubjecting even in powers more indifputably fovereign, occafional will to permanent reafon and to the fteady maxims of faith, juftice, and fixed fundamental policy, are perfectly intelligible, and perfectly binding upon thofe who exercife any authority, under any name, or under any title in the ftate. *Reflections*, 28.

At this moment, this principle *The fovereignty of power ever did, and now does, unalienably refide in the people*, exifts, becaufe it is univerfally and invariably true: and it muft for ever have exifted, with the fame force and efficacy that it now does, becaufe univerfal truth excludes all degrees. From this invariable and ever operative principle have arifen all the various changes, innovations and improvements, which have at different times been effected in our Conftitution and Government by the means of reformation and revolution. *Jura*, 130.

This avowal of the actual exercife of power by Parliament defeats the idea of a *neceffary deviation from the rule*. And Mr. Burke, by admitting this only to be a *mere abftract competence* of the fupreme power, again flies in the face of the Act of Ann, which never could have made fuch *abftract competence* the fubject of a pofitive law, and much lefs of high treafon.

So far is it from being true, that we acquired a right by the Revolution to elect our Kings, that if we had poffeffed it be-

The public fteps which were then taken by the nation were probably fuggefted and recommended by Lord Somers, and

fore, the English nation did, at that time, most solemnly renounce and abdicate it for themselves and all their posterity for ever. These gentlemen may value themselves as much as they please for their Whig principles; but I never desire to be thought a better Whig than Lord Somers, or to understand the principles of the Revolution better than those by whom it was brought about, or to read in the Declaration of Right any mysteries unknown to those, whose penetrating style has engraved in our ordinances, and in our hearts, the words and spirit of that immortal law.
Reflections, 27.

they certainly were not grounded upon our having renounced any rights at the Revolution: on the contrary, they were adopted for the express and avowed purpose of keeping alive the genuine constitutional principles, upon which the right of the people to alter the succession and government was exercised at the Revolution; and upon the presumption, that the Church of England could not be brought into danger by the propagation or maintenance of those principles.
Jura, 181.

Here Mr. Burke outsoars the highest flights of Toryism. The idea of a nation possessing a fundamental right of altering its Government at one time, and divesting itself of it at another, is truly new. Our Revolution then of 1688 not only operated a change (by necessary deviation from the rule) in the tenure and descent of the Crown of England, but also in the very essence of *social nature.* For as long as society shall last, there must be Government, and whilst there is Government, it must be in its nature alterable by the community which framed it. I should be guilty of treason were I to deny this of the British Government. For to limit the *Crown, and the descent, inheritance, and government* thereof, as the nation pleases, opens every possible avenue to alteration that human ingenuity can devise.

The two Houses, in the Act King William, did not thank

The declaration by the National Convention, of the cir-

God that they had found a fair opportunity to assert a right to choose their own Governors, much less to make an election the only lawful title to the Crown. Their having been in a condition to avoid the very appearance of it, as much as possible, was by them considered as a providential escape. They threw a politic well wrought veil over every circumstance tending to weaken the rights, which in a meliorated order of succession they meant to perpetuate; or which might furnish a precedent for any future departure from what they had then settled for ever.

Reflections, 25.

cumstances, that on this occasion summoned them to the exercise of their inherent and indefeasible rights, which I call the verdict of the nation, so far from being calculated to suppress or dissemble the matter of fact, appears to have been worded with the most cautious intention of handing down to the latest posterity a full and faithful statement of the facts, which induced them to make, and would induce posterity to approve of and support these alterations in the Constitution and Government of the Country. They make this exposition, or rather boast of the circumstances, as tending to *vivify and confirm,* not to *weaken* the the rights, which in the meliorated order of succession they meant to perpetuate. And the Acts, which they engrafted upon this declaration, are the strongest evidence of our ancestors wishes, to keep alive and active the principles upon which they passed them.

Jura, 179.

Whatever reluctance Mr. Burke may now feel to unveil or disclose the truth of facts and principles, he does much injustice to our ancestors in attempting to fix that imputation upon them.

They even boasted of the rights they then exercised; and perpetuated with all possible caution the precedent on which they acted, not only to justify their own proceeding, but to sanction posterity to follow the example, in case they should ever be exposed to the like melancholy occasion. They had no other idea of perpetuity in the Act of Settlement, than of entailing the Crown in the Brunswick line, under certain conditions. And to say, that this may not be opened, or broken in upon, by a future Act of Parliament, is treason, by the Act of Ann, which Act was passed *for the better security of her Majesty's Person and Government.*

It would be to repeat a very trite story, to recal to your memory all those circumstances which demonstrated, that their accepting King William was not properly a choice; but to all those who did not wish in effect to recal King James, or to deluge their Country in blood, and again to bring their religion, laws, and liberties into the peril they had just escaped, it was an act of *necessity* in the strictest moral sense in which necessity can be taken.
Reflections, 23.

Some persons may also formerly have been prepossessed of the idea, that the Revolution was an act of *necessity* in the strictest moral sense in which necessity can be taken; and that it never should furnish a precedent for any departure from what they had then settled for ever. Through fear and anxiety therefore, left in these prepossessions the genuine principles of the Revolution might merge and become extinguished, the Nation at different times has taken the most effectual means to perpetuate the spirit and principles of the Revolution to the latest posterity.
Jura. 180.

Even after the abdication of King James, his personal exclusion was not an act of necessity, but of choice and consent.

The nation might have recalled him either with or without new
conditions. But much less was the election of William Prince
of Orange an act of necessity. For how or why was the Nation
necessitated to give him a life estate in the crown, even after the
death of his wife, when all relation was dissolved between him
and the crown; and to open the law in his favour to the prejudice of the protestant heir at law the Princess Ann? Who
without Mr. Burke's quick and fertile conception of necessities,
and dim-sighted tardiness to discover an efficient consent in the
people, can find out by what sort of *necessity* the nation passed
over the issue male and legal heir apparent to the crown, *even
being protestant?* Was it an act of necessity to credit the tale of
the warming pan; or to wrap it up with its contents in a politic well-wrought veil? This in fact was the only circumstance
which our ancestors did not bring forward to the broadest day-
light. Was it another or the same act of *necessity* which compelled and obliged the nation to compliment the Stadtholder of
Holland with a limitation of the crown, in default of Issue of the
Princess Mary and Ann, to the heirs of his body, in preference
to the present Brunswick Family as descendants of the Princess
Sophia? But Mr. Burke has discovered the strictest *moral necessity* for the Nation's making this voluntary limitation of the
crown to the heirs of the body of a Dutch Stadtholder upon any
woman whomsoever, unqualified even with the condition of
Protestantism. A reluctance to admit of true principles will
always drive to falsity and folly.

In the famous law of 3 Car. I. called the Petition of Right, the Parliament says to the King, Your subjects have inherited this freedom, claiming their franchises, not on abstract prin- ciples *as the rights of men*, but as the rights of Englishmen,

By the Bill of Rights, the Na- tion asserts generally, that abuses and encroachments were made, or attempted by the Crown in open and direct violation of the *ancient and indefeasible rights of the people*. And there- fore the operative part of that

and as a patrimony derived from their forefathers. Selden and the other profoundly learned men, who drew this petition of right, were as well acquainted, at least with all the *general principles* concerning the rights of men, as any of their difcourfers in our pulpits or on your tribune.
Reflections, 46.

ftatute, which relates to thofe *rights and liberties,* does not enact any thing new by way of grant, or even confirmation of thofe *rights and liberties,* to the people; but it confifts of thefe fingular words: They *do claim, demand and infift upon* all and fingular the premifes as their *undoubted rights and liberties.*
Jura, 192.

What abfurdity Mr. Burke would impofe upon the public by this argument, I cannot even conjecture. Would he have *Englifhmen* claim *Englifh* liberties, as the rights of man, or even focial man, which are common to all mankind and not peculiar to Englifhmen? I defy Mr. Burke's ingenuity and eloquence to frame a more pointed, concife, and abfolute claim (even upon abftract principles) than this of our anceftor's claim of their fundamental rights and liberties. Their preface is, that their monarchs had heretofore encroached upon them. Their claim: *We claim, demand, and infift upon the premifes as our undoubted rights and liberties.*

The ceremony of cafhiering Kings, of which thefe gentlemen talk fo much at their eafe, can rarely, if ever be performed without force. It then becomes a cafe of war and not of Conftitution. Laws are commanded to hold their tongues amongft arms; and tribunals fall to the ground with the peace, they are no longer able

Since the firft inftitution of civil or political government upon earth, their never exifted, in my opinion, an inftance in which the tranfcendency of this *fovereign right in the people* was fo clearly demonftrated, as in our Revolution of 1688; for in that temporary diffolution of Government, which was occafioned by the abandonment or

to uphold. The Revolution of 1688 was obtained by a juſt war, in the only caſe, in which any war, and much more a civil war, can be juſt.
Reflections, 43.

dereliction of it by the executive power, the people in reality and practice carried their rights to an extent far beyond the ſpeculative allowances of the moſt unconfined theoriſts.
Jura, 198.

What is obtained by war, is acquired by conqueſt. Mr. Locke did not look up to conqueſt for a good title to King William. And Mr. Burke cannot be ignorant, that Parliament ordered even a biſhop's book to be burnt, for teaching that King William's right to the throne had been acquired by conqueſt.

The ſpeculative line of demarcation, where obedience ought to end, and reſiſtance muſt begin, is faint, obſcure and not eaſily definable. It is not a ſingle act, or a ſingle event, which determines it.
Reflections, 43.

In the Engliſh Conſtitution, the power of the Sovereign or King is confined or limited to that of the *law*: beyond this limitation the very relation ceaſes: conſequently where there is no King nor Sovereign, there the paſſive obedience and non-reſiſtance of the ſubject to him is out of the queſtion, as is ſelf-evident. *Jura*, 473.

Here is an open and unequivocal revival of the doctrine of paſſive obedience and non-reſiſtance. It can only have effect in abſolute monarchies. (Jur. Ang. 471.) "In *regal* Govern-
"ments was this doctrine engendered, foſtered, and reared; and
"when our Kings wiſhed or attempted to erect themſelves into
"regal arbitrary ſovereigns, they attempted at the ſame time to
"tranſplant it into this country." Woe unto ſuch attempts by
"ſovereigns or ſubjects!

Kings in one sense are the servants of the people, because their power has no other rational end, than that of the general advantage: but it is not true, that they are in the ordinary sense (by our Constitution at least) any thing like servants; the essence of whose situation is to obey the commands of some other, and to be removable at pleasure. But the King of Great Britain obeys no other person; all other persons are individually, and *collectively too,* under him, and owe to him a legal obedience.

Reflections, 41.

Those who trace the King's sovereignty from the immediate appointment of the community, undervalue and contemn the people, in proportion, as they substract from the majesty of their appointee: for the refusal of the absolute honours to the prince, is the disavowal of the relative honour to the people. I shall, therefore, hereafter consider the submission and respect due from the subject to the Sovereign as a civil duty and obligation, which every member of the community is indispensably obliged to perform, under the penalties which the State has annexed to the crime of high treason.

Jura, 218.

Here Mr. Burke dissembles no longer his doctrines; he is explicit, and formerly subjects both houses of Parliament to the absolute and sole will of the King. The Nation can only act collectively through their representatives in Parliament; and, if they collectively owe the King a legal obedience, then may he impose law upon them: the consequences of such doctrine are rather serious both to the King and People.

Unquestionably there was a revolution in the person of King William, a small and temporary deviation from the strict order of a regular hereditary succession: but it is against all ge-

The inherent rights and incumbent duties of individuals, and of the community, of which I have before spoken, will, when candidly viewed, I hope, sufficiently justify, and for ever

nuine principles of jurifpru- | eftablifh the *principles* upon
dence, to draw a principle from | which our anceftors effected
a law made in a fpecial cafe, | the Revolution, and their pof-
and regarding an individual | terity to this day cherifh and
perfon. | fupport it in its confequences
Reflections, 23. | and effects.

Jura, 193.

What Mr. Burke calls a *temporary fmall deviation*, was the moft arbitrary, wide, voluntary fettlement that ever was made of a crown. Extinguifhing the *legal* rights of an unoffending, unheard infant, giving rights to a ftranger who had neither claim nor pretenfions; and not only impofing a condition on the tenure of the crown, which depended upon the uncontroulable obligation of fubmitting the underftanding of the Sovereign to the revelations of religion, but alfo precluding the old line of fucceffion from the very poffibility of holding their ancient inheritance, by conforming with the condition of its prefent tenure. I wonder not that Mr. Burke's antagonifts denominate him truly an *unprincipled Whig*, who can difcover no *principle* in our Revolution of 1688.

I believe, Sir, that many on the Continent altogether miftake the condition of a King of Great Britain. He is a real King, and *not an executive officer*. If he will not trouble himfelf with contemptible details, nor wifh to degrade himfelf by becoming a party in little fquabbles, I am far from fure, that a King of Great Britain, in whatever concerns him as a King, or indeed as a | I have already given you to underftand, that there is a very noted fentence, a favourite maxim or rule in the civil: "That which pleafes the prince has the effect of a law." The laws of England admit of no fuch maxim, or any thing like it. A king of England does not bear fuch a fway over his fubjects as a King *merely*, but in a mixt political capacity: he is obliged by his coronation rational man, who combines his public interest with his personal satisfaction, does not possess a more real, solid, extensive power than the King of France was possessed of before this miserable Revolution. The direct power of the King of England is considerable. His indirect and far more certain power is great indeed.

Letter to a Member, 67.

oath to the observance of the laws, which some of our Kings have not been able to digest, because thereby they are deprived of that free exercise of dominion over their subjects in that full extensive manner, as *those Kings* have, who preside and govern by an *absolute* regal power; who, in pursuance of the laws of their respective kingdoms, in particular the civil law, and of the aforesaid maxim, govern their subjects, change laws, enact new ones, inflict punishments, and impose taxes at their free will and pleasure; and determine suits at law when and as they think fit. *Jura,* 319, *quoted from Fortescue.*

Here are two new paradoxes for the solution of Mr. Burke's disciples: I profess myself inadequate to their solution. I know no power in the Crown which the Constitution does not give and recognize; and which therefore must be *direct* and positive. Much less do I conceive, that an indirect power proceeding from unknown or unavowed causes, should be more *certain* than the direct power which all know and all acknowledge. But with sorrow and indignation do I hear Mr. Burke boast of the *unbounded* effects of any power in our Crown. I have been in the old fashioned habit of placing the security both of king and subject in the *direct limited power* of the Crown. This contrast of the absolute government of France against the limited monarchy of England by Fortescue, is boldly inverted by Mr. Burke, who thinks, I presume, the legislative power in the individual to be the necessary support of a modern king of England, *to whom the nation collectively owes a legal obedience.*

It has been the misfortune, and not the glory of this age, that every thing is to be discussed. (*Refl.* 17.) The British Constitution may have its advantages pointed out to wise and reflecting minds: but it is of too high an order of excellence to be adapted to those which are common. It takes in too many views, it makes too many combinations, to be so much as comprehended by shallow and superficial understandings. Profound thinkers will know it in its reason and spirit. The less enquiring will recognize it in their feelings and their experience.

Appeal, 113.

Wherever misrepresentation of truth has existed, and that misrepresentation has been attended with mischievous consequences, discussion alone can cure the evil. I openly avow this to be the intent of my making this publication; and with this view am I induced to make the most public and unequivocal profession of those principles which have engendered, nurtured and maturated our Constitution; and which, if strictly adhered to, must ever preserve it in full vigour, and so perpetuate it to the latest posterity. I am very far from wishing to draw a veil over the principles which justified the alterations in the Constitution of our Government at the Revolution. *Jura,* 168.

This veiling and mysterious principle of Mr. Burke tends first to blind, then to irritate, and finally to mislead the multitude. The knowledge of their rights will encourage them to preserve them. If they be ignorant of what they have, they will attempt to acquire what they are not entitled to. And hence the catastrophe of disorder and confusion. Mr. Burke did not always see through that hazy mist which now dims his sight.

He could formerly see, that * " In all disputes between the people
" and their rulers, the presumption was at least upon a par in fa-
" vour of the people. Experience may perhaps justify me in going
" further. Where popular discontents have been very prevalent,
" it may be well affirmed and supported, that there has been ge-
" nerally something found amiss in the Constitution, or in the
" conduct of Government. The people have no interest in dis-
" order. When they do wrong it is their error, not their crime.
" But with the governing part of the state, it is far otherwise.
" They certainly may act by ill design, as well as by mistake."
The confirmation of ignorance is a very new mode of correcting error.

Upon the publication of Mr. Burke's book, the readiness, if
not avidity, with which the majority of the country imbibed his
principles, was as astonishing to the observer as it was alarming
to the reasoner upon the consequences. The first fruits of his
extraordinary political mission, were truly superabundant: the
harvest returned a hundred fold; and if the purity of his zeal
could admit it, we should pardon the emotion of vanity that the
number and quality of his proselytes might raise in his breast.
He had the address, or the power, or the good, or the bad fortune to seduce the public into the conviction, that every variance of opinion upon the policy or propriety of every measure
of Administration, became the unequivocal and irrevocable test
of hostility or enmity to the British Constitution: hereby attempting from henceforth to divide the nation into two parties,
which he discriminated by the new and emphatical appellations
of *modern* and *ancient* Whigs. His own words will best explain
the meaning of the terms. † " The modern Whigs in Parlia-
" ment, who are so warm in condemnation of Mr. Burke and
" his book, and of course of all the principles of the ancient
" Constitutional Whigs of this country." In defiance however
of this fulminating bull of excommunication against all the dissen-

* Thoughts on the Cause of the present Discontents, sub. init.
† Appeal, 95.

ters from Mr. Burke and his book and his principles, some few who dared express their dissent and protest against them, stood firm to the principles of the ancient Constitutional Whigs of this kingdom. They were not the larger, but time and reason, and events will shew, whether they were not the sounder part of the community.

The most stupendous powers of Mr. Burke's eloquence were now experienced in the sudden and general submission of the nation to his new political paradoxes: henceforth the whole system of measures began to be directed by the newly acquired spirit of this regenerated system. It will be scarcely credited by posterity, that at the close of the 18th century, the condemnation of Mr. Burke and his book upon the Revolution of France, and of his principles, became in the eyes of the British Nation the test of turbulence, faction, and sedition. The man, who can talk of a *swinish* multitude because it is illiterate, who sets his face against the reformation of all abuses in Government, and hazards doctrines pointedly destructive of the genuine principles of the Constitutional Whigs of this kingdom, may well be expected to persecute with unrelenting rigour the different societies that had been established under the denominations of Friends of the People, Friends to a parliamentary Reform, or the Liberty of the Press, and the Whig and other Clubs for constitutional information. All these, together with the non-approvers of Mr. Burke and his book, are promiscuously involved in the general anathema, exterminated from the pale of the Constitution, and proscribed as her avowed and determined enemies. Such was the enthusiasm of this new and numerous coalition, such their confidence in their newly acquired strength, that policy and prudence were not even attended to. Instead of separating and dividing their opponents, they foolishly encreased their numbers, by connecting all the malecontents of the kingdom in one common cause of opposition to themselves, and of course, as Mr. Burke says, *to all the principles of the ancient Constitutional Whigs of this country.* I carry not my scepticism to the height of those, who have denied the existence of any enemies to our Constitution amongst us. Such I hold every man, who adopts the levelling doctrines of Paine, and every man, who supports the spirit of arbitrary power: such I hold every man, whether he attempt to establish in this country a pure republic or an absolute monarchy: but such I do *not* hold every man, who is a friend of the people, or a friend to parliamentary reform, or to the liberty of the press, or a member of the Whig club, or of the Society for procuring constitutional information.

Ministers should be more fully and more practically convinced than other men, that there is a tenacious quality of adhesion in all popular discontents, by which they entwine and incorporate upon approximation. At this hour their was a serious call upon them, to prevent the increasing union, and consequently strength of the malecontents. This could only be effected by disengaging from the general cause of murmur, all those who really had originally, and who might then still retain different wishes from others, who aimed at the total subversion of the present establishment. The nation would then have known who were friends, and who enemies to the Constitution. Then would have ceased the artful, but wicked and mischievous system, of confounding a wish to reform the popular representation in parliament with that of subverting the Constitution: of viewing all exertions to correct the abuses, as so many attempts to destroy the principles of Government; and of representing love and friendship for the people, as incompatible with respect and loyalty for the sovereign.

No human institution can be brought to that degree of perfection, that it shall not at times require some amendment and improvement; and plain reason shews us, that those are ever the most sincerely attached to the institution, who are most forward to amend and improve it, as its defects, abuses, or vices shall appear. There cannot surely be so seasonable, so proper, so necessary a time to apply the remedy, as when the disease threatens to attack the vital parts and become infectious. I have heretofore said, * " to prove that any human inftitution has attained its *ne* " *plus ultra* of perfection, is to produce internal evidence of a " radical deficiency or vice in the fyftem; and to prove a con- " tinued progrefs in the melioration or improvement of a fyftem, " is conclufive evidence, that the ground-work of the fuperftruc- " ture is in its nature firm and permanent. I have endeavoured " to trace and mark the advances which our Conftitution has " been gradually making, fince its firft inftitution, towards the " perfection of civil liberty; and in this progrefs do we find the " fureft earneft of future improvements, as the exigencies of " times and circumftances fhall require them."

It was in the direct fpirit of Mr. Burke's fweeping anathema, that every idea, every wifh, every attempt to reform the reprefentation of the people in parliament, or to befriend the general rights of the people, from which alone has arifen the Britifh Conftitution, has been holden out, as an intention, defign, and effort to fubvert and annihilate it. To condemn Mr. Burke and his book, became a renunciation of Magna Charta and the Bill of Rights; to refift the principle of arbitrary and abfolute power over the people, was the war-whoop of rebellion; and a good wifh to the happy eftablifhment of a better order of things in France, was an unequivocal determination to overthrow the whole fyftem of our prefent eftablifhment. To the magical charms, or overbearing powers of Mr. Burke's eloquence the whole nation almoft, for a time, bowed down and fubmitted. But I ftill boaft of the reluctance and indignation, with which I ever beheld him wave on his triumphant pennant, the too confident device, *Qui non eft probis contra patriam eft.* Such, however, for the (ill.-fated) moment, was the mark of the beaft. Whether Thomas Paine would level all diftinctions, Mr. Fox propagate his ideas of a revolutionary Whig, Mr. Erfkine ftand up for the rights of juries, or Mr. Grey promote a parliamentary reform, they were all equally confounded in the condemnation of Mr. Burke and his book, and of courfe equally involved in the

* Jurn Ang. p. 609.

condemnation of all the principles of the ancient Constitutional Whigs of this country. Though the dreams of Britons may be general, they are transient, and their waking reflections will do away the delusion.

The spirit of a system of Government is not only to be read in the specific acts of an Administration, but it pervades and directs every measure which the country, under its influence, pursues and adopts. In this misguided spirit of attributing the whole disasters of the country to the wishes and exertions of the friends of the people, and the promoters of a parliamentary reform, we have beholden parochial meetings throughout the kingdom, established, as their resolutions generally run, *to preserve themselves against the horrid attempts of daring and seditious men, who, under the specious pretence of reformation, wish to subvert the Constitution and Government of the country.* To such of you, my countrymen, who now see, or who ever have seen the necessity of such a reform, who now are exerting, or who ever have exerted yourselves in bringing it to bear, I apply, whether you now have, or ever had a wish, intention, or design to overturn the Constitution, or annihilate the Government of the country. If, on the contrary, you wish and expect, that the Constitution should receive strength and vigour from the adoption of the measure, in what spirit, in what principle do you vary from him who brought three several motions, to attain this great end, before parliament, and the third of them, when he was, as he still is, at the head of his Majesty's councils? Enemies to their country are liable to, and ought to be made to feel the full severity of the laws. Would not more timely rigour towards state delinquents have diminished the discontents, which still subsist in the nation? If it were not unconstitutional, if it were not seditious, but if it were commendable and patriotic, to bring motions into the House of Commons for abolishing the corruption of our popular representation, what specious reasoning, what state imposition shall convince you, that to meet with a view and intention of following up the same object, is to convene upon purposes of sedition and

F

tumult? If the end of your meeting be conftitutional, your actual affemblage is legal. Free thoughts upon political fubjects are congenial with the fpirit of a free Conftitution: they are conducive to its prefervation; they are effential to its exiftence. The prefent perfection of our Conftitution was not effected by one government, nor in one century: it boafts the tranfcendent peculiarity of gradual and diftantly progreffive formation.

Throw your eyes, my countrymen, upon the pages of paft hiftory, view the various revolutions of empires, and trace their moft ftupendous effects up to their original fources; the whole is but a vapid narrative, and a cold unintereſting fpeculation in comparifon of the prefent political ftate of Europe. Believe me, the firft and only effectual fecurity againft licentioufnefs, is the moderate and fure enjoyment of fair liberty. Dreadful are the confequences of convincing the people that they know not their own fituation; that their remonftrances are flighted; that the profpect of their grievances being redreffed, is defperate. Extenfive, ruinous, and awful are the circumftances which have forced the late difcuffions upon political and civil freedom. But truth and juftice rife out of reflection, are invigorated by difcuffion, and triumph when difplayed to the broad light of conviction. How glorious is it for our Conftitution, in this critical moment of fevere and hoftile inveftigation, to continue to command the love and attachment of thofe, who are bleft with it, and the refpect and admiration of all who know it; that no other alteration is even wifhed to be introduced into it, than a clofer conformity in the practices of popular election with its effential and unalterable principles! For the man either knows not, or wifhes to fubvert the Conftitution of his country, who queftions this elementary principle of it—That the people partake in the legiflation, and confequently are emphatically bounden to the obfervance of the laws, by the free reprefentation of their reprefentatives in parliament. As far then as the fact deviates from the principle, fo far the practice is vicious and corrupt; and whoever ferioufly wifhes to preferve the Conftitution in its full purity and vigour, muſt neceſſarily wiſh to correct the vice, and prevent the corruption. Will the friends of a reform be ſilenced and quieted, by admitting the neceſſity, and denying the expediency of the meaſure? Can they be compelled to believe the evil practical, and the remedy but an airy viſion? Will the people of England be terrified out of their conviction by the thundering *veto* of Mr. Burke? Unlimited and unknown wretchedneſs will overwhelm our country, whilſt to condemn Mr. Burke and his book, is to condemn all the principles of the ancient Conſtitutional Whigs of this country.

I will not aſſert, that the awful moment is arrived, in which the deluſive veil of art can no longer withhold the reality from our eyes: but I will affirm, that the preſent moment is of dire portent. It ſeriouſly behoves us, not only to reſcue the purity of our Conſtitution from the rude violence of anarchy, but alſo from the more dangerous, becauſe more latent efforts of miſguided zeal, or maſked defence. To ſecure to the Crown its conſtitutional prerogatives, and to ourſelves our conſtitutional rights and privileges, are purpoſes not only reconcileable, but ſo connected, that every meaſure that weakens the one, neceſſarily endangers the other. It is time to diſpel the magic of that eloquence, which has ſo long preſented, through a falſe medium, an inverted form of our Conſtitution, baſe upwards. Its undiſguiſed beauties will inſpire us with ingenuity and ardour, to give new ſecurity for the continuance of the bleſſings, which it is calculated to confer. For this purpoſe, we muſt view facts as they ariſe, we muſt explore their ſources, and follow them in their tendencies. Cool and diſpaſſionate throughout, let the voice of reaſon, and deciſion of truth and juſtice, diſplay the ſuperior excellence of a ſyſtem, which is, of its nature, proof againſt the violence of ſedition, and the more fatal attacks of eloquent miſrepreſentation.

Before I proceed, my countrymen, I feel an irreſiſtible impulſe to redouble my attempts to impreſs you with a juſt ſenſe of the conſequences, which muſt enſue from your perſeverance in

Mr. Burke's principles. I am not the voice of party, turbulence, or faction. I love and revere the Constitution of my country. When it was openly attacked, I hope I defended it upon the true and proper grounds; I see it now in more danger than I then did: and I should be justly stigmatized with the most dastardly baseness, were I now to desert the cause, because its defence had become more difficult and hazardous. In combating the open enemies of the Constitution, I was sure of the wishes, countenance, and support of all those, who professed themselves friends to their country. In attempting to secure the Constitution against the destructive measures of its beguiled friends, and beguiling (though disguised) enemies, I have to dispossess feelings, unrivet prejudices, and conquer the stubborn pride of mental error and ill directed zeal.

If, in the preservation of the British Constitution, you place your security against the anarchy, confusion, and horrors of your Gallic neighbours; it behoves you seriously to revise the political creed of Mr. Burke, which now seems to have acquired so powerful an influence on the measures of public policy. The absolute and arbitrary power of the French monarchy created and fed that volcano of abuses, which in its dreadful eruption has desolated its own, and menaced desolation to all surrounding kingdoms. This new Thaumaturgus and evangelist of royalty, has revealed a new mystery to his submissive devotees, that the *indirect power of* the King of England is *great indeed*, and more *extensive than what the King of France was possessed of before this miserable revolution.* Will you believe it, my countrymen? I will not. What the *direct* power of our King is, we all know, that know the limits and boundaries of the law. But what his *indirect power* is, which is more extensive than the arbitrary will of an individual legislator, I have not yet discovered in any ancient or modern commentator upon our Constitution. It was an anomalous planet, discovered by the penetrating sagacity of an apostate Whig, upon the verge of his grand climacteric. But if it do exist, it becomes us to make our obfervations upon its motions, with more than ordinary accuracy: it behoves us to guard againft the devouring heat of its perihelion. The very relation of caufes and effects will roufe Britons into the moft alarming cautions, how they admit the introduction, or permit the exiftence of a power in their crown more extenfive than that of the fourth Henry, or the fourteenth Louis of France*.

I fhall now endeavour to withdraw the curtain, and difplay the truth in naked (though melancholy) facts.

* I wifh Chancellor Fortefcues's xxxvth chapter of *The Inconveniencies in France by Means of the abfolute Regal Government*, to be read by all Mr. Burke's neophites: though it may too immediately concern the multitude, to intereft his attention.

CHAPTER II.

MAY, 1792.

CONTENTS.

General opening.—Resolutions in the Commons for the gradual abolition of the Slave Trade.—Free thoughts thereupon.—The flourishing state of the Revenue.—Original cause of Lord Thurlow's resignation of the Seals.—The case of the Royal Scotch Burghs, and the Riots of Dundee.—Mr. Fox's motion for repealing the penal Statutes against the Unitarians lost.—Petition of the Electors of Westminster, grounded upon the trial of Mr. Rose, against official interference in the Elections.—Introduction of Monf. Chauvelin, and his Mentor, the Bishop of Autun, as Ambassador from the King of the French.—Court Mourning for the King of Sweden.—Reflections on his Murder.—Chauvelin's Memorial to Lord Grenville about the War causes a Proclamation not to serve against France.—Publication of Paine's Rights of Man, 1st and 2d parts.—Information against him.—Proclamation against seditious writings, and warm debates upon it in both Houses.—The rights of Juries established by the Libel Bill.—Convention of the Kings of Prussia and Hungary.—They call upon all the States of the Empire for their quota against France, except Saxony and Hanover.

THE opening of this period of our History represents to us the glowing clouds of a sultry evening, that forebode a night of storm and horrors. We had, perhaps, indulged with too luxuriant a confidence the assurance of perpetuating the blessings of a long continued peace. The ingenuity, spirit, and credit of our manufacturers and merchants had so frequently poured an overflow of revenue into the treasury, that for some years it had been the new and flattering task of the Minister, to apply the welcome surplus in lightening the overgrown weight of the national incumbrance. Elated with this flattering exuberance of the revenue, Mr. Pitt, upon opening his budget for the current year*, very ingeniously profited of the circumstance to divert the dazzled eyes of the nation from the heavy expences of the Russian and Spanish armaments, which had cost the nation about 2,000,000l. to make good the damage of some few thousand pounds, done to a British Captain by the detention of his vessel at Nootka Sound; and to leave Oczakow to the imperious Catherine, which we had threatened by force to secure to the Porte. Upon this memorable occasion, the Chancellor of the Exchequer triumphantly boasted in the House of Commons, *that the intricacy and mystery of finance no longer existed:* and in a display of the most brilliant eloquence, enforced *the reasons upon which they might found a probable opinion of the permanence of such surplus.* In the unusual glow of this national prosperity, little was it to be wondered at, that the very luxuriance of the plant which produced the fruit, should for want of pruning run into some wildness and disorder.

In the present disposition of the British nation to discountenance efforts to promote the general cause of civil freedom, from an apprehension of producing unforeseen or unintended consequences, it becomes a matter more of necessary attention, than of curious observation, to reflect that the question of the Slave Trade, which had engaged the minds of the public for some years, was super-eminently liable to all the objections which have been raised by Mr. Burke, and adopted by the nation, against the discussion of any general or fundamental point of civil liberty. When this question was first started, he had not yet taught the nation † *that doctrines limited in their present*

---

* On the 17th February, 1792.
† Appeal 98.

application, and wide in their general principles, are never meant to be applied to what they first pretend. Mr. Wilberforce will not refuse to inform us, what *ulterior* views he had in introducing, nor Mr. Pitt in supporting the subject in Parliament. And who will not readily admit, that no doctrine was ever wider in its general principles, than that which inculcates the unlawfulness of the Slave Trade? Taken up upon the pure abstract rights of humanity, it evidently hazards the property of individuals, deeply affects the navigation and commerce of the nation, and immediately involves the dismemberment of the British Empire. And yet, within the lapse of five short years, the nation has beholden with rapture, the rival talents of Administration and Opposition combined in this instance, to reduce private interest and national policy under the great superseding principles of social freedom: it has seen the question supported with enthusiasm, by all that was powerful in the cabinet, and brilliant in the senate; and opposed only by the operative and persevering ingenuity of self-interest. A truly practical lesson of the propriety and advantages of extending the freedom of every oppressed part of the community, of reforming abuses, and abolishing long sanctioned usages, that militate against the principles of civil liberty. For, upon these principles alone has the abolition of the Slave Trade been taken up by Mr. Wilberforce, and supported by Messrs. Pitt, Fox, and other humane friends of their African brethren.

Upon the 1st of May, Mr. Pitt presented to the House of Commons, a string of resolutions for the *gradual* abolition of the Slave Trade, which were sanctioned by the House and carried up to the Lords. But the cause met with more opposition in this House than it had in the Commons. Many reasons have been alledged for this opposition to the resolutions in the Lords: but, as at this time, few of the Peers had been under the necessity of committing themselves upon the question of keeping up the African slavery in our colonies, many of them probably, now formed their opinions upon it, more from their feelings upon the general complexion of the times, than from the nature, reasons, and exigency of the case. However, in the debate in the Lords on the 8th of this month, those who wished to oppose, or to protract the abolition of the Slave Trade, carried the question, That the evidence upon the case should be heard at the bar of the house, and not in an upstairs committee; by which means very little progress was made in the business during the course of the sessions.

It is scarcely possible to conceive a subject of discussion more pregnant with consequences of the utmost import to the State, than the abolition of the Slave Trade. For it is obvious, that all the reasons against that traffic, which are drawn from the essential nature of human beings, or from the indispensable obligations of moral justice, or from the positive injunctions of the Christian code, militate only against the purchase of the slaves, because they ultimately militate against the state of slavery for which they are purchased. Yet has the House of Commons voted the protraction of the Slave Trade to the 1st day of January, 1800, and allowed a premium upon the importation of female slaves, with the express view of supplying the islands with a sufficient number of both sexes, to perpetuate the system of slavery, by encouraging the breed and home traffic, rather than the importation of these black herds from the coast of Africa. No legislature can sanction the means of attaining an iniquitous end. If, on the other hand, it be considered, that, in our islands, the general proportion of blacks to the number of whites, is as fifteen to one; or, in other words, that, in the island of Jamaica, three hundred thousand black human beings are the property of some hundred individuals, who compose a part of twenty thousand free inhabitants of that island; we shall tremble at the consequences of agitating any other questions concerning them, than those of regulation and tenderness. If we reflect on the nature of the individuals who compose this mass of people, and cast a melancholy eye over the now desolated and disconsolate island of St. Domingo, the Eden of the western world, we shall scarcely discover a mean point of security between the dreadful extremities of abandoning the property, and emancipating the enslaved cultivators of the soil. Yet, in defiance of all these consequences, have the humane advocates of the African slaves stood boldly forward in the cause of freedom.

Before this important question receives its final decision, it should be completely divested of the stern compulsion of conscientious morality, that shuts out the sympathy of human nature, and forbids the exercise of discretion and election. If the subject be once brought to a matter of mere civil investigation, the mist of enthusiasm will be removed, that magnifies the size of all reasons, and misrepresents the shape of every objection. Then, and not till then, will the advocates for the abolition of the Slave Trade see the full force of the reasons of their opponents for its continuance, viz. the impossibility of keeping up the culture of their plantations without it; the advantages of navigation, opulence, and industry, arising from it to their mother country; the improvement of the situation of the slaves by being removed from a more unhealthy climate, secured from cruel and despotic tyranny, and rescued from the horrors of barbarism and idolatry; the injustice of invading private property without indemnification; the danger of calumniating the acts of the proprietors, their ancestors, and the governors and legislators of the country, by supporting the system of slavery: and above all, the consequences which the slaves must draw (for they have thought) from our open declaration of the criminality of the practice of enslaving them.

If at a future day the Slave Trade shall be abolished, as an unchristian traffic, and the emancipation of our colonial slaves shall follow that abolition as a just and necessary consequence of the principle that produced it; the indemnification and satisfaction of the injured proprietors will become a serious consideration to the minister of finance. On one hand will be established claims for the loss of property resumed by the State, after the most unequivocal confirmation of it to the individual possessors;

and on the other will be heard proteſtations againſt a contribution towards reimburſing the expences of enſlaving and bartering for their fellow-creatures, in defiance of the ordinances of God; as if a ſeducer, forced by the laws from the object of his criminality, ſhould demand of the State a reimburſement for the price of her ruin. If, upon the abolition of the Slave Trade, a conſequent emancipation ſhould follow, cordial muſt be the prayers of our Weſt Indian Planters for the continuance of the preſent Miniſter. For he, who has ſo warmly eſpouſed the claims of theſe Africans to their natural rights, and who, in the year 1786, propoſed to ſaddle this nation with the ſum of one million, to buy up a right of nomination to parliament from individuals, which the Conſtitution preſumed impoſſible to exiſt, would not, without full indemnification, invade the property of individuals, confirmed to them by the ſtanding laws of the land, and the expreſs acts of the legiſlature.

The flouriſhing ſtate of our commerce at this time, cannot be more clearly aſcertained than by the actual increaſe of the revenue, which in the current week exceeded the correſponding week in the preceding year by the ſum of 118,034l. 6s. At the ſame time, a report was made by the commiſſioners under Mr. Pitt's bill for the liquidation of the national debt, that they had applied to that reduction the ſum of 8,677,850l. This increaſe of the revenue appears to be the choſen touchſtone of Mr. Pitt's popularity: it certainly is the moſt gratifying circumſtance, that can ſooth the vanity, or ſoften the labours of a miniſter of finance; but groſs is the error of thoſe, who attribute it to any other cauſe, than to the energy, ſpirit, and credit of our manufacturers and merchants. So wedded was the Chancellor of the Exchequer to his favourite plan of reducing the national debt, by the application of the annual ſurplus of the revenue, that to the diſapprobation of one part of it, is immediately to be traced Lord Thurlow's reſignation of the great ſeals of England. In a committee of the Houſe of Lords, upon the bill for appropriating a certain ſum annually for paying off the national debt, the Lord Chancellor, although approving of the object of the bill, strongly objected to that clause of it, which enacted, that no future loan should be made without being provided for at the time. He reprobated the arrogance and insolence of dictating to future parliaments, and the futility of directing how future ministers should make their loans; concluding his speech by this emphatical assertion, that *the folly of the project could only be equalled by the vanity of making the attempt.* The strong sense and integrity of the Chancellor would not permit him to lend his sanction to a clause of such a tendency, and he divided with twenty-one against twenty-seven, who, with Lord Grenville, supported it. Fortunately for the country, this great man had not been initiated in Mr. Burke's doctrines of *settling precedents for ever, from which no parliament should ever depart.* As, from this act of opposition to a favourite measure of the Minister, the public dates the loss of Lord Thurlow's abilities in the cabinet and on the bench, justice claims, from every well-wisher to his country, a tribute of grateful admiration to this true and unshaken patriot. The piteous tales of official sycophants, that attempted to shew the necessity of removing a man from his Majesty's councils, who opposed every thing, and proposed nothing, betrayed their folly and weakness in the attempt to justify the measure. The essential and important duty of the Chancellor is to examine, state, and to be in some sort responsible for the legal effects, and constitutional tendency of every bill that comes into the House of Lords. For his ability and faithfulness to discharge this duty, he receives credit from the Crown by his appointment; his peers look up to him for it in the guidance of their parliamentary conduct; the public rest their assurance and acquiescence in this same confidence. What a strange perversion of duty would it be, that because a Chancellor, in the discharge of this watchful and superintending office, should discover an illegal effect, or unconstitutional operation in a bill affecting the army, navy, finance, or commerce of the country, he should be called upon for new plans and measures in these several departments! The people of England will ever cherish and revere, as a martyr to their rights and liberties, the man who sacrifices his interest and his preferment to this rigid exercise of his constitutional duty.

Some years ago, fifty out of the sixty-six Royal Scotch Burghs had by petitions to the House of Commons demanded redress against several grievances under which they laboured; and when Mr. Sheridan brought in a bill for removing the cause of their complaints, the grievances were admitted by the House to be of the utmost magnitude; and, in order to procure full proof of their existence, the House entered into a resolution, on the 27th of May 1791, that, early in the next session, it would take into consideration the state of the Royal Burghs of Scotland. On the 18th of April, Mr. Sheridan, in consequence of this resolution, moved the House to go into a committee, for enquiring into the grievances complained of, but the motion was lost by a majority of above two to one. These Burgesses having thus failed in their attempt to effectuate the resolution of the House, which was to investigate the nature of their grievances, on the 30th day of April, Mr. Sheridan presented a petition from them, to be heard by counsel at the bar of the House, to prove the existence of the grievances they complained of. To the reception of this petition Mr. Pitt and Mr. Dundas objected, upon account of the informality of the proceeding: the Speaker, however, decided against the informality, and quoted a precedent in favour of the petitioners, of a late similar petition from the East India Company: the question having been put, that the petition be received, it was negatived. The effects of these petitioners being baffled in every attempt to bring their grievances under the fair consideration of the legislature, were as much to be expected as they were to be dreaded. On the 3d of May, at Dundee, and several other places in Scotland, the Secretary of State was burned in effigy, with several labels issuing from his mouth, emphatically expressive of the situation and resolutions of persons labouring under grievances, and shut out from all redress. Having effected this purpose, the mobs dispersed without further outrage.

The House of Commons had, in fact, come to the resolution of examining into the nature of the grievances, under which these Burgesses laboured, before Mr. Burke had warned them against any reform of abuse, or any redress of grievances.— * " *Let those who have the trust of political or of natural autho-* " *rity ever keep watch against the desperate enterprises of innova-* " *tion: let even their benevolence be fortified and armed.*" Though the abuses of the Gallic demagogues may have irritated the nerves and steeled the heart of Mr. Burke, and of his followers, and of the approvers of his books and of his principles; yet did they not lighten the burthens of these petitioners, nor convince them, that the calamities of a foreign country should prevent the removal of their own grievances. If in the cautionary view of our neighbours' wretchedness we are to seek an earnest of our own welfare, let the fatal examples of the rapid transition from the voice to the action of a discontented people, raise a serious and guarded alarm in the breast of every well-wisher to his country. Our Constitution, in guarding against the intemperate resolutions and desperate measures of irritated associations, most providently interposed the subject's right of petitioning Parliament against grievances. But the right of the subject to petition evidently imports the duty of Parliament (not to grant the prayer) but, to receive and examine into the merits of the petition. Unmeasurable will be the mischief of clogging this mode of redress with difficulties, or of throwing disrepute or suspicion upon the exercise of this constitutional right of the subject. Even Mr. Burke formerly said, with more truth and less effect than he now might, †" *Where popular discontents have* " *been very prevalent; it may be well affirmed and supported, that* " *there has been generally something found amiss in the Constitution* " *or in the conduct of Government.*"

Such a hold had the execration of the French Revolutionists now acquired upon the generality of this nation, that it had be-

---
* Appeal, 116.

† Thoughts on the present Discontents, p. 416.

come the ground of Mr. Burke's new Conſtitutional Catechiſm, that becauſe follies, crimes, and horrors were committed in France, therefore, no errors were to be corrected, no abuſes reformed, no grievances redreſſed in England. Mr. Fox, in a very full houſe, brought forward his long promiſed motion in favour of the Unitarians, for the repeal of certain ſtatutes, by which they were ſubjected to heavy and ſevere puniſhments. He grounded a ſtrong, eloquent, and ingenious ſpeech upon the injuſtice of intolerance and perſecution for religious opinions, that were purely ſpeculative. Mr. Burke, however, diſcovered in Unitarianiſm the whole volcano of a French Revolution; and in a ſpeech of uncommon animation, variety, and eloquence, diſplayed every circumſtance that had diſgraced or polluted the progreſs of that Revolution from its beginning: he proved from the toaſts given at a dinner of Unitarians, that they were deeply infected with the Revolutionary Gallomania—a ſtigma which he alſo openly attempted to affix to the Oppoſition benches of the Houſe. But the moſt ſingular of his arguments was, that the ſtatute was too bad for execution, and therefore needed no repeal. A prouder day of triumph to Mr. Burke could not have happened: a very large majority gave into his arguments, and the motion was loſt. In this debate moſt of the eminent ſpeakers took a part. The future annaliſt of the moſt credulous age would be diſcredited in reporting, that Mr. Burke had, in a full debate, excited the horror and indignation of the Houſe of Commons againſt the French Revolutioniſts, for having compleated the meaſure of their iniquities, by ſuperadding to the reſt, the crime of *religious perſecution*, in order to convince a Britiſh Senate of the neceſſity of keeping upon their ſtatute books, acts of the moſt penal rigour againſt purely ſpeculative opinions of religion*. The leading ſpeakers, who followed him, oppoſed the motion, to avoid the ſcandal which the repeal

---

* The effect of this act (9 & 10 William III.) is more extenſive than it is generally thought: for it not only applies to all thoſe who do not believe the myſtery of the bleſſed Trinity, according to the

of such an act might create in the church: and, in order to secure the Unitarians from the guilt of sedition and treason, against which the Constitution and laws have provided a full remedy, they found the necessity of holding over them *in terrorem*, disabilities, penalties, and pains, for denying revealed dogmas and mysteries of religion above the natural grasp of man's limited comprehension, to which no *human* authority can therefore demand submission.

To discountenance every idea of reform, and to check, *in limine*, every enquiry into the parliamentary representation, appears now to have become regularly systematical. The difference is wide between the acquittal of a charge after investigation, and a sullen refusal to go into an enquiry. Power may screen the culprit from trial; innocence will ever court enquiry. Mr. George Rose, one of the Secretaries to the Treasury, had, in the last Westminster election commissioned Mr. Smith, a publican, to open his house for the entertainment of the voters for Lord Hood, the unsuccessful candidate. It appears, that the faithful Secretary, upon the close of the poll, was rather less forward to make good his payments, than he had been to pledge his responsibility to the honest publican. After many fruitless applications for payment of a moderate charge, Mr. Smith wisely preferred the verdict of his countrymen to the precarious dependance upon official promises. He brought an action against Mr. George Rose in the King's Bench, which was tried before Lord Kenyon and a special jury, and obtained a verdict against the Secretary for one hundred pounds. In the course of this trial it had been proved, that an application had been made by Mr. Smith to the Secretary of the Treasury, for the remission of an excise penalty which he had incurred; but which had never been levied upon him as long as he had remained an election agent for the liberty of Westminster; yet, that when he had

Athanasian exposition or explanation of it, but against all those who do not admit of the *divine authority* of the Old and new Testament, &c.

ceased to act, it had been levied upon him. Upon the strength of these and some other similar facts, a petition to the House of Commons was drawn up, and signed by more than one thousand electors of Westminster, praying an enquiry into the reported interference of persons high in office in the election for Westminster, and into the illegal abuses of the laws, by the remission of penalties, &c. Mr. Fox, after the petition had been read, made a very long and pointed speech upon the nature, principles, and purity of popular elections, and upon the abusive influence of official power, which he ended with a motion, that the petition should be referred to a committee to examine into the matter thereof, and report the same to the House, as it should appear to them. The motion was negatived without any debate, by a division of eighty-one against thirty-four: Messrs. Pitt, Dundas, Rose, and other servants of the crown divided with the majority.

In the beginning of this month, M. de Chauvelin was introduced to his Majesty as ambassador from the King of the French. He was very young, and supposed to be warmly attached to the democratic party in France. Whether they mistrusted the inexperience of his youth, or doubted the firmness of his principles, he was ushered into the diplomatic corps under the unprecedented tutelage of an official Mentor, M. de Talleyrand, the bishop of Autun. This prelate was the first bishop in France, who by the civic oath withdrew himself from the jurisdiction and communion of the See of Rome. He was followed in his schism by three prelates only, out of one hundred and thirty-two. A rare and unprecedented example, worthy of better times, that so large a portion of a flourishing and long established clergy, should sacrifice honours, pomp, and opulence to the severe calls of duty in deprivation, exile, and indigence. The confidential letter, which was written on this occasion, by the late unfortunate monarch of France to the King of England, was strongly expressive of his pacific dispo-

H

sition, and of his hopes, that no circumstance would ever break through the amity of the two courts.

A general court-mourning was about this time announced for the death of the unfortunate Gustavus III. King of Sweden, who was murdered, on the 16th of March, at a masquerade, by Baron Ankarstrom, a military officer. This murder of a King, at a time when the prevailing power in France had expressed the most marked execration of royalty, and was generally suspected to propogate their anti-basilican spirit through every country which was open to their intrigues and treachery, was by many zealous opposers of the French Revolution, attributed to the wicked machinations of their emissaries. The representation acquired credit from the known zeal, with which this monarch had promoted the armed combination against France.

The Swedish Revolution of 1772, by which Gustavus had established an absolute monarchy upon the ruin of the aristocratical powers of his kingdom, was ever supposed to have been planned in the cabinet of Versailles, where this unfortunate monarch had spent several months previous to his accession to the throne. Being naturally fond of absolute power, he retained an affectionate regard for that court, through the influence and intrigues of which he had acquired it, and from which he received an annual subsidy, till their late financial distresses put a stop to the payment. On the other hand, many of the Swedish nobility still kept up an indignant resentment for the loss of their influence in the state, which, though silently, they determinately waited for an opportunity to regain. The King had constantly supported his power by the unpopular means of a standing army and exorbitant taxes. Averse as he was for summoning a diet, his necessities compelled him to it, in the beginning of the present year. He unadvisedly issued a proclamation for assembling the diet only three weeks previous to its meeting, for the express purpose of preventing deliberation in the choice of the representatives: and instead of the capital, he ordered them to meet at *Geffle*, a solitary town on the Gulf of Bothnia, which during the whole of their deliberations, was furrounded with mercenary foldiers. Both the Public and the King were difappointed in the refult of the meeting. No reform was effected, nor cenfure paffed upon the King for entering into a war, without the confent of the States, which was an infraction of the new as well as of the old Conftitution. In return, the diet only granted the King a part of the fupplies he demanded. Thus unfatisfactorily ended this diet, which proved fo immediately fatal to the monarch. The nobles and the people reprobated the idea of entering into the confederacy againft France; their country was then grievoufly oppreffed with taxes; and they could not be brought to confent to weaken it ftill more, by the additional wafte of its blood and treafure, in order to fupport or revive a government, which had been fo inftrumental in fettering them with the galling chains of unlimited monarchy. It is generally afferted, that fome perfonal and private refentments, from the King's having deprived one of his noblemen of an advantageous match, which he procured for a court-favourite, co-operated alfo with the general difcontent, to bring forward that confpiracy of the nobility, to which this unfortunate monarch fell a victim. I have faid thus much of Sweden, merely to detect the falfity of the affertions, that the murderer was an emiffary from the Jacobins at Paris. Are not their crimes fufficiently numerous, to withhold their enemies from fuch falfe charges?

The firft public act of the French ambaffador to our court, was the prefentation of a memorial to Lord Grenville, which ftated the reafons, why France had declared war againft the King of Hungary and Bohemia; infifting particularly upon the right, which France claimed, to change and model her own government, without the interference of any foreign power; and, upon the fame principle, holding out a guarantee to all other nations at peace with her, that the French will ever refpect their laws, their ufages, and all their forms of government. The memorial clofed with a claim of the obfervance of the treaty of commerce, of the 26th of September, 1786, on the part of England, particularly as to the refraining from any hoftilities. This memorial produced almoft immediately a royal proclamation, prohibiting any of his Majefty's fubjects to arm or act at fea againft the French, under any foreign commiffion or power whatfoever, and enjoining a ftrict obfervance of the treaty of commerce in every refpect.

Mr. Burke's Reflections upon the Revolution in France appeared in the year 1790; and early in the year 1791, was publifhed Thomas Paine's *Rights of Man, being an Anfwer to Mr. Burke's Attack on the French Revolution*. The public are too fully apprifed of the nature and tendency of thefe two works, to expect any frefh comments upon them: incredible was the avidity with which this book of Thomas Paine was read by the middling and lower claffes of people. The draught was too palatable for thofe to refift, who knew not its poifonous quality. By impunity, its credit extended; and, in lefs than a year, more than fifty thoufand impreffions of it had been circulated through the kingdom. It is a matter of notoriety, that in many places, it was fold for four pence, and in others diftributed gratis, to thofe who hefitated at paying their groat. Though Paine during this time lived publicly in London, and enjoyed the fatisfaction of feeing under his own eyes this unprecedented circulation of his book, and propagation of his doctrines, he braved and defied the arm of juftice, which had not as yet been attempted to be raifed againft him; not a fingle procefs had been inftituted againft publifher, printer, or feller of thefe libellous doctrines. Secure in his impunity, and flufhed with the fuccefs of his firft publication, he publifhed a *Second Part of the Rights of Man, combining Principle and Practice*. This work, though written perhaps with more audacity and malice, than the firft, was notwithftanding an innocuous performance, in comparifon of his firft publication. For the mifchievous effects of the firft work, were not increafed by the lecture of the fecond; nor was the Second Part of the Rights of Man fought for by thofe who had neither feen nor relifhed the firft. When, however, the fervour of the firft profelytifm had abated, and the credit of this levelling evangelift was on the wane, his Majefty's minifters, informed by Mr. Burke, that thefe * *writings deferved no other than the refutation of criminal juftice*, directed the Attorney General to file an information againft Thomas Paine for his libellous publications; which was accordingly done in Eafter term; and in order to difpofe the minds of the Nation to thefe neceffary, though late acts of juftice, a proclamation was publifhed, on the 21ft of the current month, againft the publication and fale of feditious writings, with ftrong injunctions to all perfons to inform againft thofe who fhould be guilty of fuch daring attempts, &c.

Scarcely had the proclamation been publifhed, when M. Chauvelin, the French ambaffador, prefented an official declaration to Lord Grenville, by which he complained, that certain expreffions in it appeared to give credit to the erroneous opinions, propagated by the enemies of France, both as to the hoftile intentions of Great Britain towards France, and the treacherous defigns of France, to promote fedition and confufion in the kingdom of Great Britain. It was expreffive of the moft pacific and honourable difpofitions of France towards this country, and it produced an anfwer from Lord Grenville, which was afterwards read in the National Affembly, that breathed the ftrongeft fentiments of peace and amity, with an unequivocal engagement from our King, *directly and pofitively* to maintain the treaty of navigation and commerce between the two nations.

This proclamation, fingular as it was, occafioned very warm and interefting debates in both Houfes of Parliament, and became the teft, upon which Mr. Burke's profelytes read openly their recantation of their former opinions, and enlifted formerly under the banner of his doctrines. The proclamation was more oppofed and difapproved of in the Commons than in the Lords, though the number and confequence of the perfons, who on this

* Appeal 95.

occasion seceded from those, with whom they had formerly acted, was proportionably greater in the Lords than the Commons. The arguments, by which the proclamation was opposed in both Houses, by those who had the steadiness to judge, and the firmness to act upon their old principles, in this hour of alarm, were nearly the same. That the Ministers of the Crown had, through the most criminal neglect or timidity, permitted the free circulation of Paine's books, against which they admitted the proclamations to be aimed, and were consequently responsible for all the evil consequences produced by it in the nation. That by neglecting to enforce the laws, in repressing tumult and disorder, whilst they would be effectual, they had permitted the evil to acquire such strength, that they were now justly doubtful of their efficacy, and therefore had recourse to the extraordinary and hazardous attempt, to check by royal proclamation, what they had neglected to repress by the constitutional means of legal process: by which they had vilified the Constitution, and exposed the prerogative to disgust and contempt. That they meanly attempted to screen their weakness and fear to prosecute the writer or publisher of these seditious writings, under an insidious pretence of ignorance, as if Thomas Paine were unknown to be the author, or J. S. Jordan the publisher of them. That it was establishing in a free country a system of *espionage*, widely foreign from the spirit of the British Constitution, which was never intended to be supported by spies and informers. That this proclamation was the most unequivocal avowal of the weakness and timidity of Ministers, and the direct way of ensuring to the author that consequence, which neither his merit nor his impunity would have otherwise acquired.

In the prevailing rage for discountenancing all popular attempts to enlarge or strengthen the liberty of the subject, it is a ground of surprise, though of infinite consolation to Englishmen, to reflect, that by the steady and undaunted efforts of some *real friends of the people*, the great and important rights of juries to determine upon the whole question at issue was finally established by the Libel Bill. And what in the prefent circumftances added much to the aftonifhment of the calm obferver, was, that the bill was brought in by Mr. Fox, and was the primary and favourite object of thofe affociations which had given fuch alarming umbrage to Government. In the Lords, the opinion of the twelve Judges was taken, and was decifive againft the bill. The Chancellor and Lord Kenyon fupported the opinion of the Judges with great warmth; but it was ably and fuccefsfully oppofed by Lords Camden, Loughborough, Grenville, and others. On this triumph of liberty in fo critical a juncture, juftice demands from every true Briton an honourable teftimony of gratitude to the brilliant talents, the undaunted and perfevering patriotifm of that truly conftitutional advocate, Mr. Erfkine, to whom, above any other, this country owes the invaluable boon.

Whatever fecret alliance or connection this country may have formed with the continental powers againft France, yet the appearance of neutrality was kept up. The courts of Vienna and Berlin had avowed openly their convention relative to the affairs of France, and on the 17th of this month, the Kings of Pruffia and Hungary delivered a joint declaration to all the minifters at the diet of Ratifbon, excepting thofe of Saxony and Hanover; in which they preffed the different States of the Empire for their quotas and contributions, to preferve the Empire againft the threatened invafions of France. It was ill received, and reluctantly and only in part complied with.

CHAPTER III.

JUNE, 1792.

CONTENTS.

Riots in Edinburgh—Burning of Mr. Dundas in effigy—Third reading of the National Debt Bill—The nature and fate of the New Forest Bill—His Majesty's Speech from the Throne—Parliament prorogued to the 30th August—Resignation of the Chancellor—The Seals in Commission—Outrages committed at Paris on the 20th—Proclamations in consequence—A projected union between the Dissenters and Roman Catholics in Ireland—The policy of the Roman Catholics in conducting their affairs, and particularly in securing the interest of Mr. Burke.

EVEN the late royal proclamation proved ineffectual in counteracting the popular discontents in North Britain, particularly against the Secretary of State for the Home Department. On the 4th of this month, the day annually allotted for the joyous celebration of his Majesty's birth-day, the Lord Provost and Magistrates of Edinburgh, apprehensive that the popularity of the Right Honourable Secretary Mr. Dundas would not stand the humour of the multitude, which the *feu de joie*, and other illuminations that loyalty had prepared on this festive occasion would assemble, directed all persons to keep their servants, apprentices, and workmen within doors, on the King's birth-day. It had been well known, that a complete suit of clothes, and all other external ornaments of dress had been ordered from London, to decorate an effigy of the Right Honourable Secretary, in the moſt ſcrupulous ſimilitude to the original, which they meant to commit on this night to the flames. The knowledge of this circumſtance put the magiſtrates, otherwiſe much alarmed at the diſcontented ſpirit of the people, on their guard to provide a larger military force than uſual, to ſuppreſs any riot or tumult that might break out on the occaſion. On the evening of the birth-day, the populace became much irritated by the appearance of ſo many ſoldiers parading the ſtreets, whilſt no attempts were made to break or interrupt the peace of the city. The dragoons galloping through the ſtreets, to diſperſe the curious and hitherto unoffending multitude, increaſed their numbers; they ſoon began to ſet the military at defiance, though headed by the Lord Provoſt and other magiſtrates: they drove ſeveral ſentinels from their poſts, and burnt their boxes. About midnight, they diſperſed gradually, and fourteen of the moſt active rioters were apprehended and confined in the caſtle. On the next day, every appearance of riot having ſubſided, the dragoons were ſent back to their quarters, about two miles from the town. But in the evening, a very great mob aſſembled in the neighbourhood of St. George's ſquare, whither they carried in proceſſion the effigy of Mr. Secretary Dundas, which they firſt hanged, and then committed to the flames, amidſt the ſhouts of the ſurrounding multitude. They inſulted, and pelted with ſtones and other miſſive weapons, both the military and thoſe who attempted to divert them from their riotous and ſeditious purpoſes. They had broken all the windows of the houſe of the Lord Advocate (Mr. Robert Dundas, the ſon-in-law of the Secretary), but were forced by the military to deſiſt from their apparent intent to demoliſh it. Being diſperſed from this ſcene, they ſoon rallied again in St. George's ſquare, and had actually begun to demoliſh the houſe of Mrs. Dundas, the mother of the Right Honourable Secretary, when they were fired upon by the ſoldiers, but without any effect. Upon this they grew more outrageous; and being perſuaded that the ſoldiers' muſquets had been charged only with powder, they attacked them with more aſſurance, and with every occaſional weapon which their fury adminiftered. The foldiers upon their fecond fire killed feven of the rioters, and wounded feveral. After this the mob difperfed without attempting any farther outrage. But on the third day, in the evening, they affembled again in a very riotous manner, and began to demolifh the houfe of the Lord Provoft in St. Andrew's fquare. They were interrupted in their attempt by the timely intervention of the military, who had the happinefs this night of difperfing the rioters without the neceffity of firing upon them : they fecured ten of the moft active among them. On the following day, the Lord Provoft convened a general meeting of the citizens; a ftep which had not been taken for thirty years before ; where feveral refolutions were entered into, to preferve the peace of the city, which fortunately has never been interrupted fince that time.

This mifguided rabble had, it feems, attributed the refufal of the Houfe of Commons to examine into the nature of the grievances of their free Burgeffes, after having undertaken to do it, to the fole influence of Mr. Secretary Dundas, and had therefore pointed their whole refentment againft him and his family. An awful trait of the precarioufnefs of popular favour. For if a title can be raifed to popularity, he has the fuper-eminent claim unto it, whom nature has endowed with every focial and beneficent difpofition to pleafe and gratify, and upon whom fortune has lavifhed the means of indulging it. Since the happy deftruction of the fyftem of favouritifm in this country, the rare phenomenon of the concentration of fo much royal favour in one individual, as in the perfon of Mr. Dundas, has not appeared— At one and the fame time, Secretary of State for the Home Department, Treafurer of the Royal Navy, a Lord of Trade and Plantations, and the directing Commiffioner of the Board of Control for the management of the affairs of the Eaft Indies. The Herculean labour of executing thefe numerous, arduous, and important offices, is furely more than adequate to the moderate appointments of 16,000l. which the Right Honourable Secretary is faid annually to receive from the National Treafury!

Multifarious as were the appointments of the Duke of Buckingham under James I. the patronage annexed to them was infignificant when compared to that which Mr. Dundas now commands in England, over Scotland, and throughout India and all its concerns and dependencies. But as the political exigencies of the prefent fyftem of Adminiftration feem to require very ftrong meafures, it became a neceffary part of that plan to fupply at leaft the oftenfible advifers of them with the fureft means of commanding popularity, which alone could render them palatable to the nation.

It has been before remarked, that the oppofition which the Chancellor had given to Mr. Pitt's National Debt Bill, had brought on the neceffity of his refigning the Great Seals of England. When that Bill was read a third time in the Houfe of Peers, and was paffed, Lord Rawdon, who with Lord Stormont and many others again oppofed it as a meafure of extreme prefumption, arrogance, and inefficiency, faid, " One mifchievous " confequence of it the country was already apprifed of, viz, " that it had been the means of depriving the public of the fur- " ther fervices of the noble and learned Lord on the woolfack, " whofe great abilities and known integrity had defervedly ren- " dered him the object of univerfal admiration and efteem." He had not however as yet actually refigned; when his oppofition to the third reading of the New Foreft Bill in the Lords precipitated his removal from the woolfack, before the Cabinet could negociate for a more accommodating fucceffor. His objections againft the Bill were, that it had been brought into the Houfe without the confent, and militated ftrongly againft the real interefts of the Crown, at a moment, when, if ever, the rights and prerogatives of the Crown ought, particularly by that Houfe, to be fupported; and that it contained feveral claufes of a mifchievous and unconftitutional tendency. This New Foreft Bill, which has been always looked upon as the favourite child of Mr. Secretary Rofe, was goaded through both Houfes of Parliament, under the preffure of various and weighty objections. But the strong light in which the Chancellor and others expofed the lurking defigns and anticonftitutional tendency of the Bill on the third reading, baffled all the views of its perfevering parent, and it was no more brought forward. Lord Portchefter concluded his fpeech againft the Bill in the Lords, by declaring that his Majefty had not proper materials before him, to enable him to form a judgment, and give a found and wife confent to its paffing. But the provident Secretary, from his perfonal knowledge of the claims of individuals, and the rights of the Crown upon the New Foreft, in bringing in the Bill, had given the public too large a credit for being as deeply converfant with the fubject as himfelf.

On the 15th of the month, his Majefty, after having given his royal affent to eighteen bills, made a gracious Speech from the Throne. In our principles of the conftitutional refponfibility of Minifters, the King's Speech is ever confidered as that of his Minifter; no wonder, then, that it contained fo pompous an eulogy of the *National Debt Bill*, upon which the marked difapprobation of the Chancellor had thrown fo much difcredit. " I have alfo obferved with the utmoft fatisfaction the meafures " which you have adopted for the diminution of the public " burdens, while you have at the fame time made additional " provifion for the reduction of the prefent national debt, and " eftablifhed a permanent fyftem for preventing the dangerous " accumulation of debt in future." His Majefty was alfo very emphatic in affuring his people, that it would be his principal care to preferve to them the uninterrupted bleffings of peace. He then prorogued the Parliament, to the 30th day of the enfuing Auguft.

After the refolute and pointed difapprobation by the Chancellor of fome of the favourite meafures of Adminiftration, it was not to be fuppofed, that the majority in the Cabinet fhould any longer expofe their plans to the condemnation of the man, in whofe integrity and judgment the nation had ever placed the moft unreferved confidence. The Parliament was now prorogued, and no immediate neceffity arofe for finding out a fuccessor to the woolsack; but for the sake of the equity of the nation, the Seals could not be kept up in the breast of the Minister, to await the doubtful close of the chapter of accidents, or the uncertain result of negociation, till the next meeting of Parliament. Accordingly, on the 15th of the month, his Majesty constituted Sir James Eyre, Sir William Ashhurst, and Sir John Wilson, Lords Commissioners for the custody of the Great Seals of England.

The war between France and Austria was carried on with various success in Flanders, in the different skirmishes which happened, though nothing decisive was even attempted by either party: disturbances, in the mean time, of the most alarming nature convulsed the capital of France. On the 20th of the month, the department of Paris appeared at the bar of the National Assembly, and informed them, that a multitude of 100,000 persons of both sexes, armed with pikes, swords, musquets, and even artillery, were marching towards the Thuilleries. They soon arrived, and were admitted to the bar of the Assembly, with ten or twelve pieces of cannon. They proceeded in order through the body of the Assembly, to the Caroufel, in front of the palace, repeating the civic oath as they went. Although there was a considerable military force in the palace, which could well have defended it; yet, to avoid confusion and bloodshed, about four o'clock the gates of the palace were thrown open, and immediately all the apartments were filled with the mob, to the number of more than 40,000. They placed the red cap of liberty upon the head of the King, forced him to drink out of a bottle to the health of the Nation, and grossly insulted him by the most insolent and audacious questions, assuring him that he should not long enjoy his pretended right to exercise the *veto*. The Queen, on this trying occasion, behaved with a dignified condescension, that extorted from the mob a respect and deference which was neither expected nor intended. The Mayor of Paris, with much difficulty, cleared the apartments about nine o'clock of the same night, without any further outrage having been committed. On the the 22d, his Majesty published a proclamation concerning the transactions of the 20th; in which he spiritedly represented to the Nation, that a misguided mob had, with artillery, rushed into the guard-room of the palace, broken open the doors of his apartments with axes, and endeavoured to extort from him his sanction to two decrees, which he had constitutionally refused to give; that though he were ready to sacrifice his personal repose, yet he never would sacrifice his duty, and was resolved to his last breath to afford the Constituted Authorities an example of courage and firmness, which could alone save the empire. This was followed by a cold proclamation from Petion, the Mayor of Paris, declaring that the laws ought to be respected, which prohibited the meetings of armed citizens. No enquiry was, however, instituted respecting the authors or the perpetrators of these outrages. The impunity of such public offenders bespeaks loudly the weakness or the malice of the magistracy.

In the course of this month some serious efforts were made in Ireland, to establish a political union between the body of Dissenters and that of the Roman Catholics. The former were highly indignant at the general system of government that had been carried on for years in the kingdom; the latter had long groaned under the galling pressure of the severest code of penal laws that had ever disgraced a Christian legislature, and they had been recently wounded by the most humiliating rejection of their petition to parliament, to be admitted to a participation of the elective franchise. Though the spiritual doctrines of the Presbyterian and the Roman Catholic widely differ from each other; yet such, fortunately, was their due sense of the difference between civil and religious obligations, such their improved ideas of the British (or Irish) Constitution, that one common view, one common interest, led them on to almost an enthusiastic co-operation in emancipating their country. They had both learned their respective parts of Mr. Grattan's political aphorism. *That the Irish Protestant should never be free, untill the Irish Catholic should cease to be a slave.* In the prefent fituation of the Britifh empire, and under the exifting circumftances of the Irifh nation, the difcontent and confequent irritation of three out of four millions of its inhabitants became an object of ferious alarm to Government, efpecially when there was a profpect of the body of the Diffenters coalefcing with this bulk of the nation. Such a coalition could not fail to give regular, preconcerted, and perhaps deep-planned movements to a body of men roufed into action merely by the forenefs of their prefent fufferings. There were not wanting men of folid thought, ftrong reafoning, and unfhaken determination to inftil into this vaft mafs of people, awaking from a long lethargy of inaction and wretchednefs, the pleafing and felf-convincing verities, that a free nation cannot be taxed that is not reprefented, nor bounden by laws, in the framing of which they do not concur.

By what particular manœuvre the coalition was for the prefent warded off, I cannot trace. Government was certainly very anxious to prevent it, though nothing, I believe, contributed fo much towards it, as the very warm part which the Diffenters openly took in the fucceffes of the French Revolutionifts, and the undifguifed predilection that fome of their lefs confiderate affociates profeffed for a republican form of government. Thefe fentiments ftaggered the generality of the Roman Catholics, the extent of whofe views went only to be admitted to an equal fhare of the exifting conftitution of government, from which they were excluded; but in no fhape to lend their affiftance to change or demolifh it, much lefs to frame a new one upon any other foundation.

The addrefs and policy with which the Irifh Roman Catholics conducted their efforts in every ftage to procure their freedom, have ever appeared to me truly admirable. They were fully fenfible that the frantic exceffes of the French Revolutionifts, and the unwarrantable exertions of their imitators and abettors within thefe kingdoms, had raifed an infeparable bar at at this time to every extenfion of liberty by way of reform or redrefs. They were fully aware, that Mr. Burke had founded the alarm, and *fortified and armed the benevolence of Government against the defperate enterprifes of innovation.* * *That he did not difcern how the prefent time came to be fo very favourable to all exertions in the caufe of freedom:* And they were too obferving not to remark the influence which Mr. Burke's books and principles had lately produced upon the nation. They therefore moft judicioufly committed the management of their concerns to Mr. Burke, jun. in order to fecure through their agent, the advice, the countenance, and the fupport of the father. Their moft fanguine expectations were gratified. They became exempted from his general ban and anathema againft innovators and reformers. And he was fatisfied, that the doctrines which the Roman Catholics applied to their own cafe, *though wide in their principles, were not meant to be carried further than they at firft pretended.* In a word, he wrote a moft liberal, ingenious, and eloquent letter to his friend, Sir Hercules Langrifhe, upon the reafonablenefs of the Roman Catholics' claim to the elective franchife; to the effects of which letter, perhaps, under God, that body of his countrymen owe the portion of liberty which they now enjoy. Thus fecured under the impenetrable *Ægis* of Mr. Burke's fanction, from any imputation of Gallic democracy in their efforts to procure their emancipation, they took the great work in hand, and proceeded in it with prudence, caution, and energy. They were gracioufly abfolved from the neceffity, in this inftance, of adopting the credence or following the example of their conductor and protector. They could not, like him, † *really think they lived in a free country*; nor *confider the treafure of their liberty, rather as a poffeffion to be fecured, than as a prize to be contended for.* The meafures which in this contention they purfued, will make the fubject of future pages, as they may occur in their refpective time and order.

* Reflections, p. 79.
† Reflections, p. 79.

CHAPTER IV.

JULY, 1792.

CONTENTS.

Defeat of Tippoo Sultan and peace in India—France declared in danger, and arms—Notification of the King to all the Powers of Europe—Particularly solicitous for the friendship of Great Britain—Their Ambassador's note to Lord Grenville—Evasive answer of our Court—Convention of Pilnitz—Death of Leopold—Francis declared Emperor—The Courts of Vienna and Berlin engage in open war against France—The declarations of their reasons for war. Manifestoes of the Duke of Brunswick—The principles of the Confederates in engaging in the war—Meeting and resolutions of the Scots meeting on the reform of the Burghs—Addresses upon the proclamation—Flying camp at Bagshot.

IF an unusual continuance of peace—if an un-interrupted enjoyment of power—if the unlimitted confidence of the sovereign and the people—if the daily increasing commerce, the brilliant termination of a successful war—if the very distresses of our neighbours gave additional strength to the arm of Government, they redouble also the obligation of Ministers to secure to the Nation, if not an increase, at least the continuance of the blessings which naturally flow from them.

Advices were during this month received of the signal victory gained by Lord Cornwallis over Tippoo Sultan, which produced overtures of peace from the latter: a cessation of arms between the two armies was fettled, and guaranteed by the tranfmiffion of the two fons of Tippoo to Lord Cornwallis as hoftages. By the definitive treaty of peace, three crores and thirty lacks of Sicca rupees were agreed to be paid to the allies, and one half of the dominions which had been in the poffeffion of Tippoo at the commencement of the war, were ceded to the allies adjacent to their refpective boundaries and agreeably to their election. Thefe conceffions were infifted upon and accepted by Lord Cornwallis, as effectual to preferve the future peace of India from being interrupted by Tippoo or any other power.

The political fituation of France, at this time, draws our attention to a vaft variety of circumftances, that in their confequences involve the deareft interefts of our own and every other kingdom of Europe. She was hitherto only engaged in war againft the Emperor. But the principles, or rather politics, which have fince produced the general federacy againft France, were from henceforth working a filent, though violent effect. The French forefaw the gathering ftorm, and adopted vigorous meafures to refift it. The legiflative body paffed a fet form of decrees, for arming the kingdom whenever it fhould be in danger, as they declared it then was. The King addreffed a letter to the National Affembly, to exhort them to internal peace and harmony, as the fure means of repelling the hoftile attacks of any foreign enemies. He fent a formal notification to all the powers of Europe, by which he difavowed and protefted againft all the acts which the French princes had done in his name, as to making loans of money, entering into negociations with foreign courts, and levying troops. He profeffed his attachment to the Conftitution, which he had freely accepted, and fworn to defend; and affured them of his determination to make ufe of all the force put into his hands againft the enemies of France, whatever pretexts might be employed to countenance the armed affemblies of the emigrants, or to fupport them in their hoftile proceedings. The minifter foon after announced to the Affembly the confederacy of Vienna and Berlin againſt their country, and that they would ſoon be attacked by an army of 150,000 men.

France had, on every occaſion ſince the commencement of its revolution up to this period, expreſſed the moſt anxious ſolicitude to preſerve a good underſtanding with this country. Nor were there any terms ſo humiliating or harſh, to which ſhe did not ever appear ready to ſubmit, in order to enſure this grand and primary object. Nothing can be more emphatically expreſſive of theſe ſentiments, than the note which M. de Chauvelin preſented upon this ſubject to Lord Grenville; in which, for preſerving the tranquillity of Europe, which would never be interrupted if France and England united to maintain it, the King of the French urges his Britannic Majeſty zealouſly to employ his good offices with his allies, to prevent them from granting to the enemies of France, directly or indirectly, any aſſiſtance. He complains of the meaſures taken by the court of Vienna to engage the Pruſſians in a quarrel foreign from their intereſts, and intimates that ſimilar attempts were ſucceſsfully made upon the republic of Holland. He further complains of the menaces employed to draw the different members of the Germanic body from that prudent neutrality, which their political ſituation and their deareſt intereſts preſcribe to them; and of the engagements taken with the different ſovereigns of Italy to determine them to commence hoſtilities againſt France : he laments the intrigues which have armed Ruſſia againſt the Conſtitution of Poland, and which announces a great conſpiracy againſt all free States, that threatens inevitably to plunge Europe into a general war. He invites him to employ in his wiſdom, and in the plenitude of his influence, the means compatible with the independence of the French Nation, to ſtop, whilſt yet it might be effected, the progreſs of this combination, which threatens equally the peace, the liberty, and the happineſs of Europe, and particularly to prevent from acceding to this combination, thoſe of his allies, whom the may wiſh to draw into it, or even thofe, who may already have been engaged in it by fear, artifice, and the different pretexts of a policy equally falfe and deteftable.

Whatever favourable difpofition our court might have felt towards the general armed confederacy, which it may ftill have thought prudent to diffemble, a lefs fatisfactory anfwer could not have been given to M. de Chauvelin's note. The raweft novice in politics will perceive an obvious difference between the interference with the internal affairs of an independent ftate, and the intermediation of a third power to prevent or clofe a rupture between contending fovereigns. The former as evidently incroaches upon the rights and independence of other fovereigns, as the latter acknowledges and recognizes them. The only fatisfaction, however, attempted to be given to this official note, was, " That the fame fentiments which engaged " his Majefty not to interfere with the internal affairs of France, " equally tended to induce him to refpect the rights and inde- " pendance of other fovereigns, and particularly thofe of his " allies." This evafive anfwer to the French ambaffador fufficiently befpoke the approbation with which England viewed the meafures of its allies againft France.

It has not hitherto, and perhaps never will be certainly known to the Public, what the direct and full purport was of that convention which was holden at Pilnitz, in the courfe of the year 1790. I fhall hazard no conjectures; but fhall conclude, that where I fee a vaft federative combination of great powers againft France, it muft have been formed at the only meeting which has taken place between the leading members of that confederacy, who from that time have co-operated in no other public meafures than thofe which they have purfued againft France.

The late Emperor Leopold finifhed his fhort reign by almoft a fudden death on the firft of March. Grievous fufpicions of French poifon had alfo been entertained upon his death, at fo very critical a moment; but an authentic narrative of his cafe did away that impreffion. He was fucceeded by his fon Francis I. who was proclaimed Emperor at Frankfort, on the 5th of July. The firſt act of his reign was to declare his cordial acceffion to the treaty of Pilnitz; and from henceforth the courts of Vienna and Berlin joined in public hoſtilities againſt France.

The court of Vienna publiſhed a declaration or manifeſto of the reafons which induced her to take up arms againſt France. The firſt of thefe regarded the nature of the protection afforded to the emigrants, which, through mifreprefentation, had given much umbrage to France. The next touched that fpirit of anarchy and violence now reigning in France, of which it had become neceffary for a concert of princes to check the progrefs, in order to oppofe the introduction of it into their ſtates. That it depended on thofe who reign at prefent over France to make this concert ceafe immediately, by refpecting the tranquillity and rights of other powers, and to *guarantee the effential bafis of the French monarchical form of Government* againſt the infringements of violence and anarchy. That France had fent an army of one hundred and thirty thoufand men to the borders of the Auſtrian Netherlands, whilſt Auſtria had not even ten thoufand men to defend them. In a word, that whilſt France was loudly complaining (without reafon) of other powers for interfering in the confequences of their new Conſtitution, they were endeavouring to fubvert all Governments, by fpreading all over Europe feduction and infurrection.

The King of Pruffia alfo publiſhed an expoſition of the reafons which had determined him to take up arms againſt France. His manifeſto was more diffufe than that of Auſtria, and entered more particularly into the fuppreffion and invafion of the rights and poffeffions of the German princes of Alface and Lorrain, and the violation of the treaties that united France to the German Empire. It particularly noticed the mifchievous confequences of propagating antimonarchical principles: and that the unprovoked attack of his ally, the King of Hungary and Bohemia, in his Belgic provinces, he looked upon as an invafion of the German Empire by French troops, and, confequently, as an unequivocal declaration of war by France againft his ally, with whom he had entered into a defenfive alliance.

Thefe acts or manifeftoes of the allied powers produced a confiderable fermentation at Paris. The country was publicly declared to be in danger: and the moft vigorous meafures were immediately adopted to recruit the army and ftrengthen the frontiers. A royal proclamation was publifhed, which fet forth in a very ftrong light the dangers to which the country was expofed. The confequence was a profufion of volunteers and recruits of all ages and qualities, pouring down upon the frontiers with the ardour of the moft frantic enthufiafm.

It is well known that Coblentz was the general rendezvous of all the French emigrants. Here they had affembled, to the number of near twenty thoufand; and the King of Pruffia, on his arrival, was received as their faviour. The natural vivacity of the French difpofition had already anticipated the reduction of their country to the unlimited power of their former monarch, and the whole ancient order of things. The reigning Duke of Brunfwick had the command of the combined armies, which were deftined for the great enterprife of invading France. But before he began his march from Coblentz, in order that the whole world might fully know the views and fpirit of his glorious miffion, he publifhed a declaration or manifefto, in his own name; in which he firft generally recapitulated the reafons which had induced the Emperor and the King of Pruffia to combine their forces againft France. " To thefe high interefts," fays he, " is " added another important object, and which both fovereigns " have moft cordially in view, which is to put an end to that " anarchy, which prevails in the interior parts of France; to " put a ftop to the attacks made on the throne and the altar; and " reftore to the king his legitimate power, &c." Then, as commander in chief of the two armies, he difavows any pretence to enrich themfelves by conqueft; and difclaims *any inten-*

tion to meddle with the internal Government of France. But in case of their making any resistance, when summoned to surrender, or when attacked; or of their not preventing conflagrations, murders, and pillage ; or of their removing the King and Royal Family from Paris ; or of their attempting to force or insult the palace of the Thuilleries ; or of their offering the least violence or outrage to their Majesties or the Royal Family : then does he fulminate his maledictions upon the devoted land; he denounces instant death to the rebels taken in arms; decapitation and confiscation to the members of the departments, districts, and municipalities; military execution to the members of the national assembly, magistrates, and all the inhabitants of Paris ; and total destruction to their guilty city.

Notwithstanding the raging fierceness of this thundering menace, the Duke of Brunswick was still haunted with the reproaching qualms of lenity ; and before a symptom of the effects of his first manifesto could be perceived, in less than forty-eight hours he sends forth a second to confirm and heighten the terror of the first; declaring besides, " that if, contrary to all expectation, by " the perfidy or baseness of some inhabitants of Paris, the King, " the Queen, or any other person of the Royal Family should be " carried off from that city, all the places and towns whatsoever, " which shall not have opposed their passage, and shall not have " stopped their proceedings, shall incur the same punishments as " those inflicted on the inhabitants of Paris ; and their route shall " be marked with a series of exemplary punishments, justly due " to the authors and abettors of crimes, for which there is no " remission."

However carefully the different parties to the convention of Pilnitz conceal from the eyes of curiosity and of interest, the origin, basis, and springs that set the vast federative machine in motion, yet cannot the public be blind to the measures they have actually pursued, nor ought the faithful annalist to lose sight of the principles upon which they profess to have entered into the federacy, upon which they boast of having undertaken and continued a moſt deſtructive war, and upon which they have ſucceeded in engaging this country, as well as moſt other powers of Europe, in the fatal alliance. Truth and juſtice are never at variance. All parties difavow the right, and diſclaim the intention of interfering with the internal Government of France; and in the fame breath, they inſiſt upon the abolition of that change in their internal Government which the nation had called for, and which the King himſelf had accepted and confirmed by oath. They dictate the mode and place in which theſe alterations are to be brought about, or new arrangements formed in the internal Government of the kingdom. They threaten to enforce the execution of their interfering mandates, not by the ſlow, cold, and inefficient procefs of criminal law; but by the bold energy of military juſtice, by the ſummary and indiſcriminate deſtruction of whole bodies, municipalities, towns, cities, departments, and provinces. No diſavowal of theſe principles has as yet been attempted by the confederated powers. Their inability indeed to reduce them to practice has been ſufficiently manifeſted. They boaſt of their meritorious aid in aſſiſting to check the confuſion and ſupprefs the anarchy of France. Thus did certain confederated powers force their officious ſervices upon Poland in 1773, to heal the ſufferings of that diſtracted kingdom; and they generouſly rewarded their own meritorious interference, by the difmemberment and partition of a great part of that unfortunate empire.

Great Britain had not hitherto appeared upon the ſtage in this eventful tragedy: her part, intended to be the principal and moſt intereſting of the piece, was cautiouſly reſerved for the latter ſcenes of the cataſtrophe: yet had the prompter (perhaps imprudently and prematurely) divulged too much of the ſpirit and intrigue of the plot: * *" If ever a foreign prince enters into France,*
" he muſt enter it as into a country of aſſaſſins. The mode of civi-
" lized war will not be practiſed; nor are the French, who act

---

* Burke's Letter to a Member of the National Aſſembly, p. 45.

" *upon the present system, entitled to expect it. All war which is*
" *not battle, will be military execution. This will beget acts of re-*
" *taliation from you; and every retaliation will beget a new re-*
" *venge. The hell-hounds of war on all sides will be uncoupled*
" *and unmuzzled.*" When a criminal is forewarned that there can be no remission for his crime, his remaining liberty will of course be used to ward of the threatened execution: he will be less delicate in the future means of self-preservation, than he had been in contracting the original guilt. What loss of blood have not these fatal menaces occasioned in France!

Notwithstanding the Burgesses of the royal Scotch Burghs had failed in their late attempts to bring their grievances under the consideration of the legislature, they could not thus abandon a cause which they knew to be founded in truth, and therefore entitled to justice. The steady perseverance of conscious rectitude is powerfully operative. The delegates from the different Burghs had met and deliberated for several days upon the subject at Edinburgh. The cool and constitutional spirit with which they proceeded in this grand work, was a most exemplary pattern for all persons labouring under grievances from which they think themselves entitled to be freed. On the 26th of the month, they thought proper to publish to the world at large the real views and motives for their undertaking to bring about this necessary reform in the Burghs: they were justly indignant at being represented (as the fashion had become) as turbulent and seditious men, aiming at the subversion of Government and the destruction of the Constitution. " The Convention," they say, " of Burgesses, met for the purpose of obtaining from the wis-
" dom and justice of the British legislature a reform in the in-
" ternal government of the royal Burghs of Scotland, think
" it their duty at this time to declare, that they entertain the
" most loyal attachment to our most gracious Sovereign and il-
" lustrious family, the deepest sense of the superior excellence of
" the British Constitution, to maintain for ever the principles
" on which it is established, and to defend it from every inno-

L

"vation by which it may in the flighteft degree be hurt or injured."

In this and the preceding months, addreffes upon the late proclamation were poured in from moft counties, boroughs, and towns in the kingdom. For a great part of this month, a flying camp of about five thoufand men was kept up on and about Bagfhot-Heath. The Duke of Richmond, who had projected the fcheme, was the commander in chief, and fignalized himfelf in this army by his attention to the difcipline of the men, and the feverity of the fervice which he made them undergo during this fhort campaign. It had been originally intended to have formed this camp before the 14th of the month, which was the anniverfary of the French federation; but whether it were apprehended, that fuch an appearance would argue an expectancy, and therefore infure fome riot or difturbance on that day, or that the neceffary camp equipage and other preparations were ftill incomplete, the day paffed over without a fhadow of turbulence throughout the nation. The expenfes of this encampment to the nation exceeded one hundred thoufand pounds. The Cabinet muft have known how near we were to an actual war, and were confequently impreffed with a due fenfe of the advantages of manœuvring five thoufand men for a fortnight to prepare them for actual fervice, and to inure them to the hardfhips of a continental campaign, by anticipating fome of the more common wants of water and other neceffaries on the arid heath of Bagfhot.

CHAPTER V.

AUGUST, 1792.

CONTENTS.

Case of Poland—Effects of Brunswick's manifesto in Paris—The King's letter to the Assembly—Proposals for deposing the King—The Elector of Cologne and Duke of Wirtemburgh join the confederacy—Pacific declarations of Great Britain—The impolicy of the combined Princes in proclaiming Louis insincere in accepting the Constitution—La Fayette denounced and acquitted—Jacobins move the question of the King's deposition—The horrors of the 10th of August—The King confined in the Temple—Lord Gower, the Ambassador, leaves Paris—Proposal for a National Convention—Fresh declarations of the belligerent Powers—March of the Prussians into France—Capture of Longwy—Surrender of Verdun—Mr. Pitt made Lord Warden of the Cinque Ports—Le Brun the French Minister states the dispositions of all the European powers towards France—Accession of the Landgrave of Hesse Cassel to the federacy.

WHATEVER may have been the particular stipulations of the different contracting parties in the convention of Pilnitz, it is certain that the basis of their agreement must have been some general and fundamental principle, in which they all concurred. The King of Prussia is openly acknowledged to have been a principal party in that federacy; the Czarina was also known to have acceded to it, though she had as yet taken no public measure which unequivocally bespoke her engagement. It is a fair deduction, then, that a principle of action in which both these powers have openly joined, so far from militating against the spirit of that convention, actually made an essential part of that formidable and hitherto mysterious concert of Princes. For the credit of the cause and the honour of the reigning sovereigns of Europe, let it be presumed, that no principles against the increase or stability of civil freedom formed the basis of that confederacy. Yet the lamentable case of the virtuous Polanders overpowers the mind with awful hesitation. The subscription which was set on foot about this time in England for the support of the Polish Revolution, justifies my introducing this subject; though this country has as yet taken no public step either to prevent or ensure their subjugation to a foreign yoke. The liberality of Britons towards their distant brethren, struggling in this glorious cause of civil freedom, bespeaks a zeal for liberty, which ought to be cherished and encouraged, as the very *nucleus* of the British Constitution. The views of the Conventioners at Pilnitz probably extended to all Europe, though they have hitherto been mysteriously kept behind the curtain. The actual destruction of the Polish Constitution, and the powerful efforts to crush that of France, too strongly bespeak an intention or a wish to weaken and destroy every Constitution which might enjoy a larger portion of freedom, than these federated sovereigns were disposed to measure out to the multitude.

Even the counter-revolutionary Mr. Burke has done justice to the glorious event of the Polish Revolution. * " Here was
" a state of things, which seemed to invite and might perhaps
" justify bold enterprises and desperate experiment. But in what
" manner was this chaos brought into order? The means were
" as striking to the imagination, as satisfactory to the reason and
" soothing to the moral sentiments. In contemplating that
" change, humanity has every thing to rejoice, and to glory in;
" nothing to be ashamed of, nothing to suffer; so far as it is
" gone, it probably is the most pure and *defecated* public good,

* Appeal, p. 102

" which ever has been conferred on mankind." Scarcely had Poland and its patriotic sovereign begun to taste the blessings of their happier regeneration, when the imperious Catharine, without a shadow of pretence (unless from the approximation of liberty, which she never meant to admit into her empire), invades the republic with an army of sixty thousand men, and threatens to back them in case of resistance with an additional force of ninety thousand. The Polanders, not conceiving that the internal regulation of their Government could afford any pretence to a foreign power to make war upon them, and having no hostile designs upon any of their neighbours, had totally neglected even to think of warlike preparations, Encouraged, however, by their truly heroic prince, they made a most resolute stand against these despotic invaders, and, under a great inferiority of numbers and discipline, gained some very signal and brilliant advantages. The King, however, finding the contest to be so very unequal, was unwilling to oppress his beloved subjects for resources, which now began to fail him. That same benevolent disposition which had prompted him to co-operate in the Revolution, now urged him to spare the fruitless effusion of his subjects' blood; he summoned a council of all the Deputies that were then at Warsaw, and communicated to them the last dispatches from the Empress, which peremptorily insisted upon absolute and unqualified submission. He particularly grounded the necessity of their submitting upon the unprovoked but irresistible union of Austria and Prussia with Russia, to subdue, if not to dismember, and divide their kingdom. From henceforth that unfortunate country was degraded again into her former slavery, and may thenceforth be looked upon as a province to the Russian Empire.

Since Great Britain is now in alliance with Prussia, it will be highly proper to remark, that the latter had also entered into a defensive alliance with Poland so lately, as on the 23d of April 1790: by which it had been expressly stipulated, " That the " contracting parties should do all in their power to guaran-

" tee and preferve to each other reciprocally the whole of the
" territories which each other then poffeffed. That in cafe of
" menace or invafion from any foreign power, they fhould affift
" each other with their whole force, if neceffary. That if any
" foreign power whatever fhould prefume to interfere in the
" internal affairs of Poland, his Pruffian Majefty fhould confi-
" der this as a cafe falling within the meaning of the alliance,
" and fhould affift the republic according to the tenor of the
" foregoing article, that is, with his whole force." * It will be
be readily fuppofed, that Poland, upon the firft intimation of
hoftilities, claimed from the court of Berlin the performance of
a treaty fo recently entered into, with the exprefs view of up-
holding the Conftitution, which they were then framing. But his
Pruffian Majefty, in anfwer to their application, told them that the
treaty was dated previous to the new Conftitution, which had
eftablifhed a new order of things, and that therefore he held himfelf
abfolved from his engagement. It interefts us alfo to know, that
his Pruffian Majefty had been confidentially confulted about the
formation of the new Conftitution of Poland, and that he had
actually fuggefted and recommended fome of the obnoxious acts,
which the Emprefs complained of, in her declaration againft the
Poles; and that when the new Conftitution of Poland was propofed to his Majefty he gave not the flighteft intimation, that
the new order of things would diffolve his alliance: fo far from it,
that on the 17th of May, 1791, Mr. Goltz, the *chargé des affaires*
from Berlin, was commiffioned formerly to announce to his
Polifh Majefty, the King of Pruffia's entire approbation of the
new arrangement in Poland. In the federative fpirit of this age

---

* Thofe who juftify our prefent war againft France by the refpect
we owe to treaties, will do well to examine, what we are bound by
treaties to do for Poland and Dantzic, particularly as to the pro-
tecting and preferving them whole and entire, &c. Vide Treaty
of Oliva, and thofe of 1436, 1474, 1631, 1655, 1659, 1707,
1729, &c.

of open and secret alliances, the *aptitude* of the contracting parties to perform their engagements is not the last nor the least object of diplomatic attention.

In tracing the facts and events which naturally arrest the observation of an historian, it becomes frequently necessary to recal the attention of his reader to the spirit and principles from which they proceed. In the beginning of this month, Europe beheld more than three hundred thousand men in the field, with the avowed view of supporting or subverting the Revolution of France. It must be remembered at the same time, that the Government of France was founded upon a limited monarchy; that this situation of France had given rise to the Convention of Pilnitz, had excited the philippics of Mr. Burke, and the indignation and execration of this country against that system, armed Prussia and the Empire, and cemented many private confederacies amidst subordinate powers, which the uncertainty of the grand issue still keeps locked up in prudential secrecy.

No sooner was the manifesto of the Duke of Brunswick received in Paris, than immediately the King wrote a letter to the National Assembly, expressive of his surprise and contempt of the performance, of his general love of peace, his sincere attachment to the Constitution, and his determined resolution to oppose the hostile efforts of the combined powers. The mischievous effects of this manifesto upon France are without measure or calculation. The King's letter was read in the Assembly, and a motion for sending it to the eighty-three departments was rejected. It was urged by Isnard and Thuriot to be be a mass of falsehood and insincerity, and that, in the present moment of alarm and danger, his known duplicity ought not to be trusted. At this moment were admitted to the bar of the Assembly the Envoys from the Commonalty of Paris, with Petion at their head, who demanded, in the name of the forty-eight sections, that the King should be excluded from the throne, and that the management of affairs during the interregnum should be entrusted to responsible ministers, until a new King should be elected by a National Convention. He recapitulated every circumstance, from the beginning of the Revolution, that could render the King odious and suspected by the Nation: that he too had taken a part against them in the Convention of Pilnitz, and was indefatigable in his attempts to bring about a counter-revolution. His speech, which was in writing, was delivered in to the President; but the Assembly came to no resolution upon it. In the evening of the same day, the King sent to acquaint the Assembly, that the Elector of Cologne and the Duke of Wirtemburgh had joined the armed confederacy.

On the ensuing day (August 4th) the marine committee demanded, that thirty-three sail of the line should be put into commission, in consequence of the reports of a British armament. But the Assembly rejected the application, thinking it unwise to provoke Great Britain to hostilities, after she had so recently renewed her assurances of neutrality to their ambassador. A fleet at sea and a camp, in time of peace, are not very usual sights in England: however, the Cabinet of Saint James spoke peace; and the ruling power in France gave ready credit to what it earnestly wished. The Jacobins had now acquired a decided ascendancy over the mob; and they were resolved to profit of the existing circumstances, to crush all the constituted powers. This may with propriety be called the opening scene of that dreadful tragedy of blood and horrors, the final catastrophe of which we still look up to with shuddering dread. Without flying out with Mr. Burke into enthusiastic execrations of the new Constitution of France, it must be allowed, that the small portion of power allotted by it to the supreme executive power, was but ill calculated to ensure permanency to so vast a machine. The wish and design of ruining the benevolent and ill-fated Louis XVI. could but proceed from the malice of the murderous Jacobins; but a prime intent of this history is to examine how far the conduct of the concerted princes may have provoked, forwarded, multiplied, and prolonged the barbarous enormities of those cruel men. Insulting to humanity would be the feeling for the sufferers of the prefent calamities, which was not active in bringing about a fpeedy and lafting end to their miferies.

All the meafures of the Jacobin party in France have been planned with the moft artful precautions, as they have been executed with the moft ferocious refolutenefs. Whatever may have been the principles or the plans of the princes fettled at Pilnitz, we are now to look for their effects in the open and concerted meafures of the leading parties of that convention. The unfortunate Louis had been unaccountably (if not bafely) abandoned by the bulk of the French nobility, who had embodied and embarked openly with the combined powers againft France. Whatever remained of refpectability in the nation, if they did not, like the emigrant nobility, wifh for the complete reftitution of the ancient defpotifm, yet they were more fanguine to give permanency to a Conftitution, which fhould enfure them a limited and hereditary monarchy in the perfon of their beloved fovereign. Thefe latter were more formidable to the Jacobins than the former. Both the Emigrants and Conftitutionalifts, though they cordially defpifed and execrated each other, yet agreed in the common wifh to preferve the dignity and fafety of their fovereign, whom the Jacobins were determined to ruin. They profited of the fatal errors and folly of the combined powers, who, by their proclamations, had unequivocally afferted, that *the King was not fincere in accepting the Conftitution.* The truth or falfity of the affertion was of little import. It fufficed for the Jacobins to hold him out to the nation as combining with foreign powers to reduce France by force of arms either to a ftrange yoke, or to worfe than their ancient flavery. Whatever party in France might have ftill wifhed, with the emigrant nobility, for the re-eftablifhment of the ancient unqualified power of the Crown, could not avow themfelves abettors of the immediate caufe of the enemies who were marching into the kingdom in open war. All thofe who had fworn to fupport the Conftitution, were by their oath committed to defend it, againft thofe who by an open armed confederacy were attempting to deftroy it. Thus,

M

by this ill-judged and fatal declaration, the real cause of royalty in France was irretrievably deprived of the possibility of any open or efficient support. If the assertion were true, it could but add comfort, not encouragement to a party awed and terrified into absolute inactivity: if it were false, it could but animate the real and respectable friends of the unfortunate monarch, to exert their efforts against the avowed and armed enemies of his limited powers, who countenanced and supported the abettors of his ancient unqualified authority. By the direct spirit of this armed confederacy was the ill-fated Louis deprived of any possible support either from the devotees to the old aristocracy, or the promoters of a temperate system of liberty. Thus the triumphant Jacobins found no force bold enough to withstand them, no influence sufficiently powerful to supprefs them.

The system was now brought to its crisis. The general La Fayette, who, from a real love of liberty, and not from any design or even apprehension of mischief to his country, had risqued his life and sacrificed his fortune in the cause of the Revolution, became suspected of incivism; in other words, was known to disrelish the violent and destructive plans of the Jacobins. He was accordingly denounced to the Assembly, but upon several divisions was honourably acquitted. The acquittal of this enemy of the Jacobins fermented the disappointed party into a paroxysm of despair. They unsheathed the sword, threw away the scabbard, and determined to try their force upon the desperate and decisive question of the King's deposition. No attempts of bribery, seduction, or intimidation were left untried. The falling monarch, on the 7th of the month, made his last proclamation to his subjects, which breathes the purest sentiments of a patriot King. It appeared to produce no other effect than to afford the Jacobins a fresh opportunity of holding him out to the multitude, as coalescing with the armed confederacy against the liberties of the nation.

The grand and fatal question of deposition or forfeiture stood for the 9th of the month; but the agitation of the public mind.

in Paris was too great to permit the queſtion to be fairly diſcuſſed in the Aſſembly. The purport of this hiſtory will not allow me to detail the awful and terrific events of the 10th of Auguſt, when the Thuilleries were aſſailed by the ferocious and armed mobs of the federates of Marſeilles, and deſperadoes of Paris; when the King was inveigled to quit his palace, and ſeek an aſylum for himſelf and his family in the perfidious arms of the Aſſembly; when he withdrew in his perſon from his moſt faithful ſupporters, the animating object of loyalty, and the ſanctioning ſolace of deſperate defence; when the faithful friends and body guards of this unfortunate monarch were ſacrificed in defending the deſerted ſtation of their affrighted or confuſed ſovereign; when the ferocity of a barbarous mob had been ſatiated with the bloody inſults upon the mangled corpſes of their fellow-citizens; when the declining glories of the French monarchy ſet beneath the portentous horizon of confuſion, ſlaughter, and deſtruction.

The confuſion conſequent upon the horrors of the 10th of Auguſt, continued for ſome time, and many atrocities were daily committed upon individuals. The National Aſſembly declared the King ſuſpended, and that both he and his whole family ſhould remain as hoſtages to the nation: they were accordingly committed under a ſtrong guard to the Temple, from whence there was no poſſibility of eſcape. Upon the depoſition of the King, the Britiſh Ambaſſador the Earl of Gower left Paris, having made as public a declaration, as circumſtances would permit, of friendſhip and neutrality on the part of his Court.

In order to render this change in the internal Government of France palatable and permanent, it was thought expedient to invite the French Nation to form a National Convention: accordingly the conditions for its formation were ſettled and publiſhed: and ſoon after a very minute and elaborate declaration (prepared by Condorcet) was circulated through all the departments, as an expoſition of the motives upon which the French National

Assembly had proclaimed the convocation of a National Convention, and pronounced the suspension of the executive power in the hands of the King.

All the belligerent powers presuming or pretending that they were carrying on *a war of principle*, wearied the public with declarations and manifestos, that generally set forth a partial detail or aggravated account of the measures and proceedings of the adverse parties, and seldom failed to expose their own cause by some gross inconsistency or notorious falsity. Thus, a fresh manifesto of the Emperor and King of Prussia concludes, by their solemn declaration to *Europe*, that in the just war they had undertaken, they expresly renounce all personal views of aggrandizement; and, to France, that they meant not to interfere with its internal administration: but that they were resolved to re-establish order and give protection to those who should submit to the King, (who was not deposed at the time this was written); to punish, in a striking manner, all resistance to their arms; to deliver up Paris to the most terrible justice, if any attempt of violence should be offered to any of the Royal Family; and to secure an establishment for the King and his family, and brothers, in some frontier town of his kingdom, from whence he might exercise his *ancient right and powers*, and effectually render the kingdom again submissive to his supreme authority.

The declaration of the Princes, which appeared within a few days after this manifesto, was an inflated philippic and ostentatious menace, little calculated, alas! too sooth the irritation of their incensed countrymen. In order to gain credit, and secure their confidence, they assure them, that they had left the kingdom, not so much from a desire for their own personal safety as that of the King. *The emigration from our country, was to make ourselves the safeguard of his Majesty.* They recapitulate and confirm the manifesto of the Emperor, and King of Prussia, and of their hero the great Duke of Brunswick. They introduce upon the scene new parties to the confederacy, that hitherto were not publicly known to have acceded to it; " the Kings " of the House of Bourbon, our auguſt couſins: our much " honoured father-in-law, the Neſtor of ‘ Sovereigns : the He- " roine of the North, our ſublime protectreſs: and the young " heir of the unfortunate Guſtavus." They re-echo the proteſ- tation of all theſe confederated Sovereigns againſt interfering with the internal government of the kingdom, and declare that; under their auſpices, their only object is to reſtore the ancient (unlimited) Monarchy, the ancient laws, manners, &c.

All the plans for the campaign having been ſettled, the Pruſ- ſian troops began their march from Triers, on the 11th of the month; and, by the end of it, Longwy, a ſmall, but well forti- fied town, had ſurrendered to General Clairfait, who commanded an army of about ſixteen thouſand men; it was bombarded for about fifteen hours. Some accounts ſtate, that the garriſon con- ſiſted of one thouſand five hundred; others of three thouſand five hundred men. Verdun was alſo ſummoned, and ſurren- dered to the Duke of Brunſwick, without reſiſtance. The Governor of Longwy was accuſed of having delivered up the town through treachery. The Governor of Verdun was com- pelled to do it by the inhabitants: but he would not ſurvive the diſgrace, and ſhot himſelf with a piſtol.

The adminiſtration of Mr. Pitt has ever been remarked for the frequent occaſions which he had enjoyed of extending his patronage to his friends. Such of them, in particular, who, by his bounty, were removed from the precarious ſtate of ex- pectancy, became urgent with their diſintereſted patron to ſecure, at leaſt, ſome proviſion of independence for himſelf, againſt the evil day of change or retribution. With much difficulty was he prevailed upon to break through his maiden vows of diſin- tereſtedneſs, and accept of the appointment of the Lord War- den of the Cinque Ports, lately vacant by the death of the Earl of Guildford.

Towards of the cloſe of this month, M. le Brun, the French miniſter for foreign affairs, in order to tranquillize the agitated minds of that nation, thought it advisable to lay before them their real situation, with respect to foreign powers. He stated, that Sweden was unequivocal in declaring its neutrality, and marked intention not to enter into the general league of powers against France : that Russia had been able to do no more than threaten, though she did not attempt to disguise her hostile intention: that Spain, Naples, and Sardinia were in the like situation: that the generality of the Germanic Body showed a firm reluctance to take arms against France : and that Holland and England never ceased to promise the most perfect neutrality. Such were the avowed views and open professions of these different powers: it was, however, remarked, that about this very time the Landgrave of Hesse acceded to the confederacy, and headed a body of seven thousand and ten Hessians, with a large train of artillery, to Treves. It was not credited that the Landgrave, even on this occasion, went out of his accustomed line of mercenary service: but it was generally believed, that this body of troops was paid for, by some of the powers of Europe, whose adverse wishes and hostile intentions towards France were kept concealed behind their public protestations of neutrality and forbearance.

In this general convulsion of the principal powers of Europe, the British Cabinet was in reality, or affected to be, under as little alarm or concern as if the affairs on the Continent could not even remotely affect the fate of the British Empire. The several members of administration were dispersed over the country, as widely as their different pleasures and pursuits could separate them. Mr. Pitt, however, as Lord Warden of the Cinque Ports, remained chiefly at his newly acquired castle of Walmer on the Kentish coast ; where the couriers from the Continent had occasionally orders to call in their route to town.

CHAPTER IV.

SEPTEMBER, 1792.

CONTENTS.

Effects of the Duke of Brunswick's manifesto, at Paris—Precautions taken by the Jacobins, before the massacres of September— Massacre of some thousands at Paris—Thionville besieged—Infamous treatment of the French emigrants—Proscription of the French clergy—Their reception and humane support in England —The reasons of their exile—National Convention established— Doctor Priestley and Mr. Paine chosen members—Paine examined at Dover, by the custom-house officers—Inaction and distresses of the Prussian army—The Duke of Brunswick proposes an armistice—Conferences with Dumourier—Sardinia invaded —Chamberry and Nice taken—Government of Ireland—Roman Catholics' petition rejected by Parliament—Their delegation and congress—Opposed by the Grand Juries, &c.—This an attempt to overawe the Sovereign and Legislature.

THE surrender of Verdun to the summons of the Duke of Brunswick, seems to have completed the delirium of rage which his thundering manifesto had given rise to. Paris became a scene of alarm and agitation: the ruling demagogues seized the moment of terror, to hurl destruction upon their domestic enemies; and artfully converted the threats of the confederated powers into the ready ministers of their own bloody vengeance. The fatal prediction was recalled to their minds, " * that if ever a foreign prince enter into France, he must enter it as into a conntry

* Burke, ubi supra.

of aſſaſſins. The mode of civilized war will not be practiſed; nor are the French who act on the preſent ſyſtem entitled to expect it." The confirmation of it was enforced upon them from the Prince's manifeſtos, and its verification detailed in the moſt exaggerated accounts of Pruſſian maſſacres, barbarities, and cruelties. The Duke of Brunſwick was repreſented as having paſſed Chalons: the leſs firm were intimidated with the idea of his immediate arrival at Paris, to execute his threatened vengeance upon that devoted city. The general diſmay, terror, and confuſion of the capital, ſupplied the ſanguinary Jacobins with eaſy means of glutting themſelves in the blood of all thoſe whoſe rectitude or virtue ſtood in the way of their tyrannous and licentious deſigns. The community of Paris decreed the gates of the city to be ſhut; ſummoned all citizens to arms; then, under pretence of ſearching for arms and ammunition, they inſtituted domiciliary viſits, which afforded an opportunity, in the dead of the night, of forcing away from their beds, to priſons, thoſe perſons whoſe known virtues might ſecure them reſpect and influence upon the public: and, horrid to relate! in the courſe of three days, they murdered, without accuſation or defence, in cold blood, ſome thouſands; amongſt whom were ſeveral of the moſt learned, reſpectable, and virtuous ſubjects, particularly of the clergy, of that once flouriſhing kingdom of France! Some few, who had been confined to priſon on the 10th of Auguſt, were alſo the unhappy victims of this general execution; amongſt theſe was the Princeſs Lamballe, whoſe head was carried upon a pike to the Temple, to terrify and ſhock the royal priſoners. If any circumſtance can add horror to deeds of ſuch atrocity, it was the cool, premeditated, and inſulting manner, in which they were perpetrated. The murderers impanelled a mock jury of twelve of their accomplices, before whom the wretched victims were called out in order, and underwent a ſort of ſummary examination for ſome ſeconds: the verdict or judgment generally pronounced was, *He muſt be ſet at liberty*; which was the word of command to uſher the unfortunate priſoner into the outward apartment, where he was immediately affaffinated by a band of ruffians, who were paid for their deeds of blood at the rate of twelve livres per head. In order to check inquiry, and prevent detection, the mangled corpfes were immediately ftripped of their clothes, their pockets rifled, and were then regularly carried off in carts, which had been previoufly engaged for this fervice. The favage regularity in the execution, befpeaks a preconcerted fyftem in this bloody tragedy, from perfons above the immediate perpetrators of the foul deeds. There appears not a doubt, but that the horrors of the 10th of Auguft, and the atrocities of the 2d, 3d, and 4th of September proceeded from the fame fource. In reflecting with indignation and horror upon thefe more than favage barbarities, we cannot form a conjecture where fo many hired affaffins fhould be found to perpetrate the atrocious deeds, at which a common executioner would have fickened and recoiled; we are loft in aftonifhment, that 400,000 nervelefs Parifians, petrified with fear and terror, fhould have permitted thefe murders to have been committed, without interruption, for three days fucceffively. But we can never fufficiently lament, that the mercilefs Jacobins, who gloried in wading to their tyrannous ends through the beft blood of their fellow-citizens, fhould have been fupplied by the confederates with the only fure means of executing their fanguinary project. They magnified their dangers from the external enemy; they totally fubdued the cowed fpirits of the effeminate Parifians, by convincing them that the Duke of Brunfwick was on the point of realizing his vindictive menaces of demolifhing their city, of delivering up all its inhabitants to military execution, and of oppreffing the piteous relicts of his faturated vengeance with a worfe than their ancient defpotifm. In weak and depraved minds, even the diftant view of perfonal danger eafily works off the fympathetic horror of feeing others fuffer. Thus artfully did thefe determined Jacobins impofe upon the affrighted multitude, a folicitude only to ward off the menaced carnage and devaftation of their confederate enemies. Mr. Burke has wifely faid, *that there is a boundary to men's paffions* when they act from feeling; none when they are under the influence of imagination.

It is foreign from the purpose of this History to follow the motions and successes of the combined armies, to which, as yet, Great Britain had not openly acceded. But its prime end requires me to trace, in the actions of the united sovereigns, those principles of their confederacy, which they still conceal behind the veil they had drawn over them at Pilnitz; but which must influence their conduct in the prosecution of the war, as well as the conduct of all other powers that have since become parties to the grand alliance. Dumourier, who commanded the French army, with very inferior force, contrived to prevent the progress of the enemy, and to defeat every view that had brought the combined armies into the field. The small town of Thionville was besieged, in vain, for several weeks, by the Prince Hohenloe and the chief body of the French emigrants: at this siege did these unfortunate men first find reason to lament the cause they had embarked in. Every circumstance of the war called upon their services before all others; and it would be injustice to them not to allow, that the checking of their ardour was one of the greatest humiliations they were reduced to submit to. They offered to reduce the town by themselves, if the commander in chief would supply them with proper ordnance for the siege. This was refused, and during the whole of the campaign they were constantly kept in the back ground in the most inglorious and mortifying inaction. They received no pay during their service; were disbanded at the close of the disgraceful campaign; were pillaged by the Prussian soldiery, though a part of the King of Prussia's army, and were most inhumanly excluded from the cartel for the exchange of prisoners. Having no mercy to expect from their countrymen, they had the stronger claim upon the protection of the sovereign under whose banner they were fighting. Some few, who had been surprised by the enemy, were taken and actually executed like common malefactors. This treatment of the French emigrants was little calculated to give tranfparency to the veil of the myfterious Convention of Pilnitz: it befpeaks fomething more deep and dark in the confederacy, than the public has as yet perceived or perhaps fufpected.

The execution of the decree for banifhing all the nonjuring clergymen to Guiana, who fhould not have quitted the kingdom in fourteen days from the paffing of that decree, poured thoufands of thefe venerable exiles from Normandy, Picardy, and Britanny, upon our coafts of Kent and Suffex. Mifery and diftrefs give the fufferers a full claim to the humanity of Englifhmen. Such is the amiable and juft tribute all pay to our countrymen. The tendernefs and benevolence with which thefe diftreffed exiles were received upon their landing, impreffed them with unexpected ideas of Britifh fympathy: every where they were welcomed, cheered, comforted, and relieved. The old rivality of the two Nations were forgotten, and our difference from that very religion, for which they were perfecuted, was fwallowed up in the general philanthrophy for our fuffering brethern. Never was an opportunity of exercifing heroic charity more eagerly embraced; never was benevolence conferred with more glowing fenfibility, nor received with more dignified gratitude. In the prefent melancholy variety of wretchednefs, with which, it feems, Heaven vifits moft regions of the civilized world, it will not, furely, be imputed to the prefumption of this country, that they look up with confidence to an all-merciful Being to deal out his vengeance more fparingly upon the land that has been the afylum of fuch venerable victims of prefecution. The public and private donations, upon which thoufands of thefe refpectable exiles have fubfifted in this country, fince their profcription from France, fufficiently befpeak the intereft which the Nation takes in their fufferings. Though the naked plea of wretchednefs be a precept to Britifh philanthrophy, it is but juftice to this perfecuted clergy, to apprize their benefactors of the motives and neceffity of their exile.

The test proposed to them was an oath to submit to *the civil constitution of the Clergy.* The nature and tendency of this oath has been grossly misconceived, and maliciously misrepresented, by many; to the great prejudice of those who have refused to subscribe to it. The *philosophizing* party in France, who grounded their success in abolishing every idea of Christian revelation upon the previous destruction of all the respectable clergy, were too refined to unmask their designs till the people were prepared for so daring an attempt. They knew that religion could not long survive the destruction of Church Government; and therefore, under the sanctimonious pretence of reducing it to its ancient form, they artfully transferred to the *civil* power the whole *pure spiritual jurisdiction,* which the Christian Church has uniformly, through all ages, maintained to be holden immediately of Christ, and to be transcendent to, and independent of all temporal authority. This self-created *lay* power assumed the right of deposing, displacing, and suspending from all *spiritual* powers and faculties both the Bishops and inferior clergy; of curtailing and enlarging the limits of their spiritual jurisdiction; of abolishing the old and creating new bishopricks and parishes; of conferring, by their election, the power and right of exercising the ministry of the Gospel; of superseding the authority of the Holy Councils, and annulling the primacy of jurisdiction, which, as Roman Catholics, they admitted in the Bishop of Rome. To subscribe, then, to the oath of submission to this *civil constitution of the Clergy,* was, in effect, to deny the *divine* establishment of a church upon earth; it was to renounce the spiritual hierarchy by which it has been and ever will be maintained; it was to allow that the spiritual power and jurisdiction, which they had hitherto exercised over their flocks, were usurped or invalid; it was to admit, that a self-constituted *lay* tribunal could annihilate those powers which it had not given, and absolve the flocks from their obedience to their lawful pastors; it was to subject the divine mission and ministry of the Gospel to all the changes and fluctuations of temporal governments; it was to raife the intrigues, paffions, and artifices of popular demagogues and tyrants, above the authority of œcumenical councils of the church; it was to fubftitute a profane and impious proftitution of their facred characters to *lay* ufurpers, in lieu of that fubmiffion to the fupreme Bifhop of Rome, by and through which (in the Roman Catholic tenets) they hold communion with the univerfal Church of Chrift upon earth. Such is the oath, for the recufancy of which the nonjuring clergy of France have been perfecuted, as refractory and rebellious; for which hundreds have been already martyred in that kingdom, and for which thoufands in this and many other countries of Europe have emulated the conftancy of the primitive Chriftians, in giving luftre and dignity to the fufferings they undergo for their faith. It will be well for the modern liberal deriders of fanaticifm, and fcoffers at prieftcraft, to review impartially the horrid impieties, the blafphemous atrocities with which the profane mifcreants of France, fince the expulfion of their confcientious clergy, feem to have braved the vengeance of the Almighty. The crimes and offences of the abandoned flocks proclaim the glorious eulogies of their perfecuted paftors.

In vain is this refpectable clergy calumniated by their enemies, for having refifted the civil power, and lawful conftituted authorities of the State. It is notorious, that they had peaceably fubmitted to a reduction of their livings, little fhort of annihilation; that they offered their unequivocal fubmiffion to every change or alteration which the authorities for the time being fhould choofe to make in the *civil* eftablifhment of their religion, either by the abolition or fubtraction of tithes and other temporal poffeffions, by the repeal or annulling of their temporal dignities and civil immunities or otherwife, provided they would leave untouched and inviolate that facred depofit of faith, of which, with their *fpiritual jurifdiction* they had received the guardianfhip and truft, which they could only furrender into the hands from which they had received them; and which they could not of themselves transfer nor abandon but with their lives.

On the 21ft of this month the National Convention was formally declared to be conftituted, and the fecond National Affembly was of courfe diffolved. " Thus ended," fays Briffot, " after a year's exiftence, that ftormy legiflature under which " the public fpirit made fuch a rapid progrefs, and the French " nation marched with giant ftrides towards a republic." And thenceforth commences, what the French, in boafted confidence, term the reign of liberty and equality: what their enemies, in derifion and hatred, call that of anarchy and tyranny; what the unbiaffed obferver, in fear and trembling, beholds as the refiftlefs force of a mighty empire, vitiated to the heart, by the early infection of modern philofophy; provoked to the moft cruel outrages of human nature, by the vindictive menaces of its impotent oppofers; and forced into ftrength and permanency, by the perfidious declarations, the ill-judged plans, and worfe-directed operations of their open enemies. It was the boaft of the French, to have collected from the whole univerfe, into the National Convention, whatever talent and fpirit could be found to enlighten the intellects, invigorate the freedom, and enfure the welfare of mankind. From this country they felected the Rev. Dr. Prieftley and Mr. Thomas Paine. The former very prudently declined; the latter very eagerly accepted of the nomination. If Mr. Paine had been thought guilty of feditious or treafonable practices againft the State, and if Government had been defirous of checking the progrefs of the evils which they fo loudly complained of in their late proclamation, by the exemplary punifhment of the avowed fomenter of the mifchief, he certainly might eafily have been prevented from quitting the kingdom. His election for the department of Calais was well known in England; for the cuftom-houfe officers, immediately upon Meffrs. Paine's and Froft's arriving at the inn at Dover, in confequence of an information againft them, examined their baggage for prohibited articles. This ceremony was performed by the collectors in a manner totally unknown before in this country. They examined all their papers, sealed and unsealed; and upon their remonstrating with them upon the illegality of custom-house officers' seizing private papers, which were not things under their cognizance, they replied, that they were authorized to do it by the late proclamation. Pity it is, that the impotent resentment of government should be shown against such a man, in the illegal and unconstitutional acts of their officers, when the laws and constitution fully enabled them to punish the guilt of sedition or treason (if it existed), in the most awful and exemplary manner.

Whatever perfidious policy, or weak judgment, or self-diffidence, may have induced the Duke of Brunswick to decline giving battle to the enemy, no ingenuity can justify his leading an army of seventy thousand men into the most deserted part of the enemy's kingdom, without securing for them a proper supply of provisions, and a ready and safe retreat. Two months had not expired since this thundering menacer had by his manifestos announced on his arrival, death and destruction to all that should not submit to his summons. But now, alas! his army had but advanced a few leagues into the enemy's territory to its own destruction; it had drawn upon itself their contempt for its inaction, and their detestation from its rapaciousness, plunder, and pillage: it had been four days without bread, the want of which, drove the starved soldiers to the unwholesome food of unripe grapes. The wetness of the seasons, superadded to all other causes, produced in the Combined Army a general sickness, that is said to have proved fatal to every third man, particularly of the Prussians and Hessians, who ever signalized themselves by their adroitness in pillaging, and their voraciousness in devouring the fruits of their plunder. Within three days after the meeting of the National Convention, the Duke of Brunswick proposed an armistice, and desired a conference with the French General Dumourier. Under the peculiarity of the existing circumstances, it was natural for all parties to form surmises and hazard conjectures concerning the purport of this convention. But there again, as at Pilnitz, the public was not to be initiated into the facred myfteries. As, therefore, nothing certain refpecting the conference of the two Generals can be afferted, it behoves us to be more attentive to the fubfequent movements and operations which muft in their nature have reference to it.

The King of Sardinia, who was a party to the Convention of Pilnitz, and had uniformly and fyftematically oppofed the French Revolution in every ftage, was fuppofed by France to have entered into a frefh plan and confederacy to invade that country; they accordingly declared war againft him. General Montefquieu, with a confiderable army, marched into Savoy, and was foon invited to take poffeffion of Chamberry. About the fame time General Anfelme, fupported by Admiral Truguet's fquadron of nine fail of the line, entered and took poffeffion of the city and country of Nice.

In the prefent and preceding months the internal affairs of Ireland became pregnant with importance to the Britifh empire. The whole fyftem of Government in this kingdom has hitherto appeared to me a political paradox. It enjoys the fame Conftitution as Great Britain; and from the peculiar folemnity of their celebrating the annual commemoration of the Revolution of 1688, they appear to outrun, if poffible, our zeal in profeffing their attachment to the principles of this Revolution. And yet, fays Mr. Burke, * " I fhall not think that the deprivation
" of fome millions of people of all the rights of citizens, and
" all intereft in the Conftitution, in and to which they were
" born, was a thing conformable to the principles of the Revo-
" lution. Suppofing the principles to have been altogether
" the fame in both kingdoms, by the application of thofe prin-
" ciples to very different objects, the whole fpirit of the fyftem
" was changed, not to fay reverfed. In England it was the
" ftruggle of the great body of the people for the eftablifhment

* Letter to Sir Hercules Langrifhe, p. 40.

"of their liberties, against the efforts of a very small faction, who would have oppressed them. In Ireland it was the establishment of the smaller number, at the expense of the civil liberties and properties of the far greater part, and at the expense of the political liberties of the whole. It was, to say the truth, not a revolution, but a conquest." These great truths the Roman Catholics of Ireland had long felt, and were by the increasing liberality of the times, and the sanctioning authority of Mr. Burke, now emboldened openly to claim their rights arising out of them.

The national prosperity and welfare of Ireland has been retarded in proportion as the mass of the people has been kept, *on the principles of conquest*, in a state of servitude. But from the earnestness of some men in power to continue this system, there is but too much cause to lament, with Mr. Burke, that for any consideration it should be thought " necessary to deprive the body of the people, if they adhere to their old opinions, of their liberties, and of all their free customs, and to reduce them to a state of civil servitude." Perhaps it is not the least misfortune of Ireland, that those who are immediately intrusted with the administration of its government, should possess too large a share of the confidence of the British Cabinet. It is a notorious fact, that emoluments under Government to the amount of 150,000l. per annum, are enjoyed by the three families of Foster, Fitzgibbon, and Beresford. In the scale of the Irish government these carry a large preponderancy of patronage and influence. We question not the magnitude of the services, which their country has thus splendidly rewarded; but it is natural for such a coalition to be warm and even ingenious in preserving and strengthening their political power in the state. Any alteration of the system under which it was acquired must weaken and disperse it. The real principles of the British Constitution are peculiarly unfavourable to such monopolies; resistance then to the introduction of these principles in Ireland was to be expected.

In the courfe of the laft feffion of Parliament, the Roman Catholics had prefented a petition to the Houfe of Commons, to admitted to a participation in the conftitution of their native country, which had been indignantly rejected by the Houfe. The Catholics were too fenfibly impreffed with the juftice of their claims to abandon them upon this treatment. At a numerous meeting of their body in Dublin, they voted thanks to thofe few members, who had afferted the fubjects' right to petition, and had fupported their application to Parliament; they came to a refolution of perfevering in the fame loyal and conftitutional courfe, which had hitherto been purfued for the removal of prejudices, and the attainment of that ineftimable privilege, without which all others are precarious and delufive, the right of elective franchife. There they figned a full and unequivocal declaration of their religious and civil tenets, in order to fatisfy their Proteftant brethren, that they held no principle whatfoever, incompatible with their duty as men, or as fubjects, or repugnant to liberty, whether political, civil, or religious. And that the complete fenfe of their whole body might be fairly collected, upon the choice and prudence of the meafures that fhould be adopted for effectuating this great end, a circular letter figned by Mr. Edward Byrne (the moft opulent merchant in Dublin), as Chairman of the Sub-Committee of the Roman Catholic body, was fent to every county in Ireland to choofe and appoint delegates from their refpective counties, to convene at Dublin, for the purpofe of framing a fuitable petition to his Majefty from the whole body, ftating all their grievances, and particularly praying for the right of the elective franchife, and an equal participation in the benefits of the trial by jury. This peaceable, legal, and conftitutional mode of acquiring the fenfe of the people aggrieved, in order to approach the Throne with proper energy and refpect, was too efficient a ftep towards procuring relief, not to alarm thofe whofe influence, power, and patronage muft decreafe in proportion as three fourths of the people fhould be admitted to the participation of the Conftitution.

On this occafion the oppofite junto, in their alarm, were as little delicate in their efforts to preferve, as they may have been in the means, of acquiring their power. Through moft counties, of the kingdom, the Grand Juries, upon which no Roman Catholic could ferve, were, by their intereft, eafily fo formed as to fall into the moft implicit adoption of their views and wifhes. The Lord Chancellor Fitzgibbon, whofe patrimonial eftates are in the county of Limerick, attended perfonally at the meeting of the Grand Jury, for that county; and Mr. Fofter, the Speaker of the Houfe of Commons, was Foreman of the Grand Jury of his own county of Louth, which iffued fimilar declarations, in which they expreffed, in the ftrongeft terms, their abhorrence of the *wicked and daring attempts* of circulating the letter figned by Mr. Byrne, which complains of a partial adminiftration of juftice, and of their being oppreffed to flavery, and which tended to roufe the Catholics to difturb the peace of the Kingdom, by the illegal and unconftitutional affociation of a Popifh Congrefs, in the metropolis, to overawe the legiflature. They, therefore, came to three refolutions: 1ft, That the national profperity depended upon the continuation of the Popery laws, particularly thofe which veft the right of Franchife in the Proteftants exclufively; and that fince thofe laws had been frequently called into operation, the progrefs of the national profperity had been more vigorous and rapid. 2dly. That the allowing to Roman Catholics the right of voting for members to ferve in Parliament, was deftructive of the conftitution, and fettlements of the crown, and of their connexion with Great Britain. 3dly. That, with their *lives and fortunes*, they would oppofe every attempt towards fuch dangerous innovations, &c. All the other Grand Juries, excepting two or three, iffued either the fame, or nearly fimilar declarations and refolutions. This was the laft ftruggling effort of a defperate junto, to fecure a political bias upon the country, which was not growing too large even for their own ambitious grafp. Never, furely, was a more indecent effort attempted to prejudge the merits of an aggrieved people; to interpofe the po-

litical influence of the counties between the petitions of the fubjects at large and the Crown : and to overawe and predetermine
the legiflature againft the recommendations, which his Majefty
might think proper to make, (and which he did in fact make)
in favour of his loyal, peaceful, and aggrieved Roman Catholic
fubjects of Ireland. This firft failure of men in power in their
hackneyed attempts to metamorphofe the wifhes and ftruggles
of the people for relief, into fedition and confpiracy againft the
State, was a happy omen to Ireland, and the welcome herald of
her dawning liberty. Notwithftanding this inveterate and powerful refiftance, the Roman Catholics proceeded coolly, ad-
vifedly, and firmly in purfuing the grand object of their claims.
About this time, Mr. Burke jun. arrived in Dublin, to refume
his office of Agent for the Roman Catholic Body of Ireland.

CHAPTER VII.

OCTOBER, 1792.

CONTENTS.

Great power of the Governor General of India—Mr. Shore appointed to succeed Lord Cornwallis—The conduct of the combined Princes afforded means and strength to the Jacobin party—Reports of treachery and bribery in the Prussians—Their method of carrying on the war—Fraudulent mode of acquiring provisions—Duke of Brunswick's third manifesto—His folly in negociating—His disgraceful retreat—France declared out of danger—French conquests, in Germany, of Spires, Mentz, Franckfort—Report of a letter from the King of France, that caused the retreat of the King of Prussia.

IN the present system of governing our East Indian possessions, the Governor General is invested with powers of unlimited extent and importance to Great Britain: he may involve this nation in war, and oppress the most extensive part of the British empire with all the dreadful calamities attendant upon that scourge of mankind. When upon the nomination of Lord Cornwallis, Mr. Fox, in the House of Commons, reprobated that system, as unconstitutional and dangerous, which vested such absolute and immense power in the hands of the Governors of India, his Majesty's Ministers opposed to it the well known *private virtues, worth, and dignity of the noble peer who was to exercise it.* The spirit of the British Constitution formerly knew no such grounds of engrafting absolute and unlimited power upon the virtue and discretion of the individual who was to exercise it. Blest as we now are in the perfon of the firft executive magiftrate, with the beft of Kings, the beft of Fathers, the beft of Hufbands, the beft of Friends, the beft of Men; yet the Conftitution, with this fure earneft of prudential exercife, has not, therefore, entrufted him with fuch abfolute power. It was indeed fince the inveftiture of fuch powers in the Governors of India, that Mr. Burke has taught us, that " *he is far from fure that a King of Great Britain does not poffefs a more real, folid, extenfive power, than the King of France was poffeffed of before this miferable revolution. The direct power of the King of England is confiderable. His indirect, and far more certain power is great indeed.* A fudden change feems to have taken place in the principles and fyftem of governing India. Laft year, military were the only fit men to govern India; this year, they are of all the moft unfit. Mr. Shore was the perfon fixed upon to fucceed the Marquis of Cornwallis. He had, partly from ill-health, and partly from a difguft of the meafures lately purfued in India, retired from active life, and fettled his private arrangements for ending his days in retirement upon a very moderate fortune, which, highly to his credit, he had brought with him from Afia, after having enjoyed confiderable appointments there termed *lucrative.*

Since our unhappy country is now fatally involved in the war, which, in the experiment of one fhort month, has afforded fuch a melancholy earneft of its effects, we become too nearly interefted in the turn of its events, to pafs over in filence the conclufion of its firft inglorious and deftructive campaign. The time and the manner of proclaiming this war were, perhaps, the only circumftances, in the indefinite poffibility of events, that could fo quickly and fo effectually have fecured to the Jacobin party in France the means of accomplifhing their nefarious and tyrannous defign. The Crown could not be completely deftroyed, but by the previous abolition of the ariftocracy, both in the party of the Emigrants and in that of the Conftitutionalifts; nor could this abolition be effected, but by meafures the moft violent and fhocking to the feelings of human nature. The invafion of a powerful, vindictive, and ferocious enemy, avowing themselves friends to the monarch, and declaring the monarch a friend to them, supplied them with a plea, not of plausibility but of necessity for depriving him of his liberty: the same principle sanctioned the necessity of confiscation, seizures, and murders, whilst a standard was erected on the French territories, round which their sworn enemies were encouraged, by threats and the most delusive promises, to rally. These melancholy truths were seen by all, but the infatuated persons whom they most concerned, in the instantaneous establishment of the power of the Jacobins upon the declarations and first movements of the combined armies. The overthrow of monarch, the captivity of the King with his whole family, the seizure of the forces, revenue, and authority of the whole country, were objects, which otherwise time, intrigue, and struggle could have alone secured. Thus suddenly and powerfully armed, the Jacobins were enabled to repel the efforts of their public, and crush the designs and power of their domestic enemies.

In the unexpected and unaccountable conduct of the combined armies, in the inglorious close of the campaign, it was to be expected, that the most disgraceful reports concerning their retreat should be circulated, even without full grounds for their authenticity. I cannot find sufficient vouchers to authenticate the current belief of treachery in the King of Prussia, and of bribery in the Duke of Brunswick; that the facts had been traced up to the corruption of their ministers and mistresses; and that they had openly been upbraided for it, both by the Emigrants and the Austrians. These being more interested and sincere in the cause than the Prussians, had frequently pledged their honour and lives to ensure a complete victory, if they might be permitted to engage the enemy without the concurrence or support of the Prussians. Jealousy and rivalship, it is true, might have rejected these offers, as well as corruption and perfidy. It cannot, however, be denied, that notorious advantages over the enemy were lost or neglected, and a most ignominious and destructive retreat was the conclusion of the campaign.

It was commenced by the most presumptuous declamations and vindictive menaces, and it was supported by species of fraud which had never before disgraced the warfare of a civilized nation. They had promised as ample protection to those Frenchmen who should submit to their summons, as they had threatened vengeance against those who should oppose their progress. They renounced pillage, and swindled the unresisting inhabitants out of provisions for their armies. One of these swindling and insulting instruments of fraud was sent by Dumourier to the National Convention, as a specimen of the good faith, and flattering pledge of the blessings which the success of the federated princes would heap upon France. " The village of Hans, " in Champagne, has delivered for the Prussian army 117 sheep, " the value of which his Majesty, the King of France, engages " to pay when his sacred person shall be at liberty, and order " re-established in his States. In faith of which I give the spe- " cial guarantee of his Majesty, the King of Prussia, which may " be exchanged for the value of the said in a proper time and " place." Signed, The Duke of Brunswick-Lunenbourg, Sept. 29.—But we were before told, *that the mode of civilized war would not be practised, nor were the French who acted on the present system intitled to expect it.* It was concluded by the most humiliating negociations, and ignominious retreat. The commander of the combined armies, unwilling or unable to keep the field, betrayed greater weakness in negociating with the French General, than he had in losing every advantage which he brought into the field. Having experienced the extreme mischief of his first manifestos, he was frantic enough to rest the basis of his negociation upon a third manifesto, in which he recapitulates the two former, and forebodes the immediate fall of the empire of France, from the infatuation of those who assume to themselves the title of *deputies chosen by the Nation, to secure its rights and its happiness upon the most solid basis.* He assures the French Nation, that the allied sovereigns never will depart from the the firm resolution of restoring to his most Christian

Majefty, liberty, fafety and royal dignity, or of exercifing juft and exemplary vengeance againft thofe who fhall longer dare to infringe them. That invariably attached to the principle of not intermeddling with the interior government of France, they ftill perfift in requiring, that his moft Chriftian Majefty, as well as the whole royal family, fhall be immediately fet at liberty, &c. The publication of this piece of inconfiftency and folly can alone force us to believe, that the Duke of Brunfwick could have been fo weak and rafh in the face of famine, ficknefs, impotency, defpair and difgrace.

General Manftein, on the part of Pruffia, was charged with carrying on the negociation with General Dumourier. It appears from their correfpondence, which is authentic, that perfonal interviews and conferences had been had between the Duke of Brunfwick and the French Generals. Dumourier perfifted in the impoffibility of negociating upon the bafis of a manifefto, carrying with it menace and war, that could only tend to irritate a free people; and which muft therefore break afunder the thread of negociation. " It does not," fays he, " at all enter the fenfe of " that which has been talked of between us for the laft four days, " it even deftroys it completely : it is even contradictory to the " converfation, with which the Duke of Brunfwick honoured " Adjutant General Thouvenot." The purport of thefe conferences, to which Dumourier's letter alludes, was the moft abject and unequivocal undertaking of the Duke of Brunfwick, on behalf of the combined powers, to be fatisfied with a grant of the fmalleft portion even of nominal power to the unfortúnate Louis; lefs, faid he, than that of a King of England, a King of Mahrattas, a Stadtholder, a principal Tax-gatherer, in fhort, any allowance that could afford them a pretext for retiring. Let this mendicant fupplication be compared with the language even of the laft manifefto, which had not preceded it more than three days. Then let cool reafon judge of the rectitude of principles that could be thus proftituted and abandoned. That Conftitution of France, againft which the Convention of Pilnitz had been

P

entered into, for the destruction of which above 100,000 men were then in arms, and to the execration of which most of Europe had been worked up by art and power, was a larger boon, than these humbled menacers now demanded; and in their degraded impotency it was refused. A serious lesson to Great Britain, now a principal party to the confederacy against France, to weigh the original principles upon which she embarked in the cause, the probability of failing in the attempt, and the neat sum of advantages, even in success. The want of provisions, the wetness of the season, and the sickness of the army, concurred to render the retreat of the Prussians as destructive as it was disgraceful. It is generally believed, that the French Generals, either from collusion or humanity, spared them in their retreat. Serious accusations were carried to the Convention upon this head, particularly against General Arthur Dillon. But, as Dumourier undertook to justify him, it was probably agreed upon, in the negociation between the Generals, that no molestation should be offered to the retiring army. Verdun and Longwy were given up; the siege of Lisle was raised; and thus ended this inglorious campaign. The French declared their country out of danger, as soon as the combined armies had evacuated it. They, however, pushed their conquests far into Germany: and, in the course of this month, Custine reduced the three important cities of Spires, Mentz, and Frankfort.

The King of Prussia and his General, the Duke of Brunswick, will never clear their reputations from the suspicions with which their conduct of this important campaign has covered them. Nor will the brutal ferocity of their troops be ever forgotten, who pillaged with equal barbarity the French patriots as enemies, and the French emigrants as their allies. It has, however, been said, that the late unfortunate Louis was prevailed upon to press, by letter, the withdrawing of the combined troops, as the only means of saving the lives of himself and family; and that this letter, delivered to the commander in chief in the course of the negociation between the Prussian and French Generals, was the immediate caufe of their retreat. Be it fo. Yet a letter fo recently received, and fo little expected, could not have produced the different manifeftos, or have kept the combined armies from engaging the enemy, when they commanded every advantage over them, or have driven them into difadvantageous pofts, or have deprived them of provifions, or have rendered the men and horfes fickly. The King of Pruffia and the Duke of Brunfwick are not blamed nor contemned for having retreated from France, when they were no longer able to hold the field, but for having, by their extreme folly or treachery, brought their armies and the caufe to fuch a ruinous alternative.

CHAPTER VIII.

NOVEMBER, 1792.

CONTENTS.

Succeſſes of the French in Brabant—Caſe of the Belgians reſiſting the Emperor Joſeph—Flight of the court from Bruxelles—The Archducheſs leaves behind the Emperor's grant of the Joyeuſe Entree—Effects produced throughout Europe by the ſucceſs of of the French arms—Addreſſes of Britiſh ſubjects to the National Convention—Decree of Fraternity—Our Miniſters alarmed about Holland—Lord Auckland's Memorial to the States—Diſ-poſition of the public towards France—Judge Aſhhurſt's Charge to the Grand Jury—Reflexions thereupon.

THE brilliant and rapid ſucceſs of the Republican arms in the very outſet of their career, produced the moſt ſtupendous and fatal conſequences throughout all Europe. It gave radical firmneſs to the party who had ſeized the powers and means of government in France; it emboldened them to inſult their neighbours in preſumptuous defiance, to outrage human nature with impunity, and to revile in blaſphemous impiety, the Deity itſelf. The confederated princes, whoſe ſanguinary menaces had provoked the irritation, as their diſgraceful diſcomfiture had crowned the triumphs of theſe ferocious Republicans, were ſo blinded to their infatuation, that they ſought neither to correct nor abandon the principles which had led them to the brink of ruin; but fatally ſucceeded in plunging their affrighted neighbours alſo into the devouring eddy of deſtruction. Before the cloſe of the current month, the dominion of the Republic was rapidly extended from the Alps to the Rhine, from Geneva to the mouth of the Scheldt. The victory of Jemappe secured the conquest of Brabant and Flanders; and the most numerous and best appointed armies of the universe where every where flying from the undisciplined, naked, but enthusiastic troops of the victorious Republic. How tardy are governments to see their too presumptuous confidence, to correct their mistaken measures, and to adopt remedies appropriate to the evils that threaten them!

The House of Austria had but recently secured, by the power of the sword, the allegiance of the States of Brabant and Flanders. They had risen to shake off the yoke of the Emperor Joseph, who, too confident of his arbitrary strength and power, had as imprudently as unjustly, invaded the rights of these subjects, and attempted to oppose upon them innovations in their religion, and deprive them of their fundamental privileges, upon the condition of which, they had originally put themselves under the protection of the House of Austria. The favourite, but fatal policy, of not yielding to the wishes, or claims of the people, whilst a Government thinks itself sufficiently strong to resist them by force, was here exemplified in a most striking manner. The brave Belgians, though heretofore too weak to withstand the power of the imperial arms, were too spirited to abandon their claim to their rights and privileges: they persisted in demanding in peace, what they could not maintain by war. The Government, though without ground for denying the justice of their claims, added insult to the grievance of withholding them by the mere power of oppression; they exposed their weakness and infamy in their manner and time of acceding to the demand. After the taking of Mons, all was fear and confusion at Bruxelles. The French emigrants, and every dependant upon the Court, were at one time on their flight: the latter had secured whatever boats, horses, and carriages they could, to transport themselves and their effects: and the dread of falling into the hands of the patriots, had completely cleared Bruxelles of every one who had avowed and supported the principles of the confederated princes against the Republic. The Archduchess Mary, removed with the Court to Ruremonde: her husband, the Duke of Saxe-Teschen, was with the army; and, if general accounts may be credited, had conduced not a little to the fatal disgrace of its overthrow at Jemappe. In her flight she left a melanlancholy monument, of the reluctance with which Government yielded to the just voice of the Belgian people; and in it an important lesson to all sovereigns, that to withhold the rights of their people, is to destroy at once their own power and authoriry. She addressed two dispatches to the Belgian people: one of them to announce her intention of holding her court at Ruremonde; the other to communicate to them the confirmation of the charter of their liberties, called the *Joycuse Entree*. In this disgraceful flight of the Court, from the approach of the victorious hero of Jemappe, little sagacity is wanting to trace the concessions of Government to their immediate cause. However, in the very hour of desertion and flight, she assures the people of his Majesty's intention to *make justice always the basis of his reign*, and had therefore empowered her to declare, *that he would inviolably maintain the Brabantine Constitution, and the Joyeuse Entree*. An earlier attention to this justice might have increased the regret of the Brabanters at the departure of the Archduchess, and mitigated their joy at the arrival of Dumourier.

The rapid and successful progress of the French arms, seems to have electrified all Europe with a sympathetic stroke of liberty. The cause of France was made common with every complaint of grievance, and the unwillingness to examine and redress them, an open federacy with despotism, to oppress the general cause of civil freedom. Throughout the Belgian provinces the reluctance and tardiness of the Emperor to admit and confirm the Brabantine Constitution, found a quick and palatable remedy in the success of the cause of France: the patriotic party in Holland sought, in the same source, an alleviation of their grievances against the overgrown power of the Stadtholder, which the arms of Pruffia had recently increafed. In England, particularly at Sheffield, the friends and fupporters of a Parliamentary Reform conceived that they beheld in the fuccefs of the French arms, a fure earneft of their own and fellow-citizens' free choice in the free members of a free parliament. In Scotland, the difappointed Burgeffes who had in vain importuned parliament to take under their confideration the abufes of the Royal Burghs, looked up to the happy iffue of the French invafion of the Netherlands, for the correction and redrefs of the evils they complained of. In Ireland, the Roman Catholics concluded, from the fuccefsful energy of the French Revolutionifts in giving laws to their own nation, that an united people could by no laws be excluded from the Conftitution and Government of their own State : and the Diffenters, and other friends of liberty, connected the deftruction of one abufive Government in France, with the neceffary abolition of every other Government that was fupported by any fort of abufe whatever, Thefe are the feelings of natural fympathy : the actual exiftence of the fore creates the fenfation: and the unfkilfulnefs of the phyfician drives the defpondiug patient to his own imaginary modes of relief.

Such were the fucceffes, and the effects of the fucceffes of the French arms. At home there was no party either fufficiently ftrong to refift the Jacobins, nor fufficiently refolute to attempt it. They produced feveral pretended and forged letters to criminate their unfortunate monarch of counter-revolutionary plots: and by thefe manœuvres they had difpofed a fpiritlefs public to an acquiefcence at leaft in his predetermined fate. Meafures were accordingly taken to bring on his trial.

There had long exifted at Paris, a fociety or club of Britifh fubjects, who took a very fympathetic, if not an active part in the fuccefs of the French Revolution. Upon the news of the conqueft of Brabant, they celebrated the joyful tidings in a very magnificent and general feftival ; and afterwards addreffed the Convention upon the fubject. Some other addreffes from Britifh fubjects were offered to and accepted by the National Convention, in congratulation of their successes. One of them was presented from the Constitutional Society of London, by their deputies Joel Barlow and John Frost, who, at the same time, entreated their acceptance of one thousand pair of shoes, as a patriotic offering to the brave soldiers of liberty.

The National Convention was so elated with the irresistible progress of their arms, and so confident of the propriety and rectitude of every measure proposed for its adoption, that it seems to have thought deliberation a drudgery beneath the elevated dignity of Republicans. In the inconsiderate heat of enthusiasm, it passed by acclamation, a decree, " that the National Convention " declared, in the name of the French Nation, that they will " grant fraternity and assistance to all those people who wish to " procure liberty; and that they charge the executive power, to " send orders to their Generals, to give assistance to such people " as have suffered, or are now suffering in the cause of liberty." This decree of fraternization was the most impolitic measure that the Convention could possibly have adopted; it gave the direct denial to all their former professions of not interfering with the internal governments of other kingdoms, and of not extending their own by foreign conquests. It raised just suspicions, that the fomenting disturbance and sedition in foreign countries, had become a systematic principle of the French Republic, and, consequently, afforded their neighbours plausible excuses for not admitting them to associate or settle in their dominions.

It appears that our Ministers began now to look with an eye of alarm upon the rapidity and extent of the French conquests: Brabant, Flanders, and Liege had been subdued, and seemed perfectly disposed to fraternize with their conquerors. It was well known, that in Holland a very considerable party of malecontents sought an opportunity of declaring themselves openly against the Prince of Orange. Lord Auckland was, therefore, directed to assure their High Mightinesses, that, as the theatre of war was brought so near to the confines of their republic, his

Majesty was both ready and determined to execute, with the utmost good faith, the treaty of 1788. The States, in their answer to this declaration from our Court, professed the strongest belief, that no hostile intentions were conceived by any of the belligerent powers against them. The native phlegm of the Hollander begat, in the more peaceful and steady, a real reluctance to believe activity necessary to save their country: an insuperable hatred of the court party induced the more active to dissemble their expectancies of what they most ardently wished. Hence the frequent observation, that *we* had officiously forced their High Mightinesses even into a war of defence, against their own wishes and inclinations.

It was now the determination of our Cabinet, to suppress no longer their approbation of the principles of the grand confederacy. But it was first requisite to dispose the Nation to a proper acquiescence in them. The multitude oftener act from feeling than judgment: whom they hate, fear, or contemn, they eagerly persecute, and are rarely delicate in the means, when they find the opportunity of satiating their vengeance. A supreme abhorrence of the French Government had been successfully implanted in the hearts of most persons in this country, nearly two years before the period of the current month: Mr. Burke then told them, that the French * " had put over their country an insolent " tyranny, made up of cruel and inexorable masters, and that " too of a description hitherto not known in the world. The " powers and politics by which they have succeeded, are not " those of great statesmen, or great military commanders, but " the practices of incendiaries, assassins, house-breakers, robbers, " spreaders of false news, forgers of false orders from authority, " and other delinquencies of which ordinary justice takes cogni-" zance." Unfortunately, none of their intermediate acts have tended to soften the features of this high-coloured portrait. In the excess of their horrors, lay the extremity of their folly in the

* Mr. Burke's Letter to a Member, p. 69.

mode of refifting the French Revolutionifts. Every meafure directed againft them, or their fupporters, or their admirers, however unwife, illegal, unconftitutional, or unjuft, became fanctioned in the object of its direction. Artful advantage was taken of this difpofition; every wifh, every word, and every action, that was difagreeable to minifters, was hurled into the devouring vortex of the French Revolution, and reprefented to an affrighted nation as mingling with the torrent that threatened deftruction to our political fabric.

Mr. Juftice Afhhurft, on the 19th inftant, delivered a charge to the Grand Jury, in which he very ably and pointedly fet forth the advantages of our Laws and Conftitution, and lamented that " there were men in this country of corrupt principles and " wicked intentions, who appeared to be very much diffatisfied " with our fyftem of Government, and publifhed libels on our " Conftitution daily; when this was the cafe *it was neceffary* for " the members of the ftate *to find out, and purfue, and punifh fuch* " *wicked perfons*. It would be a reformation in the ftate that fuch " corrupt members fhould be cut off, to prevent others from fol- " lowing their train." This refpectable Judge, in looking forward, fpoke the language and the fpirit of the Conftitution. But the unpunifhed and uninterrupted circulation of the *Rights of Man* for two years, was not grounded upon the recommendation which he thought neceffary for the prefervation of the State. In fact, the learned Judge, with all the delicacy that his official fituation permitted, could not refrain from noticing the inefficient meafures purfued by Government to check the evil. " The " authors who had publifhed fuch writings, however, notwith- " ftanding the proclamation, had perfifted in their conduct, which " proved that what had been done was not quite effectual to pre- " vent the further progrefs of fuch feditious writings." On the next day, however, a new, and, in the prefent circumftances, a very fingular meafure was fet on foot to encourage and countenance the execution of the laws. This was the eftablifhment of an Affociation at the Crown and Anchor Tavern, of which, in 'ts order and time, we fhall have future occafion to fpeak.

CHAPTER IX.

DECEMBER, 1792.

CONTENTS.

Great Britain openly enters into the armed Confederacy—Second Proclamation—Parliament convened within fourteen days after having been recently prorogued to January—The militia called out—The tower fortified—King's speech—Debates upon the address to the Throne—Mr. Fox's speech against the war—His motion to send over a person to treat with the Executive Power of France—Alien and Assignat Bills—The French offers to preserve peace—Maret sent over with indefinite powers—Trial of the French King—The dangerous system of establishing Clubs and Associations—Paine found guilty of libelling the Constitution—The effects of Mr. Reeves's Association brought before the House by Messrs. Fox and Grey.

WE are now come to the introduction of Great Britain upon the stage. We unfortunately are not disinterested spectators, merely to adapt our temporary feelings to the performance of the actors: we have a deep concern in the working of the plot; our dearest interests are involved in the unravelling of the piece; and the dropping of the scenic curtain will but usher into reality, the train of miseries and distresses which the performance of our part in the drama will have entailed upon us. After such recent and repeated avowals of the right of France to form, alter and model its internal Government, without the interference of any other state, after such unequivocal declarations of our intended neutrality, and the warmest professions of amity and good understanding, it was a task of no small ingenuity to engage the difpofitions, as well as to involve the interefts of this country in the armed combination againft France. The free and unchecked circulation of the worft of levelling doctrines which had brought France to its prefent ftate of violence and confufion, had operated their full effect upon thofe amongft us who were fufceptible of the mifchief: they had created in them a contempt for ariftocracy, and a diflike to monarchy: the evil was fatally augmented by the propagation of other doctrines running into the oppofite extremes, which were fure to forward the very mifchief they were (perhaps) intended to prevent. Such a war was not to be undertaken upon open principle: it was not, therefore, to be fupported by reafon. Appeal was to be made to the paffions; the pathetic cafe of a virtuous, perfecuted monarch, put in contraft with the ferocious cruelties of a licentious and frantic populace, had fuccefsfully feized the feelings of a Britifh audience: and we all know how weak is the refiftance of cool and ftern reafon, againft the pre-occupancy of animated paffion. This is in nature, and the public was prepared for it by the words and example of Mr. Burke. * *" We are fo made as to be affected at fuch fpectacles with melancholy fentiments upon the unftable condition of mortal profperity, and the tremendous uncertainty of human greatnefs: becaufe in thofe natural feelings we learn great leffons: becaufe in events like thefe, our paffions inftruct our reafon: when kings are hurled from their thrones by the fupreme Director of this great drama, and become the objects of infult to the bafe, and pity to the good."* The paffions of the public having been thus raifed, and *their reafon being fubjected to the inftruction of their paffions*, every wifh or effort to improve, ftrengthen, or preferve the rights of the people, or to keep the power of the Crown within the limits of the Conftitution, became equally feditious, difloyal, and treafonable. To a people fo impreffed, no meafure againft the object of their irritation could become a fubject of difcuffion or hefitation. Paffion is tranfient: *Veritas autem æterna.*

---

* Reflections, p. 119.

The Proclamation of the 21ſt of May, alledged that the evil which it complained of had been permitted to acquire a degree of ſtrength that threw the whole empire into a ſtate of alarm and ferment. The addreſſes, which it excited from the people, beſpoke, however, the loyal diſpoſition of the nation, and in proving the facility with which the evil could have been timely remedied, aſcertained the degree of guilt or folly of thoſe who ſaw, diſdained, or neglected the opportunity. In order, however, to render the intended meaſures palatable to the nation, it became neceſſary to deviſe ſome domeſtic urgency for entering into a war, that could be ſupported upon no political juſtice, encouraged by no proſpect of intereſt, nor undertaken without at leaſt the appearance of violating our expreſs profeſſions and promiſes. His Majeſty was accordingly adviſed to iſſue a new proclamation. The in-efficacy of the firſt proclamation ſufficiently appears from the language of the ſecond: " That notwithſtanding the royal " proclamation, evil-diſpoſed perſons were ſtill continuing, with " the utmoſt induſtry, to attempt the ſubverſion of the Laws and " eſtabliſhed Conſtitution of this realm, and to deſtroy all order " and government therein." It muſt, at the ſame time, be re-membered, that Thomas Paine, againſt whom the firſt procla-mation was avowedly aimed, was permitted to live here, with impunity, for near two years after the publication of his works, and recently to go unmoleſted to take his ſeat in the National Convention of France.

If credit be given to the words and actions of his Majeſty's Miniſters, the political ſtate of the kingdom, which depended upon the vigilance and energy of their meaſures, was, at this time, in the convulſed agonies of a mortal diſeaſe. Without any external hoſtilities either to make or reſiſt, without the conviction or even accuſation, of any perſon for attempting to raiſe internal ſedition or inſurrection, without the example of one pain, penalty, or puniſhment having been inflicted upon a perſon guilty of tur-bulence or rebellion, the Miniſters thought themſelves warranted in adviſing his Majeſty, by proclamation, to call out and embody the militia, and to convene the parliament (as in cafes of actual invafion and rebellion he is only enabled) at an earlier period than that to which it ftood prorogued. Bounties were offered to landfmen and feamen. Naval armaments were put into preparation in all the dock-yards; the army was drawn into a focus round the metropolis: and the Tower was put into a pofture of defence.* The proclamation unequivocally ftated, "that the "utmoft induftry was ftill employed, by evil-difpofed perfons "within this kingdom, acting in concert with perfons in foreign "parts, with a view to fubvert the laws and eftablifhed Confti- "tution of this realm; and to deftroy all order and government "therein; and that a fpirit of tumult and diforder, thereby ex- "cited, had lately fhewn itfelf in acts of *riot and infurrection.*" Thefe are the fuppofed facts, upon the exiftence of which the very legality of the proclamation was founded; for the Crown is only enabled to convene a parliament fooner than the time to which it ftands prorogued in the cafes of actual *invafion or rebellion*. No one ever queftioned the fact of invafion: and no one has, as yet, difcovered that of rebellion. The Legiflature, for grave reafons, reftrained the King's prerogative upon this fubject in all cafes except two, which are, in their nature, of full notoriety, and therefore feemed to have been particularly cautious that no Minifters might ever draw out the militia upon frivolous or falfe pretences. But how can infurrection or rebellion exift, but by the overt acts of individuals? And how can it be credited that thefe are known to Minifters, and that the perpetrators of them remain purpofely or defignedly concealed or fanctioned by impunity?

His Majefty's fpeech from the Throne, at the meeting of the Parliament, was a mere echo of his proclamation. In it he fays,

* If the Tower had been intended ferioufly to be put into a pofture of defence, a very different plan fhould have been adopted. At prefent it is more defencelefs than ever: the dead work of the walls is increafed, which, therefore, facilitates an attack; and the embrafures are fo conftructed, that a gun cannot be brought to bear out of them upon any point within the extent of the ditch.

" I have carefully obferved a ftrict neutrality in the prefent war
" on the continent, and have uniformly abftained from any inter-
" ference with refpect to the internal affairs of France." The
addrefs to his Majefty upon the fpeech was moved in the Houfe of
Lords by Lord Hardwicke, and feconded by Lord Walfingham:
in the Commons, by Sir James Saunderfon the Lord Mayor, and
Mr. Wallace. In both Houfes it was debated upon nearly the
fame grounds. In the Houfe of Commons, Mr. Fox, after a
very long, eloquent, and conftitutional fpeech, moved an amendment to the addrefs, which was negatived by a majority of two
hundred and forty.

As the minds of the public are now quieted upon the grounds
of alarm, which then agitated them, they may, after a year's experiment of the meafures then projected, examine them without
bias; and decide upon them without partiality or fufpicion of
difloyalty. On this occafion, Mr. Fox proved himfelf the moft
fagacious ftatefmen, the ableft fenator, and the firmeft patriot.
If there exift in the breaft of any man, at this hour, a feeling for
the actual fituation of his country, let him read over, and calmly
confider, Mr. Fox's fpeech upon that memorable occafion, and
his mind will be inftantly decided upon the awful crifis of the
prefent moment. He declared that the fpeech and proclamation
were *grounded in falfehood*, and that the Minifters who had
framed the fpeech, had made the affertion with a full conviction
of their falfehood: that they had calumniated the people of England, by accufing them of infurrections, which had no exiftence
but in the brains of thofe who had finifter views in publifhing
thefe fictions. He very pointedly enforced the danger of deftroying, as the prefent policy was, the middle order of men, who
were equally adverfe to pure democracy as to defpotifm. A
fyftem of extremes was eftablifhed, of the moft dangerous confequences. Thofe who dread republicanifm, fly for fhelter to
the crown. Thofe who defire reform, and are calumniated, are
driven by defpair to republicanifm—the evil moft to be dreaded.
He was ready to ftand in the gap between the wild projects of

new-fangled theories, and the dangerous revival of exploded and condemned doctrines, though from thefe latter he feared the worft confequences. He connected the fpirit of Government with the actions of its avowed agents. He confidered the nature of Mr. Reeves's * affociation, and quoted the doctrines publifhed and circulated by this learned chairman, that inculcated the *juro divino* right of Kings, which would have been treafonable in the years 1715, and 1745: and this in a manner perfectly new and inftructive—" *Have you not read the Bible? Do* " *you not know, that it is there written, that the King is the Lord's* " *anointed? But did you ever hear of his having anointed a Re-* " *public?*"—He preffed upon the Minifters the danger of fporting with the feelings of the people; of raifing their alarms, to draw from them the foothing expreffions of agitated loyalty; and warned them againft ftunning the public mind, with repeated fhocks of fiction, into the infenfibility of a real attack. He deprecated in the ftrongeft terms, the idea of going to war with France, becaufe we difapproved of its form of Government. He infifted that reafon required we fhould firft attempt to negociate, before we plunged the nation into war. If the ends we propofed to obtain by arms, could be acquired by negociation, the Nation demanded negociation, as an act of juftice. And the Minifters who refufed even the attempt, were refponfible to their country, for the lavifh wafte of its treafure, and the wanton and cruel effufion of its blood. Every mifery of a moft deftructive and ruinous war, would be juftly laid at the door of thofe, who, from obftinacy, pride, or folly, would not ufe the means, preffed even upon them by their very enemies, to prevent and avert the evil. It was infulting to the plain fenfe of man, and fhocking to humanity, to fport with the fate of empires, and facrifice the lives and fortunes of their citizens, to the frivolity of punctilio. Can they find a power to war againft, with whom

---

* He is Chief Juftice of Newfoundland, and enjoys fome other places under Government.

they cannot treat? Can they settle cartels and armistices, (as in war they must) with those with whom they may not prolong, and perpetuate them? Can they insure the infallible and perpetual success of their arms, and prophecy to their country, that this, or a worse executive government in France, shall not humble, and force them to sue for the peace, they now so insolently and haughtily deny the possibility of treating for? To judge from the first fruits of the crusade against France, he trembled, and blushed to look forward to the probable issue of our plunging into the disgraceful ruin. Let but negociation be attempted, and its failure would insure his vote for the war. Negociation had lately prevented a rupture with Spain. And, after his Majesty had told us in his speech, that he has uniformly abstained from any interference with respect to the internal affairs of France, what other reason can there be for not saving this country from war, by negociating with the executive power of France, (we interfere not with its form), but because the republic has not been anointed with the holy chrism of Rheims? He expected to be in a minority, but a minority had recently saved the country from a war with Russia. Were he alone, he would still raise his single voice to avert from his country the ruin and destruction, that the weak, if not wicked designs of Ministers, were bringing upon it. Whatever might be the intoxication of the moment, he saw the hour of reflection not far off, that would convince his countrymen of the preference of an honourable antitode, to an expensive, painful, and humiliating cure. In his usual manly manner he added, that he would not content himself with deprecating the acts of the Ministers, but he would pledge himself, for the system of measures that he would propose and support in hours of agitation like the present. If the Dissenters showed a tendency to discontent, on account of any partial oppression, he would repeal the Corporation and the Test Acts. They complained of nothing else: and their affectionate services were of more consequence to the state, than their exclusion from corporations was of benefit to it. If any persons

R

were tinctured with a republican spirit because they thought the representative Government was more perfect in a republic, he would endeavour to amend the representation of the Commons, and to prove that though not chosen *by all*, they should have no other interest than to prove themselves representatives *of all*. If there were men dissatisfied in Scotland, with the internal government of their Royal Burghs, he would examine their grievance, and afford redress. If in Ireland, the great body of the people stated what was the fact, that they were excluded from, and demanded to be admitted to a participation of the Constitution of their country, he would liberally admit their claim to right and justice. He lamented sorely that Government should have hitherto refused to grant, what would have been then thought the result of choice and liberal policy; but which, on the eve of a public war, must appear to be the forced effect of necessity and fear. Were he, in the present hour of alarm, to issue a proclamation, it should be to invite every man who had a grievance, to bring it to the bar of the House of Parliament, in full confidence of having it fairly investigated. These were the subsidies he would offer to Government. What instead of this was done? Complaints were suppressed, the aggrieved calumniated as seditious, redress rendered desperate, the freedom of thought, speech, and the press, subjected to the judgment of ignorant, interested, and spiteful informers, and the disapprobation of an arbitrary, unjust, and ruinous system of measures, converted into a treasonable attempt to subvert the Constitution and Government of the country. He repeatedly inculcated, what should be ever engraven on the hearts of all Ministers: That the Ministers of one country ought to treat with whomsoever they found in possession of the power of another. That those who would only treat with powers *de jure*, and not with those *de facto*, could not excuse themselves to their country for the treasure that should be lavished, and the blood that should be spilt, in the consequences of their obstinacy and arrogance. Their commission and delegation is to superintend and preserve the rights, and welfare of their own country, not to interfere with the forms and rights of the internal governments of others.

Mr. Burke, *whose passions* on this, as on some other occasions, *instructed his reason*, spoke for a considerable length of time in his usual philippic strain against France; and concluded, that the present question was not whether an address should be presented to the Throne, but whether there should be any Throne at all. He threw out as ill-founded as it was an ill-natured allusion, to Catiline's designs upon Rome. The difference of the present from the then situation of this nation, may have inverted Mr. Burke's doctrine, and taught men's *reason to instruct their passions*. When they shall impartially have reviewed the result of one year's experiment in this fatal confederacy, their reason will find conviction in the accomplishment of those predictions of Mr. Fox, to which their passions formerly prevented them from assenting. Let them now faithfully cast up the current account of the year; let them labour to counterbalance in credit the black column of debtor of *twenty* millions;* let them weigh the advantages gained over the enemy abroad, against those we have ourselves lost at home; let them compare the then flourishing state of our commerce, with the present distressed situation of our manufacturers; let them contrast the past discontents of the people with the Government, and their clamours against the necessary contributions to its support, with their present melioration of their condition, and their readiness to submit to the payment of nearly an additional million of annual taxes. Let them oppose the arrogant refusal of our Ministers to treat with the French about peace, to their vigour and exertions in supporting the war. Let them look back at our vaunting threats to crush, by anticipation, the power which the fatal experiment has increased and fortified. Let them compute the future by our past losses and misfortunes; let them cast up the sum total of

* The moneys raised last year, and what will be ultimately requisite to clear all expenses hitherto incurred by the war, cannot fall far short of this estimate.

our *sure* miseries, distresses and disgrace; let them calculate upon fair data, the improbability of obtaining the end of the war, which is the subjection of France. Let them prove, by unerring operations, the impossibility by any issue of the war, of compensating this country for the waste of blood, treasure, and happiness, even already sacrificed to the ruinous and delusive object. And then let them learn to estimate public men by the effects their measures produce upon the country.

On the third day of the Parliament, Mr. Fox made a motion in the House, to address his Majesty to send a person to treat with those, who exercise provisionally, the functions of the Executive Government in France, touching such points as may be in discussion between his Majesty and his allies, and the French nation. He observed, that the question having been narrowed by the discussions of the two former days, he made this motion with the intention that it might be entered on the Journals of the House, for the purpose of showing to the country, that an attempt had, on the first opportunity, been made by the representatives of the people, to avert the calamities of war by negociation. He was as little, as any man in that House, disposed to commend the late proceedings of France, nor did he admit the present, to be the most desirable time, for recognizing those powers; but it was an unfortunate necessity; this was the first opportunity of forwarding the measure, and the sooner it was adopted the less remarkable it would be. After a very long debate the motion was negatived without a division. The prudence and propriety of Mr. Fox's motion will only be seen and fairly judged, in the painful moment of humiliation, which will faithfully disclose the full waste of the blood and treasure, that the adoption of it would have prevented.

This system of horror and enmity against France, having been established, although no formal declaration of hostilities had been made, the Parliament proceeded to pass the Alien Bill, and the Bill to prohibit the circulation of promissory, and other notes, orders, undertakings, or obligations, for the payment of any sum, or fums of money, created and iffued under, or in the name of any public authority in France. Oppofition was given to each of thefe Bills, in both Houfes, chiefly upon the fame grounds; viz. that they were direct infringements of the Treaty of Commerce; that they were hoftile meafures whilft we profeffed neutrality towards France; and that they were founded in the falfe fuppofition of exifting danger in our own country.

In the courfe of the month, Monf. Le Brun, the French Minifter for Foreign Affairs, made feveral attempts to open a negociation with our Minifters, to preferve a good underftanding, and to prevent an open rupture between the two countries. Inftructions were given to M. de Chauvelin, and frefh agents were fent over with directions to make any overtures and conceffions that fhould be found effectual to avert the miferies of a war. All proved ineffectual; for about the clofe of the month, M. Le Brun made a report to the Convention on the ftate of affairs with England. He faid that contrary winds had kept back the refult of the laft ftep taken by the Executive Council, which was the fpecial commiffion given to M. Maret, to admit almoft of indefinite terms to prevent the war. He fpeaks flightingly of the naval armaments of England, and complains much of the Alien and Affignat Bills, as infractions of the Treaty of Commerce, which they had hitherto fcrupuloufly obferved, but from which they fhould in future hold themfelves releafed; that they had, accordingly, directed their Ambaffador to make this reprefentation to Lord Grenville. It is confidently reported, that M. Maret had it in his inftructions, unequivocally to offer to our Miniftry thefe three points: firft, that the navigation of the Scheldt fhould be given up; fecondly, that the French troops fhould not approach the Dutch territories, within a given diftance; and that the decree of the 19th of November, fhould be either altered or repealed. When the oftenfible reafons for undertaking a war are thus previoufly removed, by the conceffion of the enemy, then none but the moft fufpicious motives can induce Minifters to facrifice the peace, treafure, and welfare of the country, to their secret or wicked views. A great part of the month was taken up by the National Convention in the trial of the unfortunate Louis. His impending fate deeply affected the feelings of this whole nation. Several expedients and experiments were suggested in both Houses of Parliament, for averting the sentence which seemed doomed to be passed upon him; but none were adopted, merely from the fear of irritating the ferocious Jacobins to an earlier and severer sentence against him. It would have been difficult to provoke the Executive Council of France, more than they at this time were, at our conduct in passing the Alien and Assignat Bills, in increasing our armaments, both by land and sea, in refusing to negociate with their Ambassador, and above all, in haughtily rejecting the proposals, which they had humbled themselves in making, by their extraordinary envoy Maret.

There cannot be a more melancholy, though at the same time more incredible proof of the infatuation of Ministers, than that, with the fatal example before their eyes of France having been brought into its present situation by the means of clubs, they should countenance and encourage that very system throughout this kingdom. The motive of their meeting was indifferent as to the effect of setting the example. It would, if hereafter found necessary to forbid those self-constituted clubs, associations, or conventions, be a difficult task to rest the legality of their meeting upon the purity of the motives of the associates. Mr. Reeves's association had set out upon the most false, wicked, and dangerous grounds that could be devised. They boast of their being formed into a club for the express purpose of preserving themselves against *the horrid attempts of daring and seditious men, who, under the specious pretence of reformation, wish to subvert the Constitution and Government of their Country.* What can be more false, than that all those who wish to bring about a reform in Parliament, wish to subvert the Constitution of their Country? What more wicked, than thus to calumniate and criminate their fellow subjects, who are peaceful and loyal? What more dangerous to the state, than to establish such a system of enmity amongst citizens, and fomenting it by means obviously open to retaliation, and immediately tending to the horrid effects of irritation, revenge and despair? It was but on the 18th of the month, that Mr. Paine's trial came on, in which he was found guilty, by a special jury, for having libelled the Constitution. He had openly and unequivocally avowed himself its enemy, and exerted the full power of his talents to make what proselytes he could to his seditious doctrines; and if the evils and dangers complained of in the proclamations had a real existence, they owed it undoubtedly to the tardy and inefficient punishment of the author and propagator of the doctrines that produced them. Henceforth there appeared less zeal in punishing real delinquents, than in affixing the imputation of sedition and treason to those who disapproved of the measures of Government, or incurred their displeasure, by wishing for a Parliamentary Reform. According to the new doctrine of Mr. Reeves's association, it was holden out to the nation as *illegal and unconstitutional* to meet for the purpose of considering and discussing the state of the popular representation in Parliament, in which every voter, and every individual is in fact deeply interested. It was, therefore, judged to be the prudent, the effectual, the legal, the constitutional mode of checking and correcting the evil, to establish these counter meetings and societies throughout the kingdom, founded upon no other authority, sanction, or power, than the momentary (perhaps ill-grounded) conviction of individuals, that the present system of popular representation should be kept on foot for the improvement or preservation of the Constitution, and that the contrary opinion was a proof of an actual desire or attempt to subvert the laws, government and constitution of the country.

So seriously were the most illiberal, scandalous, and unconstitutional motives for holding these associations boasted of and propagated, that Mr. Fox and Mr. Grey thought it necessary to notice them in the House; and now perhaps, *if our passions have ceased to instruct our reason*, the real import and tendency of them may be confidered without bias or prejudice. One of the firft publications made by Mr. Reeves, the arch-patriarch of thefe affociates was, faid Mr. Grey (on the 17th) not only calculated to excite fedition, but abfolutely pointed out the clafs of perfons againft whom the loyal fury of the mob fhould be directed. The extermination of the Diffenters was their aim, and the publication alluded to afferted, *" That the Prefbyterians had been* " *the caufe of the difturbances in America; that by them the ex-* " *pences of the American war had been incurred, and that the* " *Birmingham Doctor (Prieftley) was more infamous even than* " *Paine."* Mr. Fox on the fame day, produced to the fame houfe, a circular invitation to one of thefe loyal meetings at Staines, which ended with thefe words, *deftruction to Mr. Fox, and his Jacobin committee.* On the 24th, Mr. Fox, in giving his affent to the augmentation of the army, as he had before done to that of the navy, faid that he did it upon this only principle, that we ought to be prepared either to engage in war, or to negociate with effect for peace. He then took occafion of mentioning to the Houfe, the difmiffal from the army of two officers of rank and merit, Lord Edward Fitzgerald, for being fuppofed to favour the caufe of France, when we were in a ftate of neutrality with her; and of Captain Gawler, for having refufed to withdraw his name from the Society for Conftitutional Information, to which fome of the firft characters of the nation belonged. Thefe different circumftances befpeak their own tendency, and fhew the extent of the fpirit which produced them. He queftioned not the prerogative of the Crown to difmifs any officer from the army; but thought that the exercife of it applied to fuch purpofes, became an object worthy of the confideration of that Houfe.

CHAPTER X.

JANUARY, 1793.

CONTENTS.

Maret's second mission from the Executive Power of France still rejected—Spain's treaty of neutrality with France—Carter, a bill-sticker, condemned to six months imprisonment—Crichton, a tallow-chandler, for uttering seditious words in liquor—Messrs. Erskine and Pigott removed, and Messrs. Graham and Anstruther made Attorney and Solicitor General to the Prince of Wales—Death of the King of France—Dismissal of the Ambassador, and other measures taken thereupon—Exertions in Ireland to reform the representation of the people in Parliament—The Association of the Friends of the Constitution, Liberty, and Peace, under the Duke of Leinster—Bishop of St. David's Sermon—Reflections thereupon.

FEW domestic occurrences of this month are of any particular importance to the general purport of this History. The Parliament proceeded in passing the Alien and Assignat Bills. M. Maret, who had returned again from France with enlarged powers of negociating for peace, had several conferences with our Ministers, who still rose in their tone of disdainful rejection. The example of Spain, which had, in the preceding month, entered into a treaty of neutrality with the Executive Power of France, was strongly urged as a precedent for our negociating without humbling ourselves in the eyes of Europe. The Spanish negociation was so emphatically the immediate act of the

Crown, that it was actually commenced under the administration of the Count d'Aranda, and completed under that of the the Duke d'Alcudia. All, however, was in vain: it was our inevitable fate to be plunged into the miseries and difgrace of this myfterious and ruinous confederacy. Maret returned to France under the mortification of having failed alfo in this fecond miffion to the Britifh Cabinet. Lord Loughborough, who in all the late debates upon the relative fituations of Great Britain and France, had been prominently zealous in fupporting the meafures propofed by Minifters, was honoured with the Great Seals of England, and called to fucceed Lord Thurlow on the woolfack.

As the Minifter had been either unable or unwilling to make an example of any perfon who had been guilty of thofe acts of riot and infurrection, which had induced the neceffity of drawing out the militia, they found that the prefent affection of the public mind could not be kept up without the moft exemplary and rigorous punifhment of future delinquents. The firft unfortunate victim of this regenerated feverity, which had difappeared with the memorable Jeffries in the laft century, was one Carter, who was indicted and found guilty of having unlawfully publifhed a fcandalous and feditious libel, intituled "An Addrefs from "the London Correfponding Society to the other Societies in "Great Britain, united for the purpofe of obtaining a Reform "in Parliament." The addrefs was an anfwer to that of Mr. Reeves's Affociation: and this wretched *Bill-fticker* was fentenced to fix months imprifonment for having pafted up the addrefs at the corner of St. Giles. The next example was Daniel Crichton, for uttering treafonable words againft the King: he was proved to have faid, that *he would have no King here, they had no King in Scotland*: and the fame two witneffes who proved the uttering of the words, proved alfo the intoxication of the man who uttered them: he had come up the night before from Scotland, to be bounden apprentice to a tallow chandler: honourable teftimony was made in court by a refpectable clergyman of his general good character, and he himself expressed the most sincere compunction for having, in an unguarded moment of intoxication, uttered words, which, in his full reflection, he would not ever have spoken: he was sentenced, however, to three months imprisonment. The punishment of such low and insignificant individuals, would scarcely support the system of criminating every wish for a parliamentary reform. Confidence was to be withdrawn from men of brilliant talents and tried patriotism, whose zeal for the perfection of the Constitution prevented them from abandoning even the hopes of correcting its few defects. Mr. Erskine and Mr. Pigott were removed from the honourable appointments of Attorney and Solicitor General to his Royal Highness the Prince of Wales: and Messrs. Graham and Auftruther were appointed in their lieu.

The confined plan of this History will not allow me to enter into a minute detail of the melancholy execution of the unfortunate King of France. The question for his execution was carried, in the Convention, only by a majority of five votes. In his death, which happened on the 21st of the month, he showed an example of the most heroic fortitude and christian submission to his unjust sentence. Blood-thirsty and cruel as was the conduct of the regicide party to this amiable and virtuous monarch, it is much doubted whether they would have had the boldness to attempt, or the power to carry so unjust and bloody a design into execution, if they had not been enabled to pave the way for it, under the pretext of securing their country from the imprudent and inhuman menaces of the Duke of Brunswick. Some hopes were entertained that Dumourier, who was at this time at Paris, would have profited of his influence with the people, to have attempted a rescue of the injured monarch. No shew appeared of such an attempt. Twenty thousand men were under arms: and the shocking scene was closed in the most awful fear and silence. Upon the melancholy report reaching this country, the Court was immediately ordered into mourning for his late most Christian Majesty. M. Chauvelin was, by an order of the King in Council, directed to depart this realm, on or before the 1ft of February: and a meffage was fent by his Majefty to both Houfes of Parliament, directing the correfpondence between M. Chauvelin and the Secretary of State for Foreign Affairs, together with the order of Council in confequence of the atrocious act lately committed at Paris, to be laid before them; and intimating, that his Majefty, in the prefent fituation of affairs, thought it indifpenfably neceffary to make a further augmentation to his forces by fea and land, for maintaining the fecurities and rights of his own dominions, for fupporting his allies, and for oppofing the views of aggrandizement and ambition on the part of France, which would be, at all times, dangerous to the general interefts of Europe, but are peculiarly fo when connected with the propagation of principles which lead to the violation of the moft facred duties, and are utterly fubverfive of the peace and order of all civil fociety.

Whatever may be the impreffions upon the paffions or minds of men, in the awful moment of great, wonderful, and terrific events; they are in their nature, tranfient, and momentary, as were the caufes which produced them. They may indicate the difpofitions of the perfons affected: but they can afford no ground for engrafting upon them any meafures intended to be general and permanent. Truth and reafon, which are ever confiftent and invariable, can alone fupport and juftify either the alteration or execution of laws, which were founded in their bafis. True it is, that the kingdoms of Great Britain and Ireland, are feparate and independent of each other: they have feparate legiflatures, and feparate laws: but they have an union of interefts, an union of affection, an union of allegiance to the fame Sovereign: they know but one fpirit, one principle, one form of Conftitution. *Great Britain* and *Ireland* are convertible terms. Difloyalty, fedition, and treafon, are inapplicable to one, if they be not applicable to both: the nature of the crime is common to both: the *pius* or the *minus* in the offence to the Sovereign, may be determined by peculiarity of circumftances, not by variety of foils. Let us then firft in one kingdom contemplate the British Legislature, *impervious* to every application for a reform of Parliament; let us view the Government of. Great Britain, prosecuting for sedition, every man, who speaks, or writes, or publishes his own, or others' thoughts, in favour of such reform; let us view the multifarious Clubs and Associations, regularly established through the kingdom of Great Britain, under the sanction of Government, to preserve us against the horrid attempts of daring and seditious men, *who, under the specious pretence of reformation, wish to subvert the Constitution and Government of the Country :* then let us turn our eyes to Ireland.

Here we see a regular delegation, deputed from three fourths of a people, aggrieved by being deprived (amongst other rights) of that of voting for members of parliament, (though discountenanced and opposed by most of the men in power of that kingdom) laying before their Sovereign, in respectful confidence, the sum of their grievances, and graciously received by the common father of his people*. Here we admire the tender anxiety of a truly patriot King, recommending to that very parliament, to take into their serious consideration, the case of his Roman Catholic subjects, whose petition they had the year before refused to receive. Here we behold a virtuous association of true patriots, headed by the first nobleman of the kingdom, combining their joint efforts to bring about a reform in the popular representation in parliament, entering into this, amongst other resolutions: " *that the representa-* " *tive part of our legislature is not derived from the people by the* " *free and general election which the fundamental principles of our* " *Constitution require, and the state and condition of this nation* " *would warrant.*†" Here we behold the House of Commons re-

---

* On the 2d of January, the Delegates from the Catholic Body of Ireland were introduced by Mr. Dundas at St. James's, and they presented their address, which was graciously received: they were Messrs. Byrne, Keogh, Devreux, Bellew, and Sir Thomas French.

† This respectable meeting, at which the Duke of Leinster presided, was called the Association of the Friends of the Constitution, Liberty, and Peace. The last of their resolutions was, that every person becoming a member should subscribe the following declara-

solving itself into a committee *to examine into the state of the representation of the people in parliament.* Are we hence then to conclude, that the wishes, efforts, and attempts of Britons, to improve by a temperate reform, the representation of the people in parliament, are seditious and treasonable; and that the Sovereign and Parliament in Ireland, countenance, support, and encourage these very acts of sedition and treason?

The melancholy similarity of circumstances, between the recent execution of the French monarch, and that of our first Charles, whose martyrdom is commemorated on the 30th day of January, seemed naturally to excite the public expectation of some more than ordinary exertion from the pulpit, on this solemnity, revived as it was, by the fresh application of such appropriate matter. Doctor Horsley, the Bishop of St. David's, was chosen to preach this annual sermon: and upon the motion of the Archbishop of Canterbury, he was thanked for it by the House of Lords, and desired to print it for the instruction and edification of the public. But, in the House of Commons, Mr. Sheridan, in his speech upon the reported sedition of the country, took an occasion of expressing a very different opinion of this discourse of the learned prelate: " It opened," he said, " with comments upon the vanity of political disquisitions altogether, and concluded with an anathema on those who did not " agree with him in political opinion, reviving all the slavery of " passive obedience, and non-resistance." At a time when Go-

tion: " I solemnly promise and declare, that I will, by all lawful " means, promote a radical and effectual reform in the representa-
" tion of the people in Parliament, including persons of all reli-
" gious persuasions: and that I will unceasingly pursue that object, " until it shall have been unequivocally obtained. And, seriously " apprehending the dangerous consequences of certain levelling " tenets and seditious principles, which have lately been disse-
" minated, I do further declare, that I will resist all attempts to " introduce any new form of Government into this country, or in " any manner to invert or impair our Constitution, consisting of " King, Lords, and Commons."

vernment was by proclamations, and every other exertion of power, forcing upon the nation the belief that the Conſtitution was in danger, the charge of reviving the dangerous and unconſtitutional doctrines of *paſſive obedience and non-reſiſtance* became really ſerious. At the beginning of the preſent century, the maintenance of theſe doctrines from the pulpit, had brought on the trial of Dr. Sacheverell; whoſe impeachment, as Mr. Burke ſays,* " was undertaken and carried on for the expreſs " purpoſe of ſtating the true grounds and principles of the Re- " volution, which the Commons emphatically called their *foun-* " *dation*." It is well known, that he was found guilty upon the articles of impeachment by what Mr. Burke calls *a ſteady and prevalent majority of Whig Peers.* † " The ſolemn judgment of " the Houſe of Peers, againſt Dr. Sacheverell, muſt, in my opi- " nion, make it abſolutely unlawful for any Britiſh ſubject in " future, openly to deny, or diſapprove of the Revolution prin- " ciples, or publicly to maintain thoſe, which are commonly " called the *tory* principles." As theſe articles exhibited againſt Dr. Sacheverell, are become the legal teſt of tory principles, I feel a peculiar call of duty ‡ to enable my readers to form their

* Appeal, p. 55.   † Jura Ang 185.

‡ Little did the author expect, and ſtill leſs did he deſerve, the honourable mention which this reſpectable and learned prelate has made of him in the appendix to this ſermon. The merit of intention in writing his *Jura Anglorum*, and the aim at candour in treating every ſubject which concerns the church eſtabliſhment, which his Lordſhip has ſo kindly allowed him, he particularly wiſhes to avail himſelf of, on this, and on every future occaſion that may call him before the public. It would be an abandonment of both, not to warn the public of the dangers to which he ſees the nation expoſed from the revival of Toryiſm, and not to remark, that the zeal of the reverend prelate for that part of the Conſtitution which had been openly and rudely aſſailed, had led him into a dangerous exceſs of unconſtitutional doctrines in ſupport of it. The learned prelate will allow, that ſince the author has, in the work which his Lordſhip has condeſcended to commend, ſaid, (p. 472.) " that *paſſive obedience and non-reſiſtance* could never by poſſibility " have been applicable to, or practicable in the Engliſh Govern-

own judgment upon the political doctrines delivered by the learned prelate in this difcourfe. This cannot be better effected,

" ment;" his apprehenfions and alarms of an intended change in that Government were not groundlefs, when he found thefe very doctrines enforced from the pulpit, by a perfon commanding moft defervedly the efteem and veneration of the Nation.

The immediate reafon of the author's work having been noticed by this learned prelate, was the infertion of a quotation from Calvin, cited from *Philanax Anglicus*. The quotation from Calvin appears to the Reverend Prelate to have been mifreprefented by mutilation: and he enters into a full and elaborate fcholium upon the words of Calvin, to fhew, that they import no doctrine, principles, nor fentiments againft royalty: and he fays, very juftly, *that the author will not be difpleafed, that the memory of a great man fhould be vindicated from an unfounded accufation. No injuftice of intention, nothing worfe than a very pardonable miftake is imputed to him.* The author holds himfelf equally refponfible for the quotations which he adopts from others, as for the affertions he makes himfelf. But circumftanced as he was, he felt it to be a more delicate mode of conveying certain truths to the public by the mouths of others than by his own. He thought that he could more delicately tell the public, that the doctrines of *divine right, paffive obedience, and non-refiftance,* had been the received proteftant doctrine of the Church of England, in the words of the Bifhop of Worcefter, than in thofe of a private individual, who was not a member of that church: and that " *the authority* of thofe venerable men, from whom it was " derived, gave it a firm and lafting hold in the minds of the " clergy: and being thought to receive a countenance from the " general terms in which obedience to the civil magiftrate is or-" dained in fcripture, it has countenanced in our days, and it may " be feared ftill continue to perplex and miflead the judgment of " too many amongft us." (p. 134.) For thefe reafons, the author dealt more largely in quotations throughout that work than he could otherwife have reconciled either to his inclination or judgment.

The words of Calvin which were quoted, as applied by *Philanax Anglicus*, are, " *Abdicant enim fe poteftate terreni principes dum infurgunt contra Deum: imò indigni funt qui cenfeantur in hominum numero: potius ergo confpuere oportet in illorum capita quam iis parere ubi fic proterviunt, ut velint fpoliare Deum fuo jure.*" The learned prelate undertakes to prove, that Calvin meant no more by thefe words, than

than by comparing them with thofe of Dr. Sacheverell's fermon in the year 1709.

that God was to be obeyed before man. They ever did convey to the underftanding of the author, as they ftill do, an indecent and irreverend idea of Royal Power; uttered by an overheated republican, with the exprefs view of inftilling into his followers a contempt and difguft of Kingly Power. They appeared to him falfe and dangerous, becaufe they generally made the Sovereign's offence to God, the immediate act of abdication of his own authority over his fubjects; thus converting fubjects into judges of their King's confcience, and arbiters of their own obligation to obey him. The author emphatically reprobated thefe principles as inapplicable to the Britifh Conftitution; however congenial they might be found with thofe of the Republic of Geneva or of modern France. The author cannot apply the doctrine to the poffible repetition of the circumftance at this day in this country. If he may, without offence or indelicacy, hypothetically ftate an order from a King of Great Britain to an individual to worfhip an idol, which was the cafe of Daniel, the conclufion of the author would be, that he affected a power he could not poffefs, in commanding a finful act: but not that in fo doing, he abdicated *any power* he before enjoyed. He could by no means juftify the perfonal infult to the Sovereign, on account of the moral obligation of the fubject in fuch cafe to refift the finful order. *Abdicare fe poteftate*, according to the author's conception, is the act of abdicating a power, which is poffeffed by the abdicating perfon: now, no Sovereign could have had a power to command an offence to God: and what he never had, he could not abdicate, as is evident. The author cannot, therefore, underftand, by thefe words of Calvin, a mere fpiritual exhortation to his difciples, to prefer their duty to God before the unlawful commands of man. The abdication and non-enjoyment of a power are widely different. The author allows to every defcription of perfons, who fyftematically follow the doctrines of any man, the fuperior advantage of rightly underftanding their genuine fpirit: he defends not his interpretation of Calvin's words, but merely declares, that the manner in which he underftood them, was the reafon why he introduced them as relevant to the fubject he was then treating.

T

The first Article of the Impeachment against Dr. Sacheverell was,	*Passages from the Bishop of St. Davids' Sermon.*
" That he, the said Henry Sacheverell, in his said sermon, preached at St. Pauls, doth suggest and maintain, that the necessary means used to bring about the said happy Revolution, were odious and unjustifiable: that his late Majesty, in his declaration, disclaimed the least imputation of resistance: and that to impute *resistance* to the said Revolution, is to cast black and odious colours upon the the said Revolution." The fourth and last article ends thus: " And that his said malicious and seditious suggestions may make the stronger impressions upon the minds of his Majesty's subjects, he, the said Henry Sacheveverell, doth wickedly wrest and pervert divers texts and passages of Holy Scriptures."	God to his own secret purpose directs the worst actions of *tyrants*, no less than the best of godly princes. Man's abuse, therefore, of his delegated authority is to be borne by resignation, like any other of God's judgments. The opposition of the individual to the Sovereign Power, is an opposition to God's providential arrangements. In Governments, which are the worst administered, the Sovereign Power, for *the most part*, is a terror not to good works, but to the evil, and upon the whole, far more beneficial than detrimental to the subject. But this general good of Government cannot be secured upon any other terms, than the *submission of the individual* to what may be called its *extraordinary evils*, (p. 17.) St. Pauls represents the earthly Sovereign as the vice-gerent of God, *accountable for misconduct to his heavenly master*, but entitled to obedience from the subject.

CHAPTER XI.

FEBRUARY, 1793.

CONTENTS.

France declares war against England and Holland—Our views in going to war, not avowed—The National Convention announces their reasons for declaring war—King's message to both Houses— Debates on the addresses moved thereupon—Mr. Fox's motion upon the grounds of the war—Dumourier enters Holland— Breda, and other towns besieged—Two thousand English Guards sail for Holland: and twelve thousand Hanoverian troops sent thither, to be under the command of the Duke of York—Warlike preparations general throughout the empire—Four fencible regiments in Scotland resolved upon, instead of a militia—A militia proposed and adopted in Ireland, of sixteen thousand men—Five thousand men voted to augment the forces of that Kingdom—Mr. Gratan's caution to Ministers upon this augmentation of forces.

IT is the usual reply to all complaints against the ruinous war, in which we are fatally involved, that it is *defensive*, and therefore unavoidable on the part of Great Britain. True it is, that the first actual and express declaration of hostilities proceeded from the French Republic, when on the second of the month, the Convention decreed, that on account of the multiplied acts of hostility and aggression, (which were detailed in the Convention) the French Republic was, from that time, at war with the King of England, and the Stadtholder of the United Provinces. This open and manly conduct of the republic, was certainly more honourable and just, than the system of intended insults, and avowed aggreſſions, with which this country provoked France, to the neceſſity of declaring hoſtilities. It is a humiliating circumſtance for Great Britain to be outdone in candour, by any nation: peculiarly ſo by the French in their preſent ſituation. It is beneath the ſpirit and principle of a Briton firſt to provoke, and then to aſſume the merit of being forced to the combat, by the acceptance of the challenge. The mean attempt could never have been made, but to diſſemble truth or cover infamy. If the principles and views of the confederated powers, which we have coaleſced to forward, will ſtand the teſt of honeſt inveſtigation, why not diſcloſe them to the nation that riſks its welfare in their ſupport ?. Government, to this hour, either knows them not, or dares not avow them. The late proclamation of his Majeſty, publiſhed at Toulon, which expreſſes a hope, that the other powers have the ſame moderate views in their exertions againſt France, which he has, beſpeaks the ignorance of them on one hand: and on the other, the actual confederacy in a war of ſuch magnitude, forbids the ſurmiſe of its being hazarded upon unknown principles, and with uncertain views. It is notorious, that Auſtria and Pruſſia, in making war againſt France, whilſt it had a Conſtitution, muſt have had different views, than when they declared, that their intention was to re-eſtabliſh royalty, upon the principles of that very Conſtitution. This policy of forcing France into the declaration of hoſtilities, was only for the inſidious purpoſe of avoiding a declaration of the principles, upon which we entered into the war: a purpoſe as diſhonourable to our enemy, as diſhoneſt to ourſelves. But it has been the late fatality of our countrymen, to be ſeduced by doctrines and opinions, which they cannot defend, and which they bluſh to avow. Mr. Burke has been explicit in detailing the principles, views, and motives of this war. He complained, indeed, in the debate of the 12th inſtant upon the war, that the progreſs of his opinion had been too ſlow upon the Nation ; though now the full blown miſchief had effectually alarmed them into their full adoption. * " Thefe madmen to be cured, " muft firft, like other madmen be fubdued. Never fhall I think " any country in Europe to be fecure, whilft there is eftablifhed " in the very centre of it, a ftate (if fo it may be called) found-" ed upon principles of anarchy, and which is, in reality, a col-" lege of armed fanatics, for the propagation of the principles of " affaffination, robbery, rebellion, fraud, faction, oppreffion, and " impiety." If, however, the fword be drawn to fubdue thefe madmen, to correct their morals, and to prevent the infection of their principles, the nation had furely a right to know the end to be attained by this vaft expenfe of their blood and treafure: they were entitled to examine the grounds of this extraordinary miffion, to cure difeafes, correct vice, and ftem immorality by the *dint of the fword.* This is a fpirit of chivalry very coftly, and very precarious; a crufade to be warily preached up, and encouraged. Are then the madnefs, the anarchy, the vices of the French, a reafon why Great Britain is to facrifice her peace, treafure, blood, and profperity? Is their cure or correction to terminate the war? I blufh, however, to contraft the manly, and fyftematic conduct, of thefe very madmen, with our own.

They publifhed a declaration, that the King of England had withdrawn his ambaffador from France, and refufed to acknowledge the ambaffador of their Republic; that the Britifh Government had obftructed the purchafe of corn, arms, and merchandize made by French citizens, and agents of the Republic, and laid an embargo on veffels bound for France, prohibited the circulation of affignats, fubjected French citizens to inquifitional vexations, and refufed them refidence in England, in violation of the treaty of commerce: that England had greatly increafed its forces by land and fea, whilft at peace with every power in Europe, and boafted in parliament, that France was the hoftile object of its armaments: that the Britifh Minifters had uniformly returned their propofals and offers of

* Letter, 19, 20.

peace, with haughtinefs, difdain, and arrogance: that they had fent a fquadron into the Scheldt, to interrupt their warlike operations in the Netherlands: that the King of England had concluded a treaty with Auftria and Pruffia, their enemies, fo recently as in the laft month of January, and had drawn into the league againft their Republic, the Stadtholder of the United States, who had fince taken fimilar preparatory fteps for hoftilities againft them: that they are neceffitated to look upon thefe acts of the Britifh Court, and of Holland, as acts of hoftility, and equivalent to a delaration of war. It is to be lamented, that England has not been equally explicit in avowing and declaring the reafons and motives for the acts of aggreffion, with which the French Republic fo publicly charge her.

The whole fyftem of aggreffion and defence, and the detail of the reafons, principles, views, motives, and ends of the war, were fully entered into by both Houfes of Parliament, in the debate upon the fame day on which his Majefty's meffage concerning the war, was delivered by Lord Grenville to the Lords, and by Mr. Pitt to the Commons. Similar amendments were propofed in both Houfes, to the addreffes moved for to the Crown upon the meffage. Thefe amendments went to exprefs a cordial co-operation of the refpective Houfes in profecuting a juft and neceffary war, in order to procure a fafe and honourable peace; but, which fhould import no approbation nor fanction to minifters, for having through their imprudence or obftinacy involved the country in a war, from which it might be now too late to extricate it, otherwife than by the fuccefs of their arms or the bafeft of conceffions. The chief fupporters of thefe amendments in the Lords, were the Marquis of Lanfdowne and the Earls of Lauderdale and Stanhope; in the Commons, Meffrs. Fox, Sheridan, and fome few others, whom Mr. Burke tauntingly, on this occafion, termed the dwindled phalanx * of Oppofition.

* Mr. Sheridan, in his reply to Mr. Burke, obferved, that it was but lately that the Right Honourable Gentleman had beftowed this appellation upon the Oppofition: he, however, gloried in it, for the

Here was again an accumulation of triumph to Mr. Burke, in the sure and general (though according to him, but too slow) operation of his.* great lessons : because, *in events like these our passions instruct our reason*. The servants of the Crown very successfully excited the feelings of the members against the French, as a horde of assassins, thieves, and regicides, then easily discoloured every measure that had been adopted by them. Of all the reasons reported to their Convention for their declaration of hostilities, one only was positively denied, which was the conclusion of a treaty with the Emperor in the month of January. The production, however, of the papers concerning it, when called for by Lord Lauderdale, was refused. The Ministers admitted a negociation for a general armed combination against France, but disavowed any view or intention of interfering with her internal affairs, or of imposing upon her and particular form of Government. They represented several acts of the French Government as aggressions on their part; and insisted, particularly, that their decree of *fraternization*, their entry of Scheldt, and conquests in Brabant, Savoy, and Germany, were each a sufficient ground for declaring war against them. They admitted, that even after Chauvelin had been ordered away, Maret had returned with fresh proposals for ensuring peace; but that he had not been accredited, nor his proposals received: yet they assumed the merit of more patience, indulgence, and experiment in their efforts to avert the war, than the justice of the case, or the importance of the crisis, would perhaps justify. Refusing to accredit any Envoy from the existing Government of France, with whom they possibly could treat, they boasted of a special commission sent over to Lord Auckland to negociate for peace with Dumourier, who had received his command of the French armies from that very Provisional Executive Council, to which they denied the power of deputing

---

term implied a body of men compact in its formation, and acting with union and vigour.

* Reflections, p. 119.

an accredited Envoy. Appeal was, on the other fide, made to the notoriety of facts, and the undeniable conclufions from avowed principles. The recal of our Ambaffador from Paris was ftated as a declaration of hoftilities, within the exprefs meaning of the fecond article of the treaty of commerce: that the prohibiting the exportation of corn to France, when other foreign markets were open, and the Alien Bill, were fpecific violations of the fame treaty: the difgraceful expulfion of the French Ambaffador was an open declaration of hoftilities. The queftion was forcibly put by Lord Lanfdowne, " Who are the aggref-
" fors?—They who kept a Minifter, or they who difmiffed him;
" they who offered to explain, or they who refufed to hear; they
" who offered to go on and trade in amity, or they who prohi-
" bited the exportation of grain to them, whilft open to all the
" reft of the world?" By this war we were making a common caufe with Auftria and Pruffia, who had never hitherto avowed their views and principles, and we might, perhaps, be drawn in to join them againft the will of the Nation, to impofe a government upon France, a purpofe which we had ftill the grace formally to difavow. Minifters had caufed or permitted the alarms and paffions of the Nation to be raifed and inflamed. They have committed us in a war, and they dare not avow the caufes of it, nor tell us on what terms peace might have been preferved, or may hereafter be procured. The event of the laft campaign, and the example of the American war were ferious mementos to Minifters, that we may be compelled to make peace on terms lefs advantageous than could have been obtained without unfheathing the fword. All thofe who fpoke for the amendment to the addrefs, uniformly expreffed their earneftnefs in carrying on the war vigoroufly, whilft we were unfortunately involved in it; but perfifted that they could not, in truth and juftice, join in an addrefs, which afferted it to be an unprovoked aggreffion on the part of France.

Mr. Fox and his friends were refolved to make one more effort to afford their country an unequivocal proof of their patriotifm, in difcountenancing the neceffity of the war: he accordingly propofed a ftring of refolutions, that tended fairly to difcriminate the grounds of the war, which the Minifters avowed, from thofe which they difavowed; in order that the nation might, at all times, know how near they approached to the end, which was propofed by the war, and when the propriety or exigency might arife of making either a feparate or a general peace. Mr. Fox candidly alledged, that his object for making thefe motions, was to procure a declaration of the precife grounds upon which Gentlemen had voted for the war; for, from many circumftances, he was induced to believe, that the *real* objects of our Minifters in going to war, were thofe which they difclaimed; and that *thofe* which they avowed, were only pretexts. Since, however, none of the refolutions went to the merits, but only to a manifeftation of the reafons and grounds of the war, the fame objections did not feem to lie againft them, as might be raifed againft a motion of cenfure or difapprobation of the meafure. The motion, however, produced a very heated debate, lefs interefting than any of the former debates upon the fubject, by the repetition of old arguments; but fuperabounding with invective and malevolent infinuation. The Houfe divided upon the motion, forty-four for, and two hundred and twenty-fix againft it. The war being now irretrievably entered into, and Dumourier having failed in all his efforts to negociate for peace, entered Holland with his victorious troops, and foon reduced Breda to a capitulation: Klundert, Williamftadt, and Maeftricht were befieged: and Bergen-op-Zoom, Tholem, and Steenberg were blockaded at the fame time. Two thoufand Britifh guards were fent over to Holland, under the command of the Duke of York: and a body of twelve thoufand Hanoverians were ordered to march immediately towards Holland, to be under his Royal Highnefs's command.

Warlike preparations were forwarded throughout every part of the empire. In Scotland, Mr. Dundas had propofed to eftablifh a militia: but the plan was abandoned, and four regiments of fencibles were refolved upon in lieu of it. Lord Hillfborough moved, in the Houfe of Commons in Ireland, for leave to bring in a Bill to eftablifh a militia of fixteen thoufand men: and on the fame day, the Chancellor of the Exchequer moved to raife an additional force of five thoufand men: both motions were agreed to. But upon the latter, Mr. Grattan wifhed to know precifely the purpofe of this augmentation: whether to affift Great Britain in the French war, or to guard againft the danger of domeftic infurrection. He obferved, that with this augmentation of the army, and the eftablifhment of the militia, the Irifh forces would amount to thirty-three thoufand men, a force unprecedented in that kingdom. He added, that it was in reliance upon the candour of that Houfe that they would give every neceffary redrefs to the complaints of the people, that he agreed to the augmentation. He warned them againft the fallacious hope, that the force, which they now received, would enable them to defpife or reject the wifhes and voice of the people. Ireland would never be more coerced by force.

Of all the powers that coalefced againft France, Ruffia feems to have been the moft politic and refined. She engaged to fupply large fubfidies, ten fail of the line, and whatever troops fhould be wanted to fupport the caufe. It is believed, that fhe fent fome pecuniary relief to the French Princes. She certainly paid marked honours to the Count of Artois, whilft in Ruffia, and fent him in a frigate to join his brother and the other emigrants in Germany. The fhips have not as yet appeared in our feas, and her men have been lately known to march to no other country, than to fubdue and to enflave the unfortunate Poles. And yet, within her territories, fhe has been more rigoroufly fevere in guarding againft the propagation of the French principles than any fovereign in Europe. On the 8th of this month, fhe fent off the French ambaffador, banifhed every Frenchman and woman from her ftates, who refufed, upon oath, to renounce the prefent power of Government in France, and prohibited the importation of French books, journals, and newfpapers into any part of the Ruffian Empire.

CHAPTER XII.

MARCH, 1793.

CONTENTS.

Mr. Sheridan's motion and speech concerning sedition—Secession of Mr. Burke and others from the Whig Club—The Budget—Mr. Sheridan's speech thereon—Traitorous Correspondence Bill—Money attached in the Bank, supposed to belong to the French Government—Loan of 4,500,000*l.*—12,000 *Hanoverian troops subsidized by England—The Minister charged with delay in succouring Holland—The turn of fortune in favour of the Allies—Lord Auckland's memorial to the States General upon the turn of fortune—Dumourier defeated in three engagements—Evacuates Brabant and Holland—Archduke Charles enters Bruxelles—Joy at the departure of the French—Affairs of Ireland—Defenders—Declaration of the Dungannon association—Report of the Lords on the troubles in Ireland.*

THE spirit of espionage and information, first engendered by the proclamation, since openly fostered by Mr. Reeves's association, and certainly not discountenanced by Government, had now grown into such strength as to produce consequences of the most alarming nature. The agitated minds of the public were daily more and more inflamed, by the most terrifying accounts of domestic insurrections and deep-laid plans to destroy the Constitution. The *dwindled Phalanx* of Opposition was so openly, so grosly and so confidently abused and calumniated,

that to many their very names were synonymous with the term
of traitor and enemy: even in the very houses of parliament,
prejudices, alarms, and fears, had operated upon many a conviction, that to disapprove of the war against France, was treason to
England; that to examine or enquire into the gronnds of public
measures, had almost ceased to be the constitutional duty of a
Senator; and to divide with Opposition, was but little short of
rallying under the standard of sedition and rebellion. Any scheme
against the state, in which such able men as those who composed
the Opposition had concurred, would have been truly alarming.
The rank, talents, and respectability of the conspirators, had such
been the case, were indissoluble ties upon Ministers to drag them
forth to the justice of their offended country. Now that the
fever of alarm has abated, and men are allowed to reflect
upon the tendency of public measures, without incurring the
suspicion or guilt of sedition, it will not shock the loyalty even of
Mr. Burke to assert, that known acts of *riot* and *insurrection* must
make known some criminal perpetrators of them, that conspiracies
and treasons cannot be discovered without the knowledge of the
conspirator or traitor. Will he not allow, that the severity of the
law loses its energy in ceasing to be exemplary? In justice, therefore, to the calumniated people of Great Britain, to rescue the
public mind from the agitation of imaginary dangers, and to re-
establish the confidence of a deluded people in the executive powers of Government, Mr. Sheridan moved in the House, that
an humble address be presented to his Majesty, praying that his
Majesty may be pleased to give directions, " that there be laid
" before the House of Commons, all the information which may
" have come before his Majesty on the subject of sedition, in or-
" der that it may be referred to a committee of this House, &c."
With respect to the late supposed sedition, and disposition to insurrection, and the lurking treason, of which so much was said,
and so much more seemed conjectured and suspected, there were
three circumstances to be considered, and three points of view in
which the subject ought to be placed. The first was, that the

danger had been real. The second was, that the whole was a false alarm, really entertained by Government; in which case, the propagation, although unfortunate, was yet honest. The third was, that the whole was founded on a systematic plan, laid by Government, for deluding the sense and finally subduing the spirit of the people. In any of these suppositions, the only mode of satisfying the justice of the people, quieting the public alarms, or justifying the Ministers to the Nation, was to institute a committee of enquiry. In a very long and animated speech, he entered largely and clearly into each of these distinct points. Mr. Lambton seconded the motion: a very violent debate ensued, in which Mr. Fox, Mr. Wyndham, and Mr. Burke took the chief part. The motion however was negatived without a division.

That Ministers had purposely raised these alarms, in order to seduce the Nation into a war, which in cool reason it would have reprobated, is a fact, perhaps, at all times, out of proof; in vain is it argued against the feelings of interested parties at the time, and will only gain impartial credit from a future unbiassed review of the facts, which both parties now admit, and variously represent. Certain it is, that no individual, from that time to this, has been prosecuted for any act of *riot* or *insurrection*, or for any rebellion or treason, that could have given rise to any danger, or that ought to have caused any alarm in the country. The Ministerial party admits the fact, but attributes it not to the want of guilt, but to the impropriety or danger of punishing the criminal. The Opposition rest the innocence of the country upon this very pretended forbearance of Government to punish the culprit. This spirit of forbearance, whether grounded on mildness, prudence, or policy, has not since continued very general; for there is scarcely a bookseller, connected with opposition, that has not, since that time, been prosecuted for having sold the works of Thomas Paine, at some time within the two years, during which they were so generally circulated with impunity.

Few circumstances mark more strongly the inveteracy of the political prejudice, with which Mr. Fox was at this time viewed by the public, than the fecefsion of forty-five members from the Whig Club; amongst whom were Meſſrs. Burke and Wyndham. Their pretence for feceding was, on account of the following refolution, which had been entered into on the 20th of the preceding month, viz. " That the club think it their duty, at " this extraordinary juncture, to aſſure the Right Honourable " Charles James Fox, that all the acts of mifreprefentation which " have been fo induftrioufly uſed of late, for the purpofe of ca- " lumniating him, have had no other effect upon them, than that " of confirming, ftrengthening, and increaſing their attachment " to him." Upon this refolution, no difficulty nor objection could arife againſt Mr. Fox, but in the minds of thofe, who gave credit to the calumnies; and if they really believed, or knew him to be guilty of what he was accufed, it was their duty to do fomething more than to withdraw themfelves from a club, of which he was a member. In matters of fedition and treafon, connivance, fuppreffion, and permiffion are not wholly innocuous in this country: our laws make a ferious crime of *miſpriſion* of treafon.

The Miniſter having fucceeded in plunging the Nation into a war with France, by concealing from their fight both the principle and the end propofed to be attained by it, his next concern was, to fupprefs from their view, the neceſſary hardſhips that muſt attend it. Accordingly, in opening his budget for the current year, he took the average of the laſt four years fuccefsful peace, as the foundation for his prefent eſtimate; prefumptuoufly flattering the nation with the deluſive profpect of an increaſing revenue, notwithſtanding a ruinous war. The unprecedented number of bankruptcies, which have marked the prefent as the moſt inaufpicious year to the trading intereſt of this kingdom, has but too fatally detected the fallacy of this fpeculation. And the fequel of the events of this hiſtory will prove the melancholy futility of his boaſt of the profpect of our fuccefs in the profecution of the war. Mr. Sheridan obferved on the Miniſter's fpeech of this day, that it had little novelty, except the novelty of introducing, in a day devoted to figures, all the arts of declamation. He had suddenly laid down his pencil and slate, and, grasping his truncheon, had finished with an harangue more calculated for a General of a heated army, going to storm a French redoubt, than a Minister of finance, discussing accounts, in the sober hour of calculation, with the stewards and attorneys of a burthened and patient people. Wherever he saw exertion and eloquence so misplaced, he always suspected there was some weakness to cover in the subject itself. He was the more led into the apprehension, by some very alarming hints the Right Honourable Gentleman had dropped, concerning new connections still to be formed. It seemed, the expensive corps of 12,000 Hanoverians were not the only foreign troops we were to pay. New subsidies and foreign mercenaries were announced, and in a manner that seemed to avow, that Government were adopting the general principles of the Austrian and Prussian confederacy. It requires an extraordinary degree of sagacity to find out the necessity of a more extended alliance, and more numerous forces to protect our Dutch allies from the invasion of the French, to secure to them their right by treaty to the exclusive navigation of the Scheldt, and to preserve ourselves from the menacing effects of the fraternizing decree of the 19th of November. Yet are these the *avowed grounds* for undertaking the war. The irritation of the public mind was systematically to be still kept up, and the strongest measures at home were the instruments of this fatal delusion. The plain simple law of treason, settled in the 25th year of our third Edward, which, for 500 years, had been unexceptionably found effectual against all attacks and attempts upon the Constitution, was to be opened, after the sanction of so many centuries had put its venerable seal upon it, to the admission of a variety of new crimes and offences, (as was observed by Mr. Fox in the House) framed merely for the purpose of lending support to the false alarm of sedition and treason, which Ministers had found necessary to excite in the country. The Attorney General moved for leave to bring in the Traitorous Correspondence Bill; the outline of which he opened to the House to the following effect: That it was in future to be made high treason, 1st, To supply the existing government of France, or any persons in alliance with them, with arms or military stores, or to purchase any thing for them or any of them. 2dly, To purchase lands of inheritance in France, to invest money in any of the French funds, or to lend money on any security in France. 3dly, To go from this country into France, without licence of his Majesty and the privy Seal. 4thly, For a British subject to land in Great Britain without a passport or leave, or else to deliver himself to the next magistrate, to undergo an inquisitorial examination, and faithfully to disclose where he had been, whither he was going, the reason of his journey out and home, and give surety to any amount required for his good behaviour. 5thly, To underwrite insurances upon ships and goods bounden from France to any part of the world. Messrs. Fox and Erskine very pointedly reprobated the Bill, as utterly repugnant to the principles of freedom, justice, and policy, militating against the interest of this country, and against the spirit of its fixed laws and constitution. Leave was however given to bring it in. The great superseding principle of State necessity sanctioned this and every other public or private measure that could be forced into the fatal chain of French concerns. The sacred, and hitherto unviolated deposit of property in the bank of England, was no longer a security to the individual, and the sum of 100,000l, deposited there, by the respectable house of Bourdieu and Cholett, was attached by the Attorney General, upon a supposition of its being property belonging to the persons exercising the powers of government in France. Mr Burke had long taught the necessity of these strong measures: * " There " is no safety for honest men, but by believing *all possible evil of* " *evil men*, and by acting with promptitude, decision, and steadi- " ness on that belief." Calm reason and reflection will inform

* Letter to a Member, p. 8.

us, that the hardſhip, cruelty, or injuſtice of violent *meaſures* ever reſt with thoſe who brought on the neceſſity of adopting them. The Traitorous Correſpondence Bill was hardly combated by the gentlemen of the Oppoſition in every ſtage, upon the grounds of its obſcurity, inconſiſtency, and manifeſt injuſtice; it was carried through the Houſe, though no two of the Law Members agreed in their interpretation of the operation and effects of the different clauſes; but the advocates for the war found it a neceſſary previous ſtep to reconcile the minds of the public to the war, and it had all the appearance of an attempt to engraft a general belief of paſt guilt upon this ſpecious neceſſity of preventing it in future. The Chancellor of the Exchequer has ever claimed a peculiar confidence from the public, for his minute and truſty attention to every object of finance. But Mr. Fox proved in the Houſe, ſo forcibly, that Mr. Pitt admitted, that in negociating the loan of 4,500,000l. he had ſuffered, by the terms he had made, an evident loſs to the public, and of courſe a gain to ſome individuals of 200,000l. Although in this inſtance *a great miniſter of finance* were *ex confeſſo* taken in, or over-reached in his bargain, yet it is ardently to be wiſhed that future loans may neither augment patronage, nor ſupply the Miniſter with the lubricous means of purchaſing ſupport in thoſe fatal meaſures which induce the neceſſity of taxation.

When on the 15th inſt. in the committee upon the extraordinaries of the armies, the Miniſter brought forward the firſt reſolution for ſubſidizing 12,000 Hanoverian troops, deſtined for the aſſiſtance of Holland, Lord Fielding charged him with the moſt criminal neglect in delaying to give aſſiſtance to Holland. He was ſupported by Major Maitland, who preſſed upon the Miniſter facts and dates, which are more ſtubborn arguments than thoſe of reaſon and cenſure, be they ever ſo pointed and juſt. Miniſters had expreſsly acknowledged that on the 17th of December they conſidered the French as an enemy in the ſtate of hoſtile preparation. They knew the defenceleſs ſtate of Holland, and the danger that threatened it. Yet they only entered into the negociation for fubfidizing the Hanoverian troops on the 22d of February, and 1956 guards failed from Greenwich on the 23d of February. " Was this," faid he, " an exertion becoming " a great and powerful nation, at fo critical and important a " crifis?" By the delay in fending the guards, they were nearly loft in a ftorm. They were fent out to a poft where there was, at that time, no profpect of victory; and had not the progrefs of the French arms been providently checked by the Auftrians and Pruffians, who had raifed the fiege of Maeftricht, they muft, in all likelihood, have fallen into the hands of Dumourier, as did the garrifons of Klundert and Breda. Minifters, however, could claim no credit for this turn of fortune, for, at this time, they were ignorant of it. The Chancellor of the Exchequer endeavoured to repel thefe charges of negligence, by ftating, that the neceffary preparations for fuch enterprifes, had taken up the intermediate fpace of time from December to February. The public, however, have ftill to learn, how the fpace of eight weeks can be found neceffary to tranfport fo fmall an handful of men, ready armed and formed, from England to Holland, and they fee little other preparation neceffary to put in motion this Hanoverian body of troops, than the mere ceremony of fubfidizing them; which in plain Englifh, imports nothing more than a change of paymafter. The King of Great Britain in future pays the troops, which the Elector of Hanover before maintained The Britifh treafury faving during the fubfidy, to that of Hanover, the charges of all thofe ftanding troops of the Electorate, which Great Britain takes into pay; there muft fomewhere have exifted an unaccountable rage for negociating, that could fo ingenioufly have fpun out for two month, a treaty between the King of Great Britain and the Elector of Hanover, by fifcal difficulties, diplomatic objections, or any other dilatory means whatever. It is far from my intent to derogate from the merit of our brave foldiers who went over to Holland; and I do not, as is generally done, attribute the favourable turn of fortune to their arrival; they have, and ever will, execute with

distinguished bravery and resolution every order given to them; and I glory in saying, that they have uniformly through the whole campaign, most deservedly acquired the love and admiration of their allies, and the dread and equal admiration of their enemies. On the 19th of this month, the Court published at the Hague, a detail of events, that states the fair and real cause of this change in the affairs of the armies. " After the check
" which the French invasion into our republic met with, the
" success of the allies against them, since the first of this month,
" has been so rapid, that it surpasses even the general expecta-
" tion. The French armies twice beaten by the Imperial troops,
" and once by the Prussians, have abandoned the bombardment
" of Venlo, raised the siege of Maestricht, have evacuated
" Ruremonde and its intrenchments, Aix-la-Chapelle, and Liege.
" All the French troops have retreated into Brabant; and in
" quitting the dependencies of Bois-le-duc, which they invested,
" they lost a great part of their artillery; even the siege artillery
" is in the hands of the conquerors. Their forces are reduced
" by a great number of killed, wounded, and prisoners. This
" has happened within a week's time; and according to all pro-
" bability, must change the face of affairs in such a manner, as
" to make those act upon the defensive, who, not long before,
" imagined they could carry every thing before them by offen-
" sive means. The road that lead to those advantages acquired
" by the allied powers, was the victory gained by General Clair-
" fait on the 1st of March, near Aldenhoven."

Soon after the publication of this paper, by the authority of the Court, Lord Auckland, our Ambassador at the Hague, who had been to wait upon the Duke of York, on his landing at Dort, presented a memorial to their High Mightinesses, to congratulate with them upon this successful turn of fortune. It is curious to observe, with what dexterity Lord Auckland retorts upon the French, the obvious advantage they had lately taken of the Duke of Brunswick's thundering and inefficient manifestos against their nation. His Lordship excels in profiting of the whimsical turns of fortune. He says, " That the sundry " manifestos, by which they (the French) anticipated the con- " quest of the Republic, being cruel and menacing in their " principles, would, at present, produce nothing but contempt, " if their short appearance had not been attended with violence " and cruelty, evidences of the ruin and universal destruction " which would have been most unavoidably the result of their " success."

In the course of the month, Dumourier was forced to abandon his conquests in Holland in order to rally his forces in Brabant. It was the last effort which he had to make to retain the possession of the Netherlands. Three very bloody and obstinate engagements took place between Dumourier and the Prince of Saxe Cobourg. The French were forced to retreat to Bruxelles, and on the 24th they evacuated that city, and the rest of the Austrian territories. About the same time, also, they retired from Breda and Gertruydenberg, and wholly evacuated the Republic of Holland. The month of March was an unprecedented scene of carnage. Above 30,000 men were slain in the different engagements that took place in the course of it. The re-conquest of Belgium was entirely effected without any assistance of the British troops. The Arch-Duke Charles, the brother of the Emperor, who had been lately created Lieutenant Governor and Captain General of the Low Countries, entered Bruxelles, and was received amidst the joyful acclamations of the people. It is to be observed, that the Commissioners, sent by the Convention, had, as Dumourier complains in a letter to it, " oppressed the Belgians by every species of vexation, violated " the sacred rights of their liberty, impudently insulted their re- " ligious opinions, and robbed and plundered their churches for " the sake of the pitiful lucre of the sacred vessels." They therefore exulted more in their retreat, than they had rejoiced at their first entry into Brabant.

The spirit and feelings of the people at this time in Ireland, announced serious grounds for alarm; the Dissenters and Independent party became daily more firm and resolute in their efforts to bring about a fair representation of the people in Parliament, and rested upon the emancipation of the Roman Catholics, as the corner stone of this great national object. The Roman Catholics had come before Parliament with the strongest recommendation from the Crown, and were confidently and firmly awaiting the result of their deliberations. The doctrines of Thomas Paine, which had been so generally propagated with impunity through the lowest classes of the people, were operating their destructive effects in the rapaciousness and cruelties of their wretched and infatuated proselytes *. These unfortunate wretches, who called themselves *Defenders*, were by those who dreaded the success either of the Roman Catholic petition, or the resolution to examine into the abuses of the popular representation, which were both before Parliament, most maliciously misrepresented, and were even openly spoken of in Parliament, as the hired instruments for intimidating the legislature into concession. The Dungannon Association thought proper to make an unequivocal declaration of their principles, to repel the ill-founded suspicions. They published a series of the most constitutional resolutions of their attachment to the King, Lords and Commons; and particularly, that they highly disapproved of Republican forms of Government, as " applied to this King-

---

* In the summer of the year 1791, I learnt with sorrow, that Mr. Paine's *Rights of Man* were so generally distributed about Ireland, that persons were hired to read them to such as could not read themselves, and that their adoption had become very general. I then said, *Case stated*, p. 19. " The lower class of the Irish, I un-
" derstand to be a race robust and hardy, and of a very irritable
" disposition and nature; they are now indolent in extreme poverty,
" from being debarred the common resources of industry; and are
" averse to all laws, from having felt the constant pressure of such
" only as are galling and severe. It is scarely possible for these in-
" fatuated zealots for sedition and anarchy, to have found more
" ready materials to operate upon, than persons of this description
" so circumstanced."

"dom, and they rejected with abhorrency those principles which
"have a tendency to diffolve all government, and to deftroy
"every wife and falutary diftinction in fociety." They expreffed the fatisfaction with which they beheld Parliament engaged, and pledged to look into the ftate of the popular reprefentation; that a complete reform of it was effential to the peace,
liberty, and happinefs of the people; and they folemnly pledged
to their country, and to each other, the firmeft perfeverance in
all conftitutional meafures, till that great end fhould have been
unequivocally obtained. The Roman Catholic bifhops, and feveral gentlemen of landed property, not only publifhed declarations againft thefe *Defenders*, but entered into affociations for
apprehending and profecuting them. Yet could they not do
away the fufpicion thrown upon them by fome perfons interefted
in keeping up the delufion, who had, as Mr. Burke fays, * " *a
"difpofition to carry the imputation of crimes from perfons to defcrip-
"tions, and wholly to alter the character and quality of the of-
"fences themfelves.*"

A Committee of the Lords had been appointed to inquire into
the caufes of the diforders and difturbances which prevailed
in feveral parts of the kingdom, and the Lord Chancellor was
appointed by the Lords Committees to make the report on the
7th of the month; the firft part of which confifted of an apology for bringing it forward fo early; although they had not
had time to make full enquiries (the Roman Catholic Bill was
now pending in the Houfe of Lords.) They proceeded to ftate,
that from what the Committee fhould difcover, thefe Defenders
were *all* of the Roman Catholic perfuafion, poor and ignorant,
and fworn to fecrecy; not appearing to *have any diftinct object in
view*, and yet that their meafures appear to have been concerted
and conducted with the utmoft fecrecy, and *a degree of regularity
and fyftem*, not ufual in people in fuch mean condition, as if directed by men of fuperior rank. That fums of money had

* Letter to Sir Hercules Langrifhe, p. 19.

been, and continued to be levied upon the Roman Catholics at their chapels, and elsewhere throughout the kingdom; and a circular letter was annexed to the report, which enclosed a plan for a general subscription, which had for its object the raising a fund for defraying the heavy and growing expenses incurred by the General Committee, in conducting the affairs of the Catholics of Ireland. They annexed, also, another letter from a Mr. Sweetman, to a person at Dundalk, concerning a relation of Mr. Nugent's, confined there under an indictment; and that it appeared, that this person, to whom the letter was written, had employed an agent and counsel, to act for persons accused of being Defenders. Yet after all this insinuation of Roman Catholic guilt, levying money, and giving assistance to the accused, the Committee thought it their duty to state, That nothing appeared before them, which could lead them to believe, that the Body of the Roman Catholics were concerned in promoting, or countenancing these disturbances. They further stated several facts of meetings, both armed and unarmed, at Belfast and Newry; that seditious pamphlets were constantly published, extolling the example of France; that prayers were made from pulpits, for the success of the French arms; that armed bodies had uniforms in imitation of the French, with harps on the buttons under a cap of liberty, instead of a crown; that more gunpowder had been sent to these places than could be wanted for ordinary purposes; all which circumstances were intended to overawe the legislature, and procure a parliamentary reform. The Committee forebore mentioning the names of several persons, *lest it should in any manner affect a criminal prosecution.* The Parliament proceeded in the Roman Catholic Bill, though nothing more was hitherto done upon the resolution to examine into the state of the popular representation in parliament. This system of alarming, by insinuation and misrepresentation, and calumniating a whole people, by criminating no individual, seems not to have been confined to one side of the channel.

CHAPTER XIII.

APRIL, 1793.

CONTENTS.

Proceedings on the Traiterous Correspondence Bill—Power in the Crown to prohibit British subjects from returning into their country—Mr. Sheridan's motion to address his Majesty to disavow Lord Auckland's Memorial to the States General—Five Millions Exchequer Bills issued to support Commercial Credit—General Fast—Vote of Credit for 1,500,000l.—Dumourier sends the Commissioners prisoners to Clairfait—His address to his Army—Cobourg's Proclamation in favour of the Constitution of 1789—Dumourier narrowly escapes, and goes over to the Austrians—Congress of Antwerp—Cobourg's first Proclamation revoked by a second—The war resumed—The Roman Catholic Bill passes in Ireland—The state of that Body, and their method of procuring relief—Mr. Keogh's Speech to the Catholic Convention—The Bill, with its exceptions—The Chancellor against it—Owns that he yields to necessity in consenting—Public rejoicings for its passing.

THE domestic occurrences of this month, were chiefly consequences of those measures, which had been adopted in the preceding. Strong opposition was made in the Commons to the Traitorous Correspondence Bill, and to most of the new clauses and amendments which were introduced into it: for since its first introduction by the Attorney General, it had nearly changed both its form and substance before it even passed that

House. On the third reading Mr. Fox was very emphatic in his condemnation of it: he said, "It was a Bill, which, with "one exception, was the most unjust in its principles, inadequate "in its provision, and tyrannical in its effects, that ever passed "that House—one for which there was nothing like a precedent "either in policy, justice, or humanity." In the course of the debates upon this Bill, a question was put to the Solicitor General, by Mr. Grey, *Whether the Crown was empowered by law, to issue any proclamation, forbidding the entry into this country of a British subject, not convicted of a crime?*—To which the Solicitor General answered affirmatively—for regulating the general policy of the country. At this answer Mr. Fox took fire, and in a strain of uncommon animation, proved its falsity and danger. "I am sure," said he, "the King has no such power, "and never ought to have, and never will have, unless this House "shall scandalously neglect its duty." Upon Mr. Pitt's justifying the answer of the Solicitor General, which he also did with great warmth, Mr. Fox in reply said, "I am justly alarmed when I "hear such sentiments from such a quarter; for it is not his "own opinion merely, that the Honourable Gentleman is "speaking; I say, I am justly alarmed for the liberties of my "country, when such exploded doctrines upon the King's pre- "rogative are attempted to be revived; doctrines, to explode "which the best treasure of this country was expended, and the "purest blood shed."

Well may these doctrines appear strange and alarming to those who have not subscribed to Mr. Burke's lessons upon the powers of the British crown: they cannot shock those, who, with him, see *a more real, solid, and extensive power in the King of Great Britain, than the King of France was possessed of before this miserable Revolution.* It is well known that a King of France, could by his edict, send any of his subjects into banishment; he might therefore keep them in banishment, by preventing their return into his kingdom. But it is equally well known, that the King of England cannot force any of his subjects out of the realm, he cannot even compel them to accept of a foreign Embassy, left the power of sending them upon such dignified missions, might be perverted to the purpose of keeping them in honourable exile. It is indeed known to English Lawyers, that the Crown may grant a writ of *ne exeat regno*, to keep a subject within the jurisdiction of the courts of law; but they know not the form of a writ of *ne ingrediatur regnum*. There may be cases in which a British subject ought not to be permitted to evade the rigour of the law, none in which he should be precluded from coming within its justice. Several British subjects were actually detained on board vessels at this time off Dover, by the actual exercise of this hitherto unknown power in the Crown, till they should receive passports or licences to land on their native shore. How cruel, how unjust, how unconstitutional would it not be, to detain a British senator or officer (for there is no exception) who had been upon foreign service, from landing in his own country where his presence was immediately necessary, either for public, or his own private business!

An objection was taken by Mr. Adam, to that clause of the Bill, which provided that any offence committed against the act might be laid and tried in any country, and that the party accused or impeached, should be indicted, arraigned, tried, convicted, or attainted, by such like evidence, and in such form, as counterfeiters of the King's money. He maintained, that this clause militated against all the analogies of the English law, and all principles of justice. In all crimes of high treason, for supporting or abetting the King's enemies, which was the case of the Bill, the accused was allowed a copy of his indictment ten days before trial; a list of the jury, and a list of the witnesses to appear against him, and who could not be less than two in number; he was also allowed counsel in his behalf: but in the case of counterfeiting the King's coin, the whole was considered as simple felony, of which the evidence of one witness was sufficient to convict: no counsel to address the jury, no list of jurors nor of witnesses. There was much hardship in multiplying treasons, infinitely more in thus facilitating the means of conviction. He therefore moved an amendment, the substance of which was, that persons accused under this act, should be tried according to the 7th of William III. and the 7th of Ann, which provide for trials of high treason, in case of giving aid and comfort to the King's enemies. The motion was negatived, by one hundred and ten, against thirty-two, that voted for the amendment.

In the course of the debates, the Ministers, and Law Officers of the Crown, were forcibly urged to declare, whether the Bill were declaratory of the old, or introductory of a new law of treason: this they declined answering: their refusal afforded the opposers of the Bill this unanswerable dilemma—If it be declaratory, explain in what part of the statue of Edward III. this Bill is substantially contained: if it be a new and enacting law show the facts upon which you found its necessity. It has been the spirit and practice of our ancestors, whenever they have, on any occasion, found a necessity for opening the marked and known line of treason, as settled by the statute of Edward III. in the year 1350, to state the specific ground of necessity, and not to extend the operation of the new law of treason, beyond the continuance or duration of that necessity.

Mr. Sheridan had some time before given notice to the House, that he meant to make a motion of censure upon Lord Auckland, for the memorial which he had presented to their High Mightinesses, on the 5th of the current month; and on the 24th, he moved an address to his Majesty, to express the displeasure of that House at the memorial: that it departed from the principles upon which the House had concurred in the measures necessary for the support of the war: praying his Majesty publicly to disavow so much of the said memorial as contained a declaration of an intention to interfere with the internal government of France; and which expressed menaces against the perpetrators of facts, of which neither this, nor any foreign nation can have cognizance; which compelled this country, either unjustifiably to carry

on the war, for the subversion of the present government of
France, or disgracefully to seek peace, by an ignominious negociation with the very government we have insulted and stigmatized
in our public acts: and that these menaces tended to give to the
present war, a peculiar barbarism and ferocity, by provoking and
reviving a system of retaliation and bloodshed: and finally, to
represent to his Majesty, how deeply the reputation of his Majesty's Councils was interested, in disclaiming these unjustifiable,
and, they trusted, unauthorized denunciations of vengeance, so
destructive of all respect for the consistency, and of all confidence
in the sincerity in the public acts of his Ministers, and so ma-
nifestly tending at once to render the principle of the war unjust,
the conduct of hostilities barbarous, and the attainment of honourable peace hopeless.

The memorial alluded to, is to the following purport: " It
" is known, that towards the end of the month of September
" last year, his Britannic Majesty and your High Mightinesses,
" gave, in concert, a solemn assurance, that in case of the immi-
" nent danger, which then threatened the lives of their most
" Christian Majesties, and their family, should he realized, His
" Majesty, and Your Mightinesses, would not fail to take the most
" efficacious measures to prevent the persons, who might ren-
" der themselves guilty of so atrocious a crime, from finding
" any asylum in your respective dominions. This event, which
" was foreseen with horror, has taken place, and the divine ven-
" geance seems not to have been tardy. *Some of those detestable*
" *regicides, are, already, in such a situation that they may be sub-*
" *jected to the sword of the law.* The rest are still in the midst
" of a people, whom they have plunged into an abyss of evils,
" and for whom famine, anarchy, and civil war, are preparing
" new calamities. In short, every thing we see happen, induces
" us to consider as at hand, the end of these wretches, whose
" madness and atrocities, have filled with terror and indigna-
" tion, all those who respect the principles of religion, morality,
" and humanity. The undersigned, therefore, submit to the

" enlightened judgment and wifdom of your High Mightineſſes,
" whether it would not be proper to employ all the means in
" your power, to prohibit from entering your States in Europe,
" or your Colonies, all thofe members of the *felf-titled National
" Convention*, or of the *pretended Executive Council*, who have di-
" rectly or indirectly participated in the faid crime: and if they
" fhould be difcovered and arrefted, to deliver them up to juftice,
" that they may ferve as a leſſon and example to mankind."

Mr. Sheridan made a very long, eloquent, and pointed fpeech, upon the arrogance, impolicy, and mifchief of this memorial. Mr. Pitt defended and juftified it in general: though he explicitly difavowed the principles attempted to be introduced into the war by Lord Auckland, which muſt have rendered peace impoffible. The queftion being called for, Mr. Sheridan's motion was rejected by a very large majority.

The commercial credit of this country, had, by the diftreſſes of the war, been reduced to fuch an alarming degree of embarraſsment, that it became neceſſary for Government to fupport it, by fome fpeedy and efficacious means. A committee had been appointed, to examine into the commercial credit of the country, and they had reported, that it would be neceſſary, for the fupport of it, to iſſue Exchequer Bills, for 5,000,000l. at 2¼d. per cent. per diem, which were afterwards made iſſuable to commiſſioners, to be by them made out, under certain regulations and reftrictions, for the affiftance and accommodation of fuch perfons as might apply for it, and who fhould give, to fuch commiſſioners, proper fecurity for the fums that might be advanced for a limited time. Thefe were the early effects of the war. Though the fagacious, and never diffident Secretary of State for the Home Department, roundly afferted in the Houfe, in the debate upon the report of the committee, that the evil complained of, and proved to exift, was fo far from having been brought on by the war, *that the prefent embarraſſments arofe from the profperous ftate of the country at large. The very circumftance of the prefent ftagnation was a proof of the power and energy of this country.* In the courſe of the month, his Majeſty ſent a meſſage to both Houſes of Parliament, expreſſive of his intentions to proſecute the war with vigour and energy : he proclaimed a general faſt, to draw down the bleſſings of Heaven upon the ſucceſs of our arms, in ſo *juſt a war*; and a vote of credit paſſed for 1,500,000l.

The defection of Dumourier to the Auſtrians, was at firſt ſuppoſed to have turned the whole ſcale of affairs on the continent. On the 2d of the month, he ſent eight commiſſioners from the National Convention, under a ſtrong eſcort to General Clairfait. They were, ſaid Dumourier, ſpecially commiſſioned by the National Convention, to arreſt and conduct him a priſoner to their bar, and on any reſiſtance, to have him aſſaſſinated on the road. But, ſaid he, " I have been before hand " with them, in ſecuring theſe commiſſioners and their deputies " as my priſoners." Dumourier adds, in his letter, " that he was " that inſtant about to move, with the truſty part of his army, " in order to deſtroy all thoſe who may further oppoſe them- " ſelves to the public good of France, and to give to that diſ- " tracted kingdom permanent peace and tranquillity." Bournonville headed this commiſſion. It was ſuppoſed that Dumourier would, after this, have immediately moved with his army to the interior parts of France. He addreſſed his army in a ſhort, nervous ſpeech. " It is time," ſaid he, " for our army to diſcharge its vow, to purge France of its aſſaſſins and diſturbers, and to reſtore to our unhappy country, the repoſe which ſhe has loſt by the crimes of her repreſentatives. We muſt preſerve the Conſtitution we have ſworn to maintain : we cannot be free but with good laws : if otherwiſe, we ſhall be ſlaves of crimes." He afterwards made and publiſhed a long addreſs to the French nation, in which he paints the anarchy, cruelty, and wickedneſs of the rulers of France, in the ſtrongeſt colours. " But," ſays he, " we have a rallying point which can ſtifle " the monſter of anarchy : it is the Conſtitution we ſwore " to maintain in 1789, 1790, and 1791: it is the work of " a free people ; and we ſhall remain free and ſhall recover

" our glory by refuming our Conftitution.." He tells them alfo, that their generous enemies had engaged to fufpend their march, and not to pafs the frontiers till his brave army fhould have terminated the internal diffentions of the kingdom. The cheerfulnefs, bravery, and refolution with which Dumourier had found his army execute all his former commands, gave him reafonable expectations that, in the prefent crifis, they would not abandon him. In this confidence the Prince of Saxe Cobourg backed the addrefs of Dumourier, by a proclamation in his own name, to the French nation. He firft panegyrizes the General as a great and virtuous man, who truly loves his country: he then declares, that Their Imperial and Pruffian Majefties are filled with efteem for the French nation, fo great, fo generous, &c. and that he will fupport by all the force that was entrufted to him, the generous and beneficent intentions of General Dumourier and his brave army, to give to France her Conftitutional King, *the Conftitution which fhe had formed for herfelf*, and of courfe the means of rectifying, if fhe fhould find it imperfect: he pledged his honour, that he would not come upon the French territory to make conquefts, but folely and purely for the ends above fpecified.

The peculiar misfortune of this war has been, that not one of the combined powers has ever candidly avowed the principles upon which they undertook it, or acted on any emergency with the confiftency and uniformity of a regular and honourable fyftem. This proclamation of the commander in chief in April, was little compatible with thofe of the commander in chief of the preceding month of July. Now the whole force of the combined armies was to co-operate in re-eftablifhing that very Conftitution which they were then pledged to abolifh and deftroy. On the other hand, we beheld in the French an uniformity of principle, and an invariable fource of enthufiafm, always tending with fuperior and unprecedented energy to the fame open and avowed point. Of the many thoufand men, of which the army of Dumourier confifted, he found not one thoufand, upon experiment, to fecond his design. He was, therefore, obliged to consult his own personal safety, and with some hundred dragoons went over to the Austrian army. This was a serious lesson to the confederated powers, of the spirit which pervaded the French Republic. It should have taught them, that an external enemy served but to rally their divided interests, and resistance to give energy to their united efforts. The first impressions of this fond delusion committed the Prince of Saxe Cobourg in undertaking to re-establish the Constitution of 1789: and betrayed Lord Auckland into that incautious and arrogant memorial, which was so warmly debated in the Commons. It was natural for his Lordship to foresee a most prosperous harvest in Dumourier's coming over: he had not long before negociated with him in secret: it is not then surprising that the lustre of such an example, should have elevated his sympathy into this high tone of address. The real state of the case appears to be, that whilst Dumourier's army thought that the Convention had sent to arrest him on account of his retreat, which they knew he had made in a most masterly manner, they resented it as an insult to themselves, and made it a common cause with their General: but when they discovered, that by sending Bournonville, and the other commissioners, to the Austrians, he was in concert with the enemy of their country, they turned upon him, and endeavoured to seize him. He was covered in his flight by his dragoons, fourteen of whom were shot by their fellow-soldiers.

When Dumourier had arrived at Mons, he requested to attend the congress that was then assembling at Antwerp: but the interest even of Lord Auckland could not procure him that honour. At this congress were present, the Prince of Orange and his two sons, and his excellency Vander Spiegel; the Duke of York, and Lord Auckland; the Prince of Saxe Cobourg, and Counts Metternich, Starenberg, and Mercy Dargenteau, with the Prussian, Spanish, and Neapolitan Envoys. The particulars of this congress were brought over by Sir James Murray, but have never yet been made known to the public.

From the [measures adopted after the meeting, it appears, they resolved to *commence a plan of active operations against France*, and not to entangle themselves with the engagements so very recently entered into by the Prince of Saxe Cobourg: for within four days from the publication of his first proclamation, he revoked and annulled it entirely by a second, by which he declared a cessation of the armistice, and that he had given orders for recommencing the war with all the energy and vigour of which victorious armies are capable. The total repeal of the first proclamation of the Prince of Saxe Cobourg, can leave no doubt, but that the re-establishment of the Constitution of 1789, was no longer the object of the confederates: it concerns Great Britain not lightly, to know the new object, for which the war from this time was carried on. Was it the restoration of the ancient unlimited monarchy, or the dismemberment of the kingdom by the combined sovereigns? Our Ministers have denied it to be a war of extermination, or of vengeance.

During this and the preceding month, the Roman Catholic Bill passed through the two Houses of the Irish Parliament. It was brought in by Mr. Secretary Hobart, which bespoke it to have been first framed and modelled according to the wishes and intentions of Government, who certainly could afterwards be no more responsible for the fetters with which it was clogged in its progress through the Houses, than for any other measure, which is carried by a decided majority of a free and independent Parliament. After the honourable and paternal recommendation from the Throne, of the case of his Majesty's Roman Catholic subjects, a very different expression was to be traced in the features of the public, than what was observable during the preceding sessions. It is to be remarked, for the fair understanding of this notable act of legislative justice, even at a time, which—Mr. Burke *did not see so peculiarly favourable to the extension of civil freedom*, that the Roman Catholic body (which they themselves assert to consist of 3,500,000 persons) had, in their first exertions, entrusted the mode and management of

Z

their application for relief to Lord Kenmare, and about threescore gentlemen of landed property, who were, or at least were supposed to be, under his direction and influence. The slow progress which was made towards the attainment of their emancipation under this commission, was attributed by the body at large, to the want of judgment, firmness, and energy in those who had undertaken it. The act in favour of the Roman Catholics, which was boasted to have been lately procured by the influence of these Gentlemen, extended only to the right of catholics taking apprentices and of keeping schools, the power of protestants intermarrying with catholics, and of catholics being called to the bar; a removal certainly of some hardships, to which some of the body were certainly exposed. But it left about their necks the millstone of slavery, the want of the *elective franchise, and fair trial by jury:* without these, all buoyancy in the element of freedom was impossible. The body at large felt an aggravation of their disappointment after the passing of this act, which affected so few of them, in the insult of being called upon for a vote of thanks to the indulgent legislature for the liberal boon; which was, notwithstanding, both in and out of Parliament, hinted and sometimes expressly asserted to have been a bill granted to sixty eight addressing Gentlemen, not to three millions of an oppressed people. Hence originated the measures of collecting the full sense of the Catholic body, by delegates from each county, and of applying no more to the Castle, but immediately to the source of mercy and justice, to the common Father of his People. They confided with reason, that his Majesty's ear would be ever open to hear the complaints, and his heart disposed to relieve the sufferings of his affectionate and loyal subjects. I cannot so justly express the spirit and views with which the Roman Catholics proceeded in their efforts to attain this revival of their liberty, as in the words of the Gentleman, who was the most active in devising and prosecuting the means of their attaining it: in these we shall not only read the facts and circumstances, but we shall also learn the impreſſion which they made upon the body itſelf. Mr. Keogh, a man of that ſtrong and firm mind, which could cheriſh and improve the true ſpirit and ideas of civil freedom, in the deprivation of all its enjoyments, was deputed to England, to negociate an opening in their future meaſures: and when, upon his return to Ireland, he met his brethren, at their Convention in Dublin, amongſt other things moſt worthy of attention and conſideration, he ſaid:

"It would be tedious to relate the various ſtruggles of the
"Catholics of Ireland, to preſent to parliament their petition:
"that numerous and diſtreſſed body, could not find acceſs, and
"this too was a new triumph to thoſe, in whom we uſed to con-
"fide. What ſhall we think of that man, who might be adored
"by three millions and a half of people, who might be of the
"utmoſt importance in the ſtate, and even to our gracious mo-
"narch, by the confidence of the people; yet was contented
"to deſcend from that ſtation, in order to ſtrut at a levee, the
"contempt of every ſpirited man, to live deſpiſed, and die ne-
"glected, aud to have his name only known to poſterity, as the
"enemy and traitor to the Catholics of Ireland? The ſtate of
"the Catholics was indeed melancholy—no ray of hope from any
"quarter. The loyal and reſpectable, and ſpirited Catholics of
"Cork, thoſe men, who, though borne down by the penal code,
"when hoſtile fleets were on the coaſt; came forward to expoſe
"their lives in defence of their country, diſdaining then to ſpeak
"of relief; theſe men offered an humble addreſs to the preſent
"Lord Lieutenant, in which they expreſſed a *hope* that their paſt
"conduct might procure them ſome relaxation of that dreadful
"code of the laws. His Majeſty's repreſentative in this kingdom
"declined to receive this humble expreſſion of loyalty, becauſe
"it was accompanied with a *hope* of relief. A ſecond application
"was made—a deputation waited on the Secretary, with the
"Penal Laws, and humbly entreated ſome relaxation from *any*
"*part* of that dreadful code: this application never was ho-
"noured with any anſwer whatſoever. Speaking of the Penal

" Code, I muft digrefs to fay, it was a fketch that was pre-
" fented to the Secretary, and we now find a very imperfect one.
" For a late publication, ' The Digeft of the Popery Laws,'
" the United Irifhmen, and their refpectable chairman, the Ho-
" nourable Simon Butler, demand our warmeft gratitude. I own,
" feeling as I did, reftraint and difability, on every fide, our rich
" degraded, and our poor oppreffed, yet my idea of that dread-
" ful fyftem was imperfect until I faw that publication. But to
" return to the fubject: Every application failing here, the Ca-
" tholics proftrate without hope: the General Committee
" thought it a duty they owed their Sovereign, to endeavour,
" through his confidential fervants, to make known their fitua-
" tion, to try that laft effort, before they fhould refign their
" truft, and tell the Catholics of Ireland, that the refult of all
" their loyalty and exertions, to obtain a reftoration to the
" common advantages of the focial condition, was defpair, total
" and unqualified defpair. Accordingly, one of their body was
" deputed to go to London, in September laft; there an applica-
" tion commenced, and continued till Chriftmas, in which the
" perfon deputed received the exertions and able affiftance of a
" refpectable Gentleman, well known to them, (Mr. R. Burke.)
" From the appearance of this negociation, there was every rea-
" fon to expect, that although a great and vaft catalogue of re-
" ftrictions would be retained, yet fufficient would be removed
" to afford protection to all the claffes of our people, to our
" houfelefs peafantry, to give a pledge of future benefits, and
" to render it unanimoufly and fincerely grateful. The ob-
" jects were, the Bar without reftriction; High Sheriffs and
" Magiftracy in counties, and Grand Juries, and a fhare in the
" elective Franchife. Our applications were favourably attended
" to, and we had flattered ourfelves all decided in our favour.

" In this ftage of the bufinefs, when the negociation was car-
" ried on three months—when it was juft clofed—a certain
" noble Lord, who had ufed every effort, for four years, to keep
" us back—dreading left the people fhould be relieved, notwith-

" ftanding his conduct, then came forward, to promote that fa-
" mous addrefs—and to induce the *fixty-eight* to fubfcribe, many
" of whom were totally ignorant of the negociation going on
" at the foot of the Throne.

" Thus ftands our obligation to thefe Gentlemen, and to the
" Bill, with which the promptitude and obfequioufnefs of their
" loyalty has been rewarded.

" It muft be faid, indeed, on their behalf, that they were pro-
" mifed a Bill to contain much greater benefits. How were
" they treated? An outcry was fet on foot, by men under *influ-
" ence* of the Caftle, againft our relief. Thefe *fixty-eight* DUPES
" were told, Gentlemen, ' you fee there is a great outcry, we
" cannot do what we *promifed*—we can only now open the Law,
" and that with many and degraded reftrictions. I believe the
" other objects contained in the Bill, will not be much in-
" fifted on.'

" Having ftated fome paft tranfactions, I now come to what
" is more pleafing—that is, to ftate my opinion, that the time
" is not remote, when we fhall meet to join with heart and
" voice, in the fincereft gratitude to Parliament, and to Govern-
" ment. However unfavourable fome things appear, I am per-
" fuaded it is not intended to doom you to flavery, and that a
" wife government will adopt the patriotic meafure of reftoring
" you to the Conftitution of your country.

" When that day arrives, and it will foon arrive, you will
" then prove your juft and unfeigned gratitude to your deliverers,
" to Government, to the Legiflature, to the illuftrious men who
" efpoufed your caufe in parliament—to the virtuous, patriotic,
" and enlightened citizens of Belfaft—the firft, (let it never be
" forgotten) who came forward in a body, to apply to Parliament
" for our relief.

" While we pretend to honour, gratitude, or virtue, or have
" any claim to freedom, let this live in our memory, and be im-
" printed on the memories of our children.

" To Derry, we owe much: their decifions, though more

" limited, yet were honourable teftimonies of their good will,
" and expreffions of their fentiments, in the previous debate,
" breathed liberal and manly principles.

" My reafon for thinking the time of deliverance approaches
" is, that it is impoffible, on any other principle, to account for
" the conduct obferved towards us. The proceedings of thofe
" who made the Penal Code, were confiftent and fyftematic:
" they might be unjuft and cruel, but they acted like men who
" had a plan. When they deprived us of liberty, they alfo doomed
" us to ignorance, and prevented our receiving education at
" home, or daring to receive it abroad.

" Indeed, they went a little farther, or rather laid the founda-
" tion for our disfranchifement, by the furrender of their own li-
" berties. The plan was but the more fyftematic. But, as
" things ftand at prefent, unlefs our emancipation is intended,
" all is incongruous.

" Why, in God's name, year after year, were the eloquence
" and abilities of Ireland, exerted in giving lectures in College-
" Green (reduced into practice by the eftablifhment of an inde-
" pendent legiflature)—to prove the bleffings of liberty, and the
" curfe of flavery?

" And, left we fhould miftake, both are defined: we are told,
" that flavery confifts in being governed by laws, to which we
" do not confent by ourfelves, or reprefentatives.

" We look to ourfelves, and our expiring peafantry, and fee
" the truth verified.

" They tell us, taxation and reprefentation fhould be infepa-
" rable: we feel the effects of the contrary. We are told, that
" every man is born free, and that wealth, nay life itfelf, is not
" worth poffeffing without liberty. We fee, indeed, the gentle-
" man who ufed thefe very words (one of the firft in talents and
" connections of this country) vote for rejecting our petition
" for the right of franchife. But the truth is, if his conduct be
" inconfiftent, his doctrine is unqueftionable, and, though in-
" ftilled with *lefs* ability, would work conviction. Every Catho-

" lic in Ireland, whose library only extends to a magazine, or an
" old newspaper—reads their beautiful orations—we are to a
" man convinced.

" We look to America—to France—to the Netherlands—
" to all Europe—and ask each other, why it is, that we, who are
" as faithful subjects as any King in Europe can boast—why
" are we thus reduced to *slavery?* for *slavery it is*—as defined
" to us by high authority—and that without crime—Why have
" our equals, our inferiors, our tenants, and even our servants,
" privileges which are denied us?

" Is it that we disagree about the elements in the sacrament?
" With equal justice might the Copernican system be set up,
' and sworn to, as a test for civil and political liberty. From
" those considerations I am convinced, that it is not their inten-
" tion, nor can it be, to doom you to a perpetual deprivation of
" the elective franchise: were it so, another and a very different
" mode would govern the conduct of our rulers. They continue,
" indeed, to talk of something which we are told, is to exclude
" us from the Constitution for ever, and which they call *the*
" *protestant* ascendancy—which they assert was founded on the
" principles of the Revolution of 1688, though the word was
" never heard of till 1792."

The paternal recommendation of the Catholics' case from the Throne, operated instantaneously in their favour. The general good and happiness of the Kingdom, conquered in the breasts of most, the bias of early prejudices. Intolerance and oppression, after a faint struggle, ceded the palm to liberality, reason, and justice. The inveteracy, however, of some, was not to be overcome even in the agony of their despair: whatever could be saved to them from this wreck of their monopoly, they secured by exceptions from the broad and liberal relief which the first form of the Bill held out. Some of these exceptions were admitted, others were rejected. It is curious to observe, to what a degree of sublimation, the boon of the granting clause is refined by being thrown into the alembic of exceptions, introduced to rectify the spirit of the Bill. This enacted, "that it shall, "and may be lawful for Papists, or persons professing the Popish "or Roman Catholic Religion, to hold, exercise, and enjoy all "civil and military offices, and places of trust or profit, under "his Majesty, his heirs, and successors in this kingdom." However liberally the capacity of enjoyment is conceded to the Catholics, very singular caution has been taken to cramp the liberality of his Majesty, in dealing out the favours. For it is particularly enacted, that nothing in the act shall extend to enable any Roman Catholic, to sit or vote in either House of Parliament, nor to be Lord Lieutenant, Lord Deputy, or other chief Governor of the Kingdom, Lord Chancellor, Keeper or Commissioner of the Great Seal of the Kingdom, nor to enjoy a seat on any of the Benches of the three Courts of Record, nor to be a Judge of the High Court of Admiralty, nor Master or Keeper of the Rolls, nor Secretary of State, Keeper of the Privy Seal, Vice Treasurer, or Deputy Vice Treasurer, Teller and Cashier of the Exchequer, nor Auditor General, Lieutenant, or Governor, or Custos Rotulorum of Counties, Secretary to the Lord Lieutenant, Lord Deputy, or other Chief Governor of the Kingdom, nor Member of the Privy Council, nor Prime Sergeant, Attorney General, Solicitor General, Second and Third Sergeants at Law, nor King's Counsel, nor Masters in Chancery, nor Provost or Fellow of Trinity College, nor Post-Master General, nor Master and Lieutenant General of the Ordnance, nor Commander in Chief of his Majesty's Forces, nor a General on the Staff, nor Sheriff, nor Sub-Sheriff of any County; nor to hold any office or employment of trust, or confidence, that can be established by the Lord Lieutenant and Council, under the 17th and 18th of Charles II. Notwithstanding this tantalizing exclusion from the encouraging rewards of every profession and calling, which were now opened to them, the Roman Catholics were gratefully sensible of the inestimable blessing they were admitted to, in the *elective franchise*, and *fair trial by Jury*.

The debates upon this important subject, were too copious to report, and too interesting wholly to omit. I shall therefore notice but such parts of the speeches of the different Gentlemen, who took part in them, as disclose or confirm the detail of facts, which it is the duty of the impartial annalist to record.

The spirit and disposition of the Chancellor towards the body of the Roman Catholics, cannot be so impartially known, as from his own words in the debate upon the address to the Throne. They will also speak for those, who, like the Grand Jurymen of the Counties, could be dictated to, and influenced by his authority. " I did not," said he, " expect that any set of " men, would have dared to approach the Throne, with a gross " and malignant deception upon the Father of his People. I " therefore seize this first opportunity, to reprobate and de- " tect it." Then, in a very long and heated philippic against the body and doctrines of the Roman Catholics, he added: " If any man can be so wild, as to look to a total repeal of " the Popery Laws of this kingdom; if any man can be so " wild, as to desire to communicate the efficient power of a " free Protestant, to a great majority of the people of Ireland, " professing the Popish Religion ; I do not scruple to say, that " it is an absurd, and a wicked speculation. I am satisfied, " that as long as the nature of men continues to be what it is, " it is utterly impossible that a zealous Catholic can exercise the " efficient powers of Government in suppport of a Protestant " establishment in Ireland, or in support of her connection with " the Protestant Empire of Great Britain; and therefore, if I " am the single man to raise my voice against such a project, I " *will* resist it."

This irritation and soreness of mind upon the effects of the Catholics' Petition to the Throne, seem to have been equally felt by the Speaker of the House of Commons, though he did not express himself so strongly upon it as his colleague in opp- sing the Roman Catholic claims. As the Bill proceeded, it w s indeed observed, that the opposition to it was not so violent and determined even from the Chancellor, as upon the first agitation of the queſtion: for reports after this were rumoured, that doubts had been conceived in the Britiſh cabinet, of the policy of granting the Seals of Ireland to any other than an Engliſhman; and ſome extravagant notions began to gain credit in that kingdom, that the acceptance of appointments, involved a call of concurrence with the wiſhes of thoſe who granted them.

At the ſecond reading of the Bill in the Commons, the Right Honourable Mr Foſter, after apologizing for breaking ſilence, undertook in the firſt place to prove, that the conduct of the Grand Juries, in declaring againſt the admiſſion of the Catholics to the participation of the Conſtitution, *had not only been proper, but neceſſary and perfectly conſtitutional*. He further ſaid, " Gentlemen have thanked the Iriſh Miniſter for this meaſure; " he could not thank him for it, though he could for many " others: from his ſoul he conſidered it as the prelude and cer- " tain forerunner of the overthrow of the Proteſtant Eſta- " bliſhment. The *Britiſh Miniſter was the firſt to rouſe this queſ- " tion, and he was not well adviſed*." He then attributes the fall of the country from unknown proſperity to the preſent ſtate of alarm, miſery, and danger, not to " *French tranſactions*; they " have not been felt here, at leaſt not till very lately: it ariſes " from the fears and agitations into which this kingdom has been " thrown, by the *rouſing and ſupporting this claim*." The oppoſition to the Bill in both Houſes, was confined to very few: five or ſix made up the formidable number in the Commons: there were, in fact, but two diſſentient voices againſt bringing in the Bill; and in the Lords, the Archbiſhop of Caſhell alone, openly ſupported the oppoſition of the Chancellor: his grace had committed himſelf to this oppoſition, by his formal declaration in the Houſe, that the *Roman Catholic religion was a religion of knaves and fools*. The ſame principle ſeemed to affect the whole oppoſition to the Commons; for Mr. Ogle expreſsly ſaid, that the introduction of the Bill was, " *the mandate* " *of the Britiſh Miniſter. Let that Miniſter make his experi- " ments at home, where he may be ſuppoſed to know ſomething

" of the country, Let him try, will an English Parliament
" abolish the Test Act? He knows they will not. Why then
" should he presume to direct the Protestant Gentlemen of Ire-
" land to abandon their situation in the State?" This situation was the monopoly of the whole power of the country.

The situation of the Catholic body up to this time in Ireland,
was compenduously described by Mr. Hardy: " The major part
" of the people of Ireland, at one time leaning on the Crown
" for support, then looking for protection from some enlightened
" Protestants: then following some persons of rank of their
" own persuasion, then fixing their eyes on Dissenters, then on
" both Houses of Parliament: and after all, turning their backs
" on the Ministry of their own country, and flying to the foot
" of the Throne for relief." Mr. Egan, after having stated, that
he had formerly presented a loyal and dutiful petition from the
Roman Catholics to that House, and that on the very next day *the
Administration expunged it, and its reception from the journals, with
reviling calumny and precipitation.* " But," said he, " we now hear
" his Majesty's paternal benignity and liberality recommending
" from the Throne, those complaints which you rejected from
" the House of Parliament. I see the Sovereign of his people,
" in effect, the vindicator of my conduct, the reprover of his Ad-
" ministration and the advocate of his oppressed subjects." And
Mr. Curran, adverting to these very circumstances, said, " Their
" petition was rejected by those who called themselves their Re-
" presentatives: the next year that petition passed over that par-
" liament, and approached the Throne. Had it been rejected
" there, there remained only one other Throne for misery to in-
" voke; and from that last and dreadful appeal, let it never be
" forgotten by Irish gratitude, that we have been saved by the
" piety and compassion of the Father of his people." The
Honourable T. H. Hutchinson said, " He would not state the
" resolutions of the different Grand Juries, or what had passed
" at the meetings of several of the counties, in consequence of
" this plan; but would only remind the House, that their gene-

"ral tendency went to form a perpetual bar againſt the Catholic
"to all his pleas, and all his expectations, and to exclude him
"forever from the pale of the Conſtitution. He did not lament
"thoſe proceedings, becauſe they had produced the ſcene, in
"which the committee were then engaged: the Catholics, firm
"in the purſuit of their object, had not yielded even to the au-
"thoritative opinions of thoſe very reſpectable bodies. Too
"bold to be intimidated, and too proud to be coerced, they be-
"came animated, not awed; they ſought protection at the foot
"of the Throne, and had returned under the ſtamp of the royal
"recommendation, through whoſe wiſe and benevolent interpo-
"ſition, we had now adopted their complaints." Beſides theſe
ſpeakers, Mr. Grattan, Sir Hercules Langriſhe, Mr. Conolly,
Mr. D. Browne, Major Doyle, the Provoſt of the College,
Mr. Secretary Hobart, and ſeveral others, delivered themſelves
in ſentiments of the moſt admirable humanity and conſtitutional
love and zeal for their country, in favour of the recommendation from the Throne. Doctor Duigenan, almoſt alone, vented
the moſt embittered horror of the Roman Catholic Religion and
Body, that could be expreſſed in an exaggerated detail of every
falſe, ſcandalous, or malicious report, that had ever been raiſed or
publiſhed againſt them. Such, however, was the liberality of
the Houſe, as to be little affected by the narrative.

Before this Bill was committed in the Houſe of Lords, the
Lord Chancellor, though his firſt efferveſcence had rather cooled,
in a ſpeech of conſiderable length, and of uncommon virulence
againſt the Roman Catholics, pointedly animadverted on their
paſt conduct, which he endeavoured to prove, by a long ſtate-
ment of hiſtorical facts, ought to be the moſt powerful induce-
ments to the Houſe, to reject all their demands. If he conſented
to the Bill, it was becauſe the ſituation of the country now rendered *it neceſſary*. He then endeavoured to prove, that the religious fury and bigotry of Papiſts in Ireland, was now as great
as it ever had been; and that there was a moral impoſſibility for
Proteſtants and Catholics to agree in political intereſts, He

accufed them of wifhing to annihilate the prefent fyftem of re-prefentation, and to found it on a baftard King. " In earlier " periods of Governments," faid he, " the Irifh never thus " loudly complained of any one Englifh act of oppreffion. It " was of late, the prefent moft fantaftical idea that now prevails " among them had its birth, fo that it seemed to him, that the " heavy hand of God was at this time ftretched over the land. " Every one now looks upon his neighbour with a jealous eye, thinking him an impediment *in his own way to power and pre-" eminence."* The Archbifhop of Cafhell vehemently oppofed both the fpirit and principle of the Bill. It was, however, ably and humanely fupported by other Prelates on the Bench. The Bill was paffed, to the general joy and fatisfaction of the kingdom at large, and the Catholic Delegates prefented an addrefs to his Majefty, and to the Lord Lieutenant, expreffive of their gratitude for its having paffed into a Law. Amidft the general and peaceable teftimonies of the public joy, for the emancipation of the bulk of the Irifh Nation, the Corporation of Dublin granted the freedom of their city to Dr. Duigenan, as an honourable teftimony of their gratitude to him, for his fteady zealous, and perfevering oppofition to the Bill, in every ftage of it.

CHAPTER XIV.

MAY, 1793.

CONTENTS.

Mr. Grey's motion for a Reform in Parliament—Twenty-three petitions presented for it; some of them signed by 15,000 *persons— Two days debate thereupon—Rejected by* 282 *against* 42*—Scotch Catholic Bill—Mr. Dundas declares his intention of establishing a Scotch Militia—The Irish Militia—Opposition at first against it—Penalties on Catholics entering into the service of Great Britain, by Land or at Sea—Battle of Maulde—Camp at Famars taken by the combined forces—Furnes taken by the French— Tobago taken from them—Mentz invested by the King of Prussia —The emigrant legion of the De la Chatre.*

FEW things could have more clearly proved the prevalence of the present spirit of opposing public petitions against grievances, than the division upon Mr. Grey's motion for a Reform in Parliament, after two days debate; the numbers being 42 for the reform against 282 who opposed it. It would be useless to attempt to follow the different speakers upon this great and important subject. Their arguments upon it can receive no additional force, no further elucidation; *whilst our passions continue to instruct our reason,* we must patiently look for the change of reason in the turn of events that may excite a difference of passions. Circumstances may happen that will dispose some, and alarm others to *act* upon truths, that have hitherto remained mere speculative and inoperative affections of the mind; when the dread of meeting conviction will be lefs than that of rejecting invefligation; when the feelings of the people fhall mark more pointedly the proper time for confidering their grievances, than the judgment of their reprefentatives. The attempt has been made at all times; in times of war, and in times of peace; when commerce flourifhed; when its credit was expiring: when the minds of men were eafy and free; when they were foured and vacillating; in the hour of invafion and rebellion; in the glow and tranfport of loyalty and triumph. Ingenuity can fcarcely devife a poffible novelty of circumftance under which this reform has not been brought forward and rejected. Mr. Pitt's fpeech on the fecond day of thefe debates, chiefly refted upon the impropriety of the prefent moment for attempting any fort of reform. Many others alfo refted their oppofition to the motion upon the fame ground. Twenty-three petitions were prefented to the Commons on the firft day of thefe debates, by different members; fome of them figned by many thoufand names (as far as fifteen thoufand). Mr. Burke was amongft the moft forward to oppofe Mr. Grey's motion; and vehement as he is in warning *this country* againft every fort of innovation or reform, he could, with undeniable reafons (though with unaccountable inconfiftency) encourage and forward in his own country, without danger of following the example of France, the ftrongeft meafure of reform that has been effected fince the eftablifhment of the Britifh Conftitution; the admiffion of above three out of four millions to vote for their reprefentation in Parliament. In England he could not fee what was fo clear to him in Ireland, that * " *becaufe wicked men of various defcriptions are* " *engaged in feditious courfes, the rational, fober, and valuable part* " *of one defcription, fhould not be indulged their fober and rational expectations.*"

The body of Roman Catholics in Scotland, which confifts of about twenty thoufand, chiefly of the lower order of fociety, had

* Letter to Sir Hercules Langrifhe, p. 8.

made frequent applications to Government, to be relieved from the hardships of a very severe penal code, under which they laboured. A deaf ear had been constantly turned to their application; generally upon pretext of the inveteracy of the prejudices of that kingdom against them. This illiberal idea was kept up much longer than necessary, not only to the prejudice of the suffering Catholics, but to the scandal and calumny of the Scotch nation. Mr. Dundas, however, upon being persuaded that such a measure of liberality might now insure him some popularity in the country, consented to the introduction of a Bill, which passed without any opposition, by which the Roman Catholics of Scotland were put nearly upon the same footing as those of England, upon taking the same oaths of allegiance prescribed for English Roman Catholics. The news of its passing into a law, gave general satisfaction and joy throughout the kingdom.

At the beginning of the session, mention had been made in the House of Commons, by Mr. Dundas, of an intention of establishing a Militia in Scotland. Nothing had been done since that time upon the subject, and Major Maitland now put the question to the Right Honourable Secretary, whether he had, or had not abandoned the idea? He answered, that late as it was in the session, he assuredly should take some step towards effecting it. None, however, was openly taken.

The Militia Bill passed the Irish Parliament with little opposition. An attempt, however, was made by that party, which had so zealously opposed, and so reluctantly yielded to the Roman Catholic Bill, to exclude the Roman Catholics from appointments in the Militia. Though the system was cordially adopted in many counties; yet in others, serious effects were apprehended from the resistance which was offered against it. These difficulties were, however, but of short duration; obvious reasons occured to persuade the people of every description to enter freely into the Militia; the steady and peaceable were eager to lend their aid to strengthen the hands of Government, and secure the peace and tranquillity of the country; the discontented and active found in the legal poffeffion and ufe of arms, the fure defence againft oppreffion, and the ready means of redrefs. The crooked policy of the party, from whofe tenacious gripe as much power feemed to be wrefted, as was conferred upon the Roman Catholics, had nearly expofed the country to very ferious danger. Unable to prevent the liberality of Parliament from admitting the Roman Catholics upon an equal footing with the Proteftants into the Militia; they at firft fuccefsfully exercifed their influence and power in the country to fill up all the appointments with Proteftants, to the utter exclufion of the Roman Catholic gentlemen, in thofe very counties where they were moft numerous. This grofs partiality began to operate very ferioufly upon the Catholic peafantry, from amongft whom the Militia-men were principally ballotted; the partial fyftem was neceffarily abandoned, and the different corps of Militia were then quickly and peaceably completed.

The importance of this populous nurfery of ftout and valiant recruits both for the land and fea forces of Great Britain, is too great to juftify my filence upon a fubject of fuch national confequence, upon which the public feems to have given into an error of no fmall moment. It is a generally received idea, not only throughout Great Britain, but in Ireland itfelf, that fince the paffing of the Roman Catholic Act, the army and navy of Great Britain are as open to Irifh Roman Catholics, as to any other defcription of his Majefty's fubjects. The Irifh Parliament has, indeed, declared Roman Catholics capable of any military office and employment: but it is to be remembered, that Ireland has no permanent military body (except now the militia) fubject to their conftant jurifdiction; the troops of Great Britain upon the Irifh eftablifhment are merely fubfidized, as it were, by Ireland; they are paid out of the Irifh treafury, and during their refidence in that kingdom, are under the temporary controul of the Irifh Parliament. There is no Irifh navy. Every Irifh as well as Englifh Roman Catholic, who wifhes to ferve his country, either in the army or navy of Great Britain is prohibited by the ſtatute (1 Geo. I.) to do it, without renouncing his religion by oath: if he refuſe to take this oath of renunciation within a limited time, he is not only expelled from the ſervice, but he incurs alſo a civil death, by being rendered incapable of bringing any action at law, or ſuit in equity; of being a guardian, executor, or adminiſtrator; of taking a legacy or deed of gift; of being in any office in Great Britain; of voting at any election for members to ſerve in parliament; and ſhall, moreover, forfeit the ſum of 500l. to any perſon that will inform againſt him. If candour and good faith be to be holden with the loyal ſubjects, who tender their ſervices to their country, preſs-gangs and recruiting ſerjeants ſhould be preceded by heralds, to announce the pains and penalties which thoſe who retain the faith of their anceſtors, will incur, by being forced or enliſted into the ſervice of their country. It is well known, that upwards of ſeventy thouſand recruits were raiſed in Ireland during the American war; and, as the Legiſlature has now declared the Iriſh Roman Catholics capable and worthy of ſerving their King and Country, theſe obſervations will not be found irrelevant to the ſubject of this Hiſtory.

There would be little need of offering bounties of fifteen guineas per man for enliſting recruits, if the recruiting ſerjeants were properly inſtructed to diſplay the liberal and noble and irreſiſtible terms of the Iriſh Roman Catholics' engagement. " Welcome, brave, loyal and free ſoldiers! Long live
" the King, the happy and free Conſtitution! Welcome into
" your long loſt rights; your liberty of perſon, of property, of
" ſervice, and of conſcience. Your loving, your generous, your
" glorious country calls for your ſervices, to cruſh the tyranny,
" ſlavery, and wickedneſs of your Gallic neighbours. Which of
" you can withſtand the enthuſiaſtic glow of ſuch a call? To
" cruſh tyranny, and give to mankind that liberty which you
" yourſelves enjoy in ſuch an eminent degree. Live the cauſe
" of Britiſh freedom! Once *enliſted*, my brave fellows! you
" will be happy to ſacrifice your *all* to ſupport it. For the mo-

" ment of your engagement, is the word of command to re-
" nounce your religion; the practife of it you will be difpenfed
" with, or marfhalled by beat of drum to a better and purer fer-
" vice. Whilft you remain under the jurifdiction of the Britifh
" Parliament you fhall be civilly dead, that you may fully know
" the benefit of returning into your own free and bleffed country;
" and fhould fortune blefs you with prize-money, five hundred
" pounds of it will reward the good fervices of a neighbourly
" informer, that you did not make a timely renunciation of
" your religion."

On the 22d of February, in the Houfe of Peers, Lord Farnham propofed an amendment to this claufe of the Roman Catholic Bill, by rendering its operation conditional, until Great Britain fhould pafs a fimilar law, to open the army and navy to Catholics throughout the whole Britifh empire. But the Chancellor oppofed the amendment; " for," faid he, " it could " not be fuppofed, that his Majefty would appoint a man to fuch " a poft, until the laws of the empire fhould fully qualify him " to act in every part of it. It was more than probable, a fimi- " lar law to this would be adopted in England before the lapfe " of two months; and on this ground the amendment would be " wholly unneceffary." The learned Lord forgot, that the Act of Geo. I. applies its rigorous effects exprefsly to *foldiers and feamen*, as well as to officers. Eleven months are now elapfed fince this liberal promife was holden out, and the feverity of the law is ftill fully operative againft every Roman Catholic who renders himfelf liable to it, by engaging in the military or naval fervice of his country.

On the 8th of the month, the combined armies engaged the French near Maulde, in which the Britifh troops turned the fate of the day in their favour; and on the 25th, the combined forces under the command of the Prince of Saxe Cobourg and of his Royal Highnefs, defeated the enemy, and drove them from the ftrong and important camp of Famars, of which they took poffeffion. The French entered without refiftance the fmall town of Furnes, and threatened Oftend. The ifland of Tobago was taken from the French. The king of Pruffia had been for a long time before Mentz with an immenfe army. The Royalifts rofe in a formidable body in Britany, and gained feveral advantages over the Republicans. About the clofe of the month, a body of 600 French emigrants was raifed in England, and taken into our pay; they were commanded by the Count de la Chatre, but were not embodied till they arrived at Oftend. An offer was made by Government to embody five legions of French emigrants, of 600 men each; but the difagreements among themfelves, their objections to the commanders intended to be placed over them, or their coldnefs or defpair in the caufe, defeated the intentions of Government, and this fingle legion of Monf. de la Chatre, was in the courfe of feveral months, with great difficulty formed.

CHAPTER XV.

JUNE, 1793.

CONTENTS.

Mr Birch's motion in the Commons, about a rumoured scarcity of arms—Debates in the Lords upon Lord Auckland's Memorial—Lord Stanhope's motion for printing our Treaties with the Continental Powers—Dumourier in London—Valenciennes besieged—Support given in Ireland to Commercial Credit—Traitorous Correspondence Bill passed in Ireland.

FEW things of any material consequence occurred during the course of the current month, either in or out of Parliament. Mr. Birch, in consequence of the rumoured scarcity of arms, and knowing the fact to be, that several regiments of militia and regulars had applied unsuccessfully for arms, moved in the House of Commons, that an account be laid before the House, of the quantity of small arms in store in the Tower. Mr. Rose opposed the motion; and Mr. Birch consented to defer it. On this occasion, Mr. Sheridan asserted, without being contradicted, that it was rumoured and credited, that there were not, at that time, more than two or three thousand stand of small arms in the Tower, which, if a fact, was a criminal neglect that ought to be enquired into, and traced to those who had been guilty of such neglect. It was, to him, an additional proof, that the whole of the late tremendous preparations and formidable entrenchments of the Tower, againſt internal dangers, were mere fiction and pretence.

The confideration of Lord Auckland's memorial to the States General had been feveral times attempted to be brought before the Lords, by the Earl of Stanhope: on the 17th inſtant, he made his promiſed Motion in a very full houſe. His ſpeech, on this occaſion, was chiefly grounded on the idea, That all Memorials, holding language of ill-timed menace, only ſerved to irritate and provoke retaliation. Such had been the proclamation of General Burgoyne to the Americans; ſuch thoſe of the Duke of Brunſwick to the French. He pointedly reprobated the idea of appropriating to our cauſe the avenging arm of Divine Providence: the ſucceſs of war was not to determine the juſtice of the cauſe in the decrees of the Almighty, any more than the morality and virtue of individuals were to be eſtimated by their temporal proſperity in this life. Lord Grenville defended the Memorial, as grounded in the ſpirit of the Ambaſſador's Inſtructions, the Speech of his Majeſty, and the Addreſſes of both Houſes of Parliament upon it. His Royal Highneſs the Duke of Clarence took an opportunity, in this debate, of expreſſing his ſentiments upon the war. Not conceiving that any thing cruel in its tendency, or oppreſſive in its nature, could originate with a Britiſh ſubject, he had been willing to attribute the compoſition of this Memorial to the Auſtrian Miniſter, who had ſigned it jointly with our Ambaſſador. He was ſorry that his conjecture was groundleſs. With regard to the war, though he thought it had commenced on the principles of juſtice and neceſſity, he found neither of thoſe principles to warrant its continuance; he had the ſatisfaction to ſee the avowed object of the war obtained. The danger which had threatened Holland, was completely removed; there had ceaſed, therefore, the immediate and only avowed cauſe, for which we had undertaken the war. Lord Auckland offered nothing new in his own defence, which he reſted upon what had fallen from the Secretary of State. The Chancellor was very animated in ſupport of his *old friend's* Memorial, and pointedly decisive for carrying on the war at all risks (though with Lord Scarborough's reserve upon its prosecution) till the honour of this country to its allies were, in its fullest extent discharged, and their security ensured. In reply to the Chancellor, and the other servants of the Crown, who had spoken upon the subject, the Earl of Guildford said, " he rose to answer " a question that had been that day more than once put by dif- " ferent noble Lords. It had been asked, with whom were Mi- " nisters to treat for peace? In answer, he would say, that their " situation was as extraordinary as it was lamentable; if they " found enemies to send armies against, and could not find out " persons fit to negociate a peace with." An amendment of Lord Grenville's to the Earl of Stanhope's motion, which went to approve of the Memorial, was put and carried without a division.

With the same vigilance with which the noble Lords, who reprobated the Memorial of Lord Auckland, attended to the honour of the Country, did they, on a future day, exert themselves in endeavouring to secure its safety. The Earl of Stanhope moved for the printing of certain Treaties, which this country had entered into with the powers of the Continent. This was opposed by Lord Grenville, to whom the Duke of Norfolk replied, and forcibly reprobated the unprecedented and dangerous delay of laying such important papers before the House, for the opinion of their Lordships: there were no less than three treaties, offensive and defensive, entered into between this country and considerable continental powers, signed in May last, and not presented to the House till within two or three days of the close of the session. His Grace was desirous that they should be printed, that the country might know to what extent the war was about to be carried; and that Ministers were hazarding a long continuance of calamitous evils, by entering into the views of a variety of continental powers. The motion was lost. Thus closed the session of a parliament, convened upon the strength of facts, which are univerfally known not to have exifted;* and fupported throughout by an implicit confidence, and unlimited credit to Minifters for an equal neceffity of enforcing and fuppreffing the grounds of the ftrongeft meafures.

Nearly about the time that the combined armies laid regular fiege to Valenciennes, Dumourier came to London. Whether any public or private fpeculation brought him over is not afcertained; he remained but two days in town, and was forced to quit the kingdom under the provifions of the Alien Act.

The ruinous confequences of the war fpread over every part of the Britifh empire; Government found itfelf obliged, in Ireland, to lend fupport to the drooping credit of the very firft commercial powers; and Parliament undertook to make good the fum of 200,000l. which the Bank had advanced to mercantile perfons, with intereft at five per cent. The Parliament of Ireland paffed alfo a Traitorous Correfpondence Bill, fimilar to that paffed in Great Britain.

* The words of the Act (30 Geo. 2. c. 25. fec. 46) by virtue of which this parliament was convened, and the militia drawn out and embodied, are *in cafe of actual invafion, or upon imminent danger thereof, or in cafe of rebellion.* It is then correct to ftate, that neither of thefe cafes was known to have exifted.

CHAPTER XVI.

JULY, 1793.

CONTENTS.

Mr. Reeves's affociation—Their publications and doctrines—Upwards of two thoufand fuch affociations formed—Lord Hood's Fleet in the Mediterranean—Lord Howe has the command of the Channel Fleet—Condé, Mayence, and Valenciennes taken—Unfuccefsful defcent at Martinico, by Admiral Gardner—Convention Bill in Ireland—Thoughts relative to it—Libel, Civil Lift, and Penfion Acts paffed in Ireland.

ALTHOUGH the Parliament had clofed the feffion, it was ftill found requifite to keep awake the fpirit of alarm and agitation, which had feized the Nation from the month of December. The means of attempting this, were as fingular as they were new. As the meafure was not in its nature tranfient, but is, in fome degree, ftill operating its effect upon the public, it is peculiarly incumbent upon me, to apprize my reader of its origin, nature, and tendency. Mr. Reeves's affociation now thought proper to bring before the public, a collected fum of their meritorious fervices to the country, with an unequivocal avowal of their views and proceedings. They, accordingly, publifhed a confiderable volume of their affociation papers, with a well written preface, which befpeaks the pen of talent and information. And when we throw our eye over the lift of the eighteen names, which form their committee, from the known abilities, knowledge, and refpectability of the individuals who compofe it, I will readily own, that an implicit credit might have been expected from the Nation for every measure they should adopt. It is therefore certainly a hazardous, and, probably, an invidious task, to speak otherwise than in commendation of the proceedings of such respected members of this community. But, *amicus Plato, magis amica veritas.* In the collected view and review of the late public measures, I cannot help seeing a concerted league to introduce or revive, in this country, a spirit and principle disavowed since the æra of our Revolution, in order to engraft upon them a system of measures, that would have received neither life nor vigour from the old stock of the British Constitution. I view Mr. Burke, as the Æolus of this league. He formally anathemises every man who condemns *him and his book, as condemning, of course, all the principles of the Constitutional Whigs of this Kingdom.* His zealous colleagues or imitators set out upon he same claim of infallibility of doctrine, and confidently announce to the public * that *they can have no enemies, but such as the law would term offenders.* Their chief aim in this preface, is to convince the public, † that none of the King's Ministers " knew, or heard of this association, till they saw the first ad- " vertisement in the public prints. It was planned without their " knowledge, and has been conducted, to the present moment, " without their aid. The Minister had no more to do with this " association, than of the *two* thousand, and more, that were " formed in other parts of the Kingdom." So peculiar a solicitude to deprive his Majesty's Ministers of any share or merit in establishing and forwarding an institution, to which *none but public offenders of the laws of their country, could be enemies,* bespeaks a degree of doubt, either as to the truth of the assertion, or the propriety of the fact. If, however, we reflect upon the closeness with which Ministers were urged in the House of Commons, to state the grounds of the strong measures, they were then taking, and that they were either unable, or unwilling to admit, or disclose them; we must necessarily allow some closer,

---

* Preface, p. iv.   † Ibidem.

and more intimate connection with Ministers, than ordinary, that could have authorized men of so much respectability, to declare unequivocally to their country, that * it *was known*, " that " *emissaries were paid by France, to stir up sedition; and engineers* " *sent to assist in military operations; that a revolt was planned in* " *the beginning of December, when the Tower was to have been* " *seized: the agents in these designs, whether French or English,* " *were likewise known.*" If such things *were known*, either through Ministers to these associators, or through these associators to Ministers, the country had a call, an irresistible call for example and vengeance against the delinquents. These acts, which are so publicly declared *to be known*, were acts of the highest and rankest treason: and by the 1 Ed. 6. it is enacted, *that concealment or keeping secret any high treason, shall be from henceforth adjudged, deemed, and taken misprision of treason, and the offender therein, shall forfeit and suffer as in cases of misprision of treason, as heretofore hath been used.* I wish not to throw responsibility where none is assumed. The associators have very explicitly undertaken to avow and defend their different publications, and have boasted not lightly of the effects they have already produced. † " These papers consist of two classes. The first are " such publications as the society ordered to be printed, after " they had been perused and approved by the committee. The " second consists of tracts that were put to the press, without the " special direction or approbation of the committee, by a person " in whom the committee confided. It was endeavoured, by such " publications as the present, to counteract the poison that had " been disseminated, and to restore the minds of the people to " that tone of good sense, which had ever been the characteristic " of this country. The success fully answered the expectation: " by these means falsehood was refuted; sophistry exposed, and " sedition repelled: the peculiar happiness of our Constitution " was displayed; designs of pretended reformers were examined;

* Preface vi.   † Page xi.

"and the principles of civil fociety were fully opened and ex-
"plained."

As the different papers are not publifhed in the order of their refpective claffes, the public may be at a lofs to know to what clafs each paper ought to be referred. The Committee has, however, generoufly undertaken the refponfibility of both claffes. The re-publication of a work written by an author of no mean repute, evidently argues a more unequivocal, and reflected approbation of the doctrines contained in it, than the firft publication of a new production. More ferious inference is, therefore to be drawn from the Committee's adopting and re-publifhing the doctrines of Mr. Soame Jenyns, upon the bafis of our Conftitution, than from their inftructing the nation, through the mouth of Thomas Bull, that the oily chrifm gives civil power, and that God alone makes Kings*. No man who wifhes to preferve the fpirit and being of the Britifh Conftitution, will furely at this day be hardy enough to deny, that the democratical part of that Conftitution confifts of, and is fupported by the *free reprefentation of the people in Parliament*. To what other end can the people be told, that fuch reprefentation is impoffible, and that it is no part of the Englifh Conftitution, unlefs it be for the wicked purpofe of deftroying all confidence in the Houfe of Commons, depriving it of its refpect, and diverting the people from looking up to their reprefentatives for redrefs in all their grievances? Was this, above all others, a time to teach the people of Great Britain, that † "the corruption of the Members of

---

* *Vide* No. I. Second Part of Affociation Papers, p. 4.

† No. IX. Affociation Papers, p. 129. Thoughts on a Parliamentary Reform, by Soame Jenyns, Efq. Having committed myfelf to the public laft year, upon this, amongft other conftitutional queftions, I cannot help quoting from my work, the doctrine I there adopted, by way of an apology for having faid fo much upon thefe publications of Mr. Reeves's Affociation. The danger becomes really ferious, when we are told, that above two thoufand *fuch* Affociations are already formed. *Appendix to Lex Parliamentaria, p.* 433.

" the House of Commons will always increase in proportion to
" their power, because they have more to sell, and are more ne-
" cessary to be bought? Those who cannot make a shift with
" such a Parliament, *must have none.*

" Let us now see what would be the effect of this independent
" Parliament, if obtained. By an independent Parliament, in
" the language of the present times, is to be understood a Par-
" liament, in which the majority would oppose any Administra-
" tion: now no arguments are necessary to prove, that with
" such a Parliament, no public business whatever could be trans-
" acted, nor any Government subsist. But it will be said, This
" is not what is wished for, but one in which the Members
" shall be always ready to support the measures of Ministers
" when right, and to resist them when wrong, unawed and unin-
" fluenced, and guided only by the dictates of their own judg-
" ment and conscience. This, indeed, is what every wise man
" would desire, but no wise man will expect to see, as no such
" assembly, if numerous, ever existed in this or in any country,
" from the beginning of the world to the present hour; nor ever
" can, unless mankind were melted down and run in a new mould:
" as they now are formed, in every numerous assembly, there

quoted in Jura Ang. p. 450. " There is nothing ought to be so dear
" to the Commons of Great Britain, as a free Parliament; that is,
" a House of Commons every way free and *independent* either of
" the Lords or Ministry, &c. *free* in their persons; *free* in their
" estates; *free* in their elections; *free* in their returns; *free* in
" their assembling; *free* in their speeches, debates, and determina-
" tions; *free* to complain of offenders; *free* in their prosecutions
" for offences, and therein *free* from the fear and influence of others
" how great soever; *free* to guard against the encroachments of
" arbitrary power; *free* to preserve the liberties and properties of
" the subjects; and yet *free* to part with a share of those properties
" when necessary, for the service of the public: nor can he be
" justly esteemed a representative of the people of Britain, who
" does not sincerely endeavour to defend their just rights and
" liberties, against all invasions whatsoever.

" muft be fome who have no judgment, and others who have
" no confcience, and fome who have neither: take away felf-
" intereft, and all thefe will have no ftar to fteer by, but muft fail
" without a compafs, juft as the gales of favour or refentment
" of popular abfurdity, or their own, fhall direct them: a Mi-
" nifter, therefore, muft be poffeffed of fome attractive influence
" to enable him to draw together. thefe difcordant particles, and
" unite them in a firm and folid majority, without which he can
" purfue no meafures of public utility, with fteadinefs or fuc-
" cefs. *An independent Houfe of Commons is no part of the Eng-
" lifh Conftitution.*" Such are the ideas of the neceffity of the
corruption and venality of a Britifh Houfe of Commons, taught
and maintained in this new palladium of our Conftitution. Un-
due influence over the judgment of the reprefentatives is neceffary, according to them, to the very exiftence of the Conftitution. * *Parliaments have ever been influenced, and by that
means our Conftitution has fo long fubfifted.*

As to the doctrine of Thomas Bull, which thefe leaguers
revive, adopt, and inculcate, if it mean any thing, it means, in
the common and accepted terms of the Englifh language, that
the King of Great Britain reigns over his people *jure divino*, or
that he is immediately appointed King by *God*, and not by the
people: and which of the eighteen members of the committee
will ftand forth, like Sir Robert Filmer, the avowed champion
of this doctrine, and rafhly attempt to *Un Locke* thofe revolution
principles upon which alone the Conftitution ftands? Confident as
thefe leaguers are, in *denouncing all their enemies as offenders againft
the law*, it is proper to weigh their loyalty in the fcale of their
pretended doctrine. On the 11th of December, 1792, this *Club
de Surveillance*, kindly undertook to remind the good people of
England, whom they had taken in tow, to conduct fafely into
the haven of the Conftitution, that *the notion of a libel may be
applied to any defamation whatever.* Hawk. P. C. *l.* 1. *c.* 73.

* Ibidem.

That *a Libel is a contumely or reproach publiſhed to the defamation of Government.* Com. Dig. *Libel* A. *That malicious defamations of any perſons, eſpecially a magiſtrate, made public by either printing, writing, ſigns or pictures, in order to expoſe him to public hatred, contempt, or ridicule, are puniſhable as libels.* Bl. Com. l. 4. c. 4. —And theſe Conſtitution-mongers tell the ſame good people of England, that their repreſentatives in Parliament are neceſſarily corrupt, and muſt be both bought and ſold. That it is phyſically impoſſible that their repreſentatives ſhould be ſo unawed and uninfluenced, as to be ready to ſupport the meaſures of Miniſters when right, and to reſiſt them when wrong. That the greateſt part of the Houſe of Commons can have no other ſtar to ſteer by, than ſelf-intereſt; and that majorities in that Houſe muſt neceſſarily be formed by the miniſterial influence; that an independent Houſe of Commons is no part of the Engliſh Conſtitution; that the Conſtitution has hitherto ſubſiſted by the miniſterial influence of the Commons; that the reaſon why we cannot preſerve the wealth, honour, power and dominion which we once enjoyed is, becauſe the means of miniſterial influence are no longer ſufficient to ſatisfy the demands of ambition and the hunger of faction. If the Commons of Great Britain, who have ſometimes exerciſed their power in puniſhing a ſevere or diſreſpectful obſervation in a newſpaper, ſhall chooſe to acquieſce in this exaggerated maſs of calumny and diſgrace, there needs no great ſagacity to foretell the early extinction of the reſpect, dignity, and power of their Houſe; and the immediate and neceſſary miſtruſt, contempt, and ridicule of the conſtituents for their repreſentatives.

Leſs dangerous to the Conſtitution of this country were the doctrines of Thomas Paine, which denied its exiſtence, than of theſe aſſociated leaguers, which teach the neceſſity of ſuch abuſes. Dangerous at all times is a ſyſtem of Clubs and Aſſociations under the blind influence of any demagogues: but what is not to be apprehended from the joint efforts of two or three thouſand Aſſociations, eſtabliſhed for the avowed purpoſe of diffuſing, through the Nation, such dangerous and false doctrines concerning the Sovereign's title to the Throne, and such base and scandalous calumnies and libels, against the House of Commons?

The attention of the Cabinet was now drawn chiefly to the operations of the fleets and armies, by which the power of the Gallic Republicans was to be crushed. They had long before sent out a confiderable fleet to the Mediterranean under Lord Hood. And in order to secure every advantage to this country, which could be procured at sea, they committed the command of the Channel fleet to Lord Howe, an officer of uncommon skill in naval tactics, who had already signalized himself in America, by the superiority of his abilities and the warmth of his zeal, in crushing the powers of a nascent republic. They were flattered with the accounts of the various successes in different quarters. The settlements of Miquelon and St. Pierre had surrendered, without resistance, to the British arms. Condé had surrendered, after a long blockade, to the Duke of Wirtemburgh, as had the city of Mayence to the King of Prussia, who permitted the garrison to march out with all the honours of war, carrying their arms, baggage, and other effects, on condition of not serving for one year against the allied armies. They, accordingly, marched immediately against the Royalists in the Vendée and elsewhere. Valenciennes capitulated after a siege of near two months. The garrison was reduced from 11,000 to 4,500 men; and the allies during the siege, threw 489,800 shells and balls into the town. Accounts not so flattering were at this time received from the West Indies. Admiral Gardner had on the 14th of June, landed some troops on the island of Martinico; he had taken a fort, and had been joined by a confiderable number of Royalists: a most unaccountable mistake had happened, considering the small number of men which he had landed; the British troops fired upon each other, and killed above one hundred and fifty men. A dispute also arose between the Admiral and the General; and they disgracefully quitted the island on the 17th of the same month. Sufficient details of this unfortunate expedition have not reached us, to enable us to point out the immediate cause of its failure. It seems to have been either too long deferred, or unadvisedly undertaken, without any preconcerted plan or preparation. When the Admiral sailed from the island to America, to avoid the hurricanes, the beach was covered with the unfortunate Royalists, who had joined him upon his landing, imploring him to transport them out of the reach of their cruel enemies: they were inhumanly left to their fate, and, it is supposed, that our appearance upon the island for three days had caused the greatest part of them to be executed. Of such dire consequences are either dilatory or half-planned measures against so irritable and determined an enemy.

The collecting of the sense of the Roman Catholic body in Ireland by election of delegates, and their deputation to the Throne, although attended by no symptom of turbulence or insurrection throughout the kingdom, was a measure so unexpectedly efficacious in procuring their relief, that the Chancellor was determined to prevent a possible repetition of such a surprise. He accordingly brought in a Bill *to prevent the election or appointment of unlawful assemblies, under pretence of preparing or presenting petitions or other addresses to his Majesty or the Parliament.* This most extraordinary act recites, that the election or appointment of assemblies purporting to represent the people, or any *description or number* of the people, under pretence of preparing or presenting petitions, complaints, remonstrances, declarations, and other addresses to the King, or both or either of the Houses of Parliament, for alteration of matters established by law, or redress of alledged grievances in church and state, may be made use of to serve the ends of factious and seditious persons, to the violation of the public peace, and the great and manifest encouragement of riot, tumult, and disorder : and it enacts, that all such assemblies, committees, or other bodies of persons, elected or otherwise, constituted or appointed, are unlawful assemblies: and that all persons giving or publishing notice of the election to be made of such persons or delegates, or attending, voting, or

D d

acting therein, by any means, are guilty of a high misdemeanor. The act ends with a declaration, that nothing in it shall be construed to prevent or impede the *undoubted right* of his Majesty's subjects to petition the King or Parliament for redress of any public or private grievance.

It behoves every man to abstain from irreverent observations upon a public act of any Legislature, to which his Majesty has given his Royal consent. This act of the Irish Parliament is expressly founded upon *the possibility* of those actions being abused, which are thereby rendered unlawful, and which were, therefore, lawful before its passing. A British subject, to whom they are still lawful, may be allowed to throw out some few remarks upon the nature of that liberty, which Englishmen enjoy, of petitioning against grievances, and the rights which that liberty necessarily bestows. The example of a sister kingdom may, possibly, render some preventative reflections upon the subject not wholly nugatory.

It always was the undoubted right of Englishmen to petition the King, or both or either of the Houses of Parliament against any public or private grievance: this right is founded in the very essence of the Constitution: it cannot, therefore, be extinguished without a grievous violation of the Constitution. If, on any occasion, it has been found necessary by the legislature to impose certain conditions upon the exercise of it, they were only calculated to preserve the right itself in greater security. Thus we see after the restoration of Charles II. that the Parliament were of opinion that *tumultuous and other disorderly* soliciting and procuring hands by private persons to such petitions had been made use of, to serve the ends of factious persons, and had been a great means of the late unhappy wars, confusion, and calamities in the Nation. It therefore provided, that no person should procure above twenty names to any one petition, without the consent of three justices, or of the major part of the Grand Jury and that no petition should be actually presented by a larger number than ten, under the penalty of one hundred pounds and nine months imprisonment. Even these checks upon the exercise of this right were so jealously viewed by the nation, that it was declared, by the Bill of Rights, at the Revolution, *that it is the right of the subjects to petition the King, and all commitments and prosecutions for such petitioning are illegal.*

Where the end is lawful, all necessary means of attaining it are also lawful. The subjects of England, who, by this act of 1 William and Mary, have a general unqualified right to petition the Crown, cannot know the nature of a public grievance but by communication with each other upon the subject; nor can this be had without assembling or meeting: if, therefore, the meeting of any number of subjects for this purpose were to be declared an *unlawful meeting*, and the persons so meeting, or promoting such meeting, were to be arrested, and become guilty of a high misdemeanor, Englishmen would be then liable to commitments and prosecutions for petitioning the King, against the express provision of the Bill of Rights. The drawing up and signing of the petition is evidently included in *the right of petitioning*. To render the inchoate act unlawful, is to make the completion of it criminal.

If the most sacred rights of Englishmen, that can only be exercised by the assemblage of several persons, can be wrested from them upon *the bare possibility* of some mischief happening from any number of persons meeting together, there will be an end of their Constitution, and they may bid an everlasting farewell to all the rights and liberties they now enjoy. However it may be thought by some, that in Ireland licentiousness is of nearer kin to liberty than in England, we Englishmen have full confidence in our Legislature, that the peaceful and temperate manner in which we have, for this last century, exercised that right, shall not ground a pretext for depriving us of it, merely because there is a possibility of our abusing it hereafter. As well might we be deprived of the right of choosing our representatives in Parliament, because popular elections *may be made use of to serve the ends of factious and seditious persons, to the violation of the public peace, and the great and manifest encouragement of riot, tumult, and disorder.* By that very spirit, in which our ancestors thought, for a time, that the exercise of the right should be somewhat restrained and regulated, because it had been used in a *tumultuous and disorderly* manner, do we confide that it would be enlarged and confirmed (were it desirable) to us for the regularity and order with which we have uniformly exercised it.

When we reflect, that the patrons of more than two thousand associations have, under the countenance and rewards of the British Ministry, broached doctrines so emphatically consonant with the spirit and words of the Irish Convention Act, the apprehension of a like experiment in this country cannot be groundless. It is notorious, that several meetings of the societies called *the Friends of the People,* and *Friends of the Liberty of the Press,* were had, at which, resolutions and declarations were published as the acts of these societies. Those who admitted of their reasons, of course found them constitutional; those who thought them seditious or treasonable, condemned the Government of the most criminal timidity or neglect, for not executing the rigour of the laws against the delinquents, who were all known and open to the justice of their offended country. This superintending association of Mr. Reeves has made the avowal of having formed itself *for the preservation of the public security, and of the Constitution itself; for uniting and engaging to lend assistance to the civil Magistrate, in discovering and bringing to justice, offenders of the most dangerous description, those who endeavour to subvert the very basis of our civil rights and of our social happiness.* Association Papers, No. IV. *Bowles's Answer to the Declaration of the Friends to the Liberty of the Press:* And instead of forwarding or procuring the prosecution of any of those who were ready to avow the publication, and stand the trial of its loyalty by their peers; it assumes a power of general accusation and general condemnation of their countrymen, without the form or pretence even of a public trial. " Wicked men," say they, " by the means of clubs " and associations, have been spreading among the simple and ig-

" norant, seditious opinions, destructive of good government and
" the happiness of us all. Good men associate to counteract these
" evil designs, to support good Government and to continue to
" us our present happiness. To associate in the forms in which
" they do (as appears by the printed papers exhibited to this so-
" ciety) is always seditious and very often treasonable: *they all
" appear to be offenders against the law.* To meet as is now pro-
" posed, for suppressing sedition, for propogating peaceable opi-
" nions, and for aiding the magistracy in subordination to the
" direction of the Magistrates, the law allows it, and the time re-
" quires it. Then, as if a *public grievance* could by possibility
exist but in the effect of some act of the Legislature or of Government, against which they have a right to petition, and, consequently, to consult about, they very dictatoriously assume to
pronounce, that. " *the Society, after full consideration of the na-
" ture of private meetings, formed with a design to take cognizance
" of what is transacted by the Executive or Legislative Powers of
" the country, are of opinion, that all such meetings are irregular.*"

Notwithstanding leave had been given by the House of Commons, in Ireland, upwards of two months, to bring in a Bill to
improve the representation of the people in Parliament, still no
farther progress had been attempted to be made till within very
few days of the close of Parliament; when Sir Hercules Lan-
grishe observed, " it was submitted to the discussion of Parlia-
" ment at a period of the session so far advanced, that must preclude
" all possibility of its present success." He complained, that it
had too long kept up the agitation of the people, and he was unwilling " it should be laid by, as it were, to ripen by fermenta-
" tion. He could not prevail on himself to let it go in reference
" to the people with the authority of such respectable Members
" as those who patronized it, altogether unquestioned and uncon-
" troverted; at least without stating some of those arguments
" which had impressed upon his mind a conviction of the inexpe-
" dience and danger of the measure." When we reflect upon
the confident assurance with which the people of Ireland looked

up to Parliament at the commencement of the seffion for a reform in their reprefentation, we cannot but shudder at the poffible confequences of an animated people being so severely difappointed in their fondest hopes and proudeft expectations. If ever they again meet in any number, to devife or concert meafures for conveying the fenfe either of that difappointment, or of their original grievances to the Throne or Parliament, it muft be in contempt and violation of the Convention Act: an awful alternative, which muft quickly decide the policy of this new and ftrong meafure.

In order, however, to meet the wifhes of the people to a certain extent, the Parliament paffed a Libel Bill, fimilar to that paffed in England: they alfo granted to his Majefty, a civil lift eftablifhment of 225,000l. per annum, by which they limited the power of the Crown to grant penfions in the whole amount to 80,000l. per annum, and not to exceed in any one grant 1,200l. unlefs to the royal family, or on an addrefs: by this act, alfo, the allowance for fecret fervices was ftinted to 5000l. per annum. They likewife paffed a very popular act, for excluding from the Houfe of Commons, certain officers and penfioners under the Crown.

CHAPTER XVII.

AUGUST, 1793.

CONTENTS.

Domeſtic effects of the war in France—The French riſe in arms—Their forces amount to 1,0,22,902 men—Lord Howe's and the French Fleet at ſea—Our trade unprotected, at ſea—Plan of the Britiſh Cabinet for attacking Weſt Flanders—Order for artillery, ammunition, and ſtores by the Duke of York—Demurred to by the Duke of Richmond—Three weeks interruption to the plan—The camp of Cæſar taken—The redoubt of Lincelles ſtormed by the Guards—The Duke of York arrives before Dunkirk—Summons it—General O'Meara's anſwer—Operations before the Siege.

POWERFUL and unprecedented as was the preſent combination of armed forces againſt France, which, at this time, amounted to more than four hundred and ten thouſand men, beſides the navies of England, Spain, and Holland, it appears incredible and unaccountable, that the French Republicans ſhould have refiſted even to this hour. But the melancholy truth is, that the combination of their enemies is the very circumſtance that gives them ſtrength, and our proſecution of the war defeats its own ends, if thoſe ends really be, as they are avowed, for cruſhing the power of the French Republic. Strong, violent, and ſanguinary meaſures, are the only means by which they can forward and ſtrengthen their preſent revolutionary Government;

and the war alone can fupply them with plaufible pretexts, and ready opportunities for carrying them into execution. Whatever may be the ultimate views, or in whatever point of novelty they may wifh to reft their future Government, the previous neceffary ftep is a total and radical change in the principles and habits of the Nation. The war enabled them to confifcate the property of every man they chofe to fufpect: it fupplied the treafury with all the *fpecie* that was above ground in the kingdom; the war drew off from fober induftry, the active citizens; it infpired them with a fpirit of barbarifm and ferocioufnefs: the war united all jarring interefts at home; it infufed into men a pride in becoming unlike their enemies; it prompted then to renounce and revile every idea of religious worfhip, and fhake off the laft link of the chain, that had hitherto connected moral virtue with their focial engagements: the war had cheapened the value of their lives, and worked them up into a delight in bloodfhed; the war had converted the moft tyrannous acts of cruelty and injuftice, into the neceffary exertions of republican virtue and energy. Barrere, in the Convention, reported from the *committee of public welfare*, that they would, on the next day, prefent to them a new and efficient plan of military meafures. " Tactical wars," faid he, " do not fuit a free Nation. The wars of Kings refemble " tournaments, which laft as long as the patience of the people " can fupport them. The war of the people ought to be a tor- " rent, a flood of liberty." On that day, therefore, (Aug. 16) the people of France declared, by the mouth of their reprefentatives, *" that they would rife in one body, in defence of their liberty, of " equality, and of the independence of their territories, and their " Conftitution."* Their new and laft Conftitution they had accepted *indivifibly*, on the 10th of the month. Their forces, which were at this time either embodied, or ordered to be immediately embodied, amounted to the incredible number of 1,022,902 men.

Under all thefe difficulties from their external enemies, the French Republicans were, at the fame time, preffed with the moft alarming infurrections from the Royalifts in the Vendee, and the defection of the city of Lyons, which had declared itfelf openly againft the Convention. Marfeilles had followed the example of Lyons; and Bourdeaux was generally fufpected of the fame difaffection towards the reigning powers in France. In the acceffion of every enemy, foreign or domeftic, a new pretext and opportunity arofe for pillage and flaughter.

The expectations of this nation were greatly raifed upon the knowledge of Lord Howe's being at fea, when a French fquadron was certainly out of Breft. There is an innate confidence of fuccefs in Englifhmen, whenever their fleets have an opportunity of engaging the enemy. This affurance is often pufhed beyond reafon and prudence, but it is always grounded on the fair prefumption of the fuperior conduct and difcipline of Britifh feamen. It was reprefented in the French Convention, that the Britifh Admiral had declined meeting a republican fleet, and had bafely returned into port. It is generally fuppofed, that this French fleet was fuperior in number to the Britifh, but it is certain, that our prudent Admiral did not expofe his fleet even to the chance of fuffering from the fuperiority of the enemy. Though the Nation had been now upwards of fix months at war, as little attention appeared to be given either to the protection of our own trade, or to the annoyance of that of the enemy, as if we were in the fecurity of a profound peace. Whatever difference of opinion there might have exifted upon the propriety or the neceffity of beginning the war, there was but one fentiment of carrying it on with vigour in every department, when it was once begun. At one and the fame time, Julien de Thouloufe announced to the National Convention, that one hundred, and forty-three merchantmen had arrived fafe from the colonies, in the different ports of the republic, and that they had brought home fix thoufand foldiers; and a deputation from our Jamaica merchants waited upon the Lords of the Admiralty, to reprefent to them the defencelefs ftate of that ifland, and to learn, if poffible, what force had been fent by Admiral Gardner, to convoy the homeward bound trade, then on their paffage, worth more than four millions; they had the piteous confolation of learning, that the fafety of this valuable fleet had been confided to the protection of a fingle fifty gun fhip. But credit feemed to be given to the affertion of many divines, that Providence had acceded to the combination againft France; eighty-nine veffels from Lifbon and Oporto had been waiting for convoy fince the beginning of May, and they were entrufted at laft to the protection of the Flora frigate; both fleets, however, arrived fafe.

In confidering the progrefs of our arms on the continent, lefs attention will be paid to the motions of the armies, than to the general views and plans of the campaign, which can be traced up to our Cabinet at home. Both our officers and men have invariably behaved, upon all occafions, with the refolution and bravery which have ever diftinguifhed the Britifh troops. There can be no other anxiety for them, than left their valour fhould be wantonly facrificed to the unavailing projects, ill-judged plans, or the rafh enterprifes of the prime rulers of the war. No fooner had Valenciennes capitulated, than the Britifh Miniftry communicated to the heads of the armies, their peremptory orders for that part of the combined forces, which were in the pay of Great Britain, to attack the weft fide of French Flanders, in order to become mafters of the towns of Dunkirk, Bergues, Graveline, and Calais. This command of the coaft would keep open all fupplies, and effectually prevent the poffibility of being either furprifed or furrounded. Whereas, at prefent, the line of communication, which the enemy commanded from Lille to the fea, afforded them every opportunity of harraffing the Auftrian Netherlands, and obliged the allies to keep up a very confiderable force in thofe parts, to prevent a furprife. The fole objection to the enterprife was the latenefs of undertaking it. Had the campaign opened with this plan, the allied armies might then have proceeded, fafely and regularly, from the fea-coaft, in their progrefs into their enemy's country, and have avoided the fatal loffes and difgraces, which they afterwards fuffered. It is ufelefs to notice the difference of opinion upon the propriety of this plan, fince the wifhes of the Britifh Cabinet were in fact fubmitted to, though decidedly, it is faid, againft the opinions of every General, to whom the project was communicated : it will be fruitlefs to fpeculate upon the probable refult of better plans, that never were adopted.

The welfare of the public is too deeply engaged in the fate of the prefent war, not to feel feverely, not to reflect deeply, not to fpeak freely upon its effects and confequences. *They enjoy a privilege of fomewhat more dignity and effect, than that of idle lamentation over the calamities of their country.* The Englifh Nation has an innate predilection for their Royal Family ; it is their boaft, to be led on to victory by the gallant iffue of their beloved Sovereign. They know no referve to their confidence, no boundaries to their credit, for his intrepidity, refolution, and bravery. But they look to the combination of councils, as well as of forces, for a fupply of that experience, which the bleffings of a ten years peace have deprived the warlike youth of an opportunity of acquiring. The candour and fympathy of the Englifh Nation will not permit his early laurels to be blighted by the ftorm which others raifed, and which he could not avoid.

The war on the continent, from this time, affumes a new and unprecedented form: the plans of operations were dictated to the commanders of the armies by a diftant cabinet, neither on the fpot to feize the advantages of the ever-fhifting turns of fortune, nor compofed of men of any military knowledge or experience. Too great, however, were the dependencies of the allies upon the Britifh Government for fubfidies, for fupplies, and for fhipping, not to receive, though with reluctance, the plans impofed upon them by the Britifh Cabinet. In all human events and circumftances, one principle of action is invariably and unexceptionably to be followed. Though the adoption of a plan be flow or doubtful, its execution muft be ever prompt and vigorous. No fooner had it been determined, in council, that the armies were to be feparated, and that the Duke of York was to undertake the attack of Weft Flanders, with the Britifh, Hanoverian, Heffian, Dutch, and fome Auftrian troops, than he inftantly fent over to the Mafter of the Ordnance, an exact lift of the ordnance, ammunition, and ftores, which were requifite for the fiege of Dunkirk, and which he particularly directed to be ready for the time at which his Royal Highnefs intended to be, with his army, before that town; and without which it was impoffible for him to attempt the fiege with any profpect of fuccefs.

The noble Duke, at the head of the ordnance, though no man's ideas had been fo extended as his own, in the plans of home fortifications and felf-defence, it is faid, was ftartled at the magnitude of the order: he inftantly fent for the principal ftore-keeper, and other officers of the Warren, to know if they had the quantity required, and could embark it within the time mentioned. They undertook the order, and actually on the next day, by uncommon exertions, the whole demand of ordnance, ammunition, and ftores, was on the water edge, ready for embarkation. But his Grace, ftill doubting of the fafety of thus difarming the country, which he faw in real, or would reprefent in imaginary danger, remonftrated to his Royal Highnefs upon the inexpediency of fupplying his demand at that time. Three weeks were confumed in the correfpondence between the Commander in Chief of the Britifh Forces, who had ordered what ordnance and ammunition he found requifite for the moft urgent fervice of the country, and the Mafter General of the Ordnance, who chofe to demur to the command. In the mean time the ammunition and ftores were again depofited in the ftorehoufes, left they fhould be damaged by lying thus expofed on the open fhore. His Royal Highnefs, to avoid warning the enemy of his intentions, filled up the time of this extraordinary negociation, with the army of the Prince of Saxe Cobourg. But in vain; for the enemy during this very period, either knowing or fufpecting the views of the Britifh Cabinet, increafed the garrifon of Dunkirk, by an augmentation of twelve thoufand troops.

In this interval, the combined armies drove the French from the famous ftrong camp of Cæfar, at Bourlon, behind Cambray, which they took poffeffion of, and immediately abandoned. The Auftrian General fummoned the republican Governor of Cambray to furrender, which he refufed. The combined armies then marched towards Menin, where the Britifh troops gave a fignal proof of their cool bravery and refolution. Three battalions of the guards, confifting of one thoufand one hundred and twenty-two men, were ordered under General Lake to march to the fuccour of fome Dutch troops at Lincelles. Upon their arrival, they found a redoubt of uncommon fize and ftrength, occupied by five thoufand French, who had diflodged, and routed the Dutch from that poft. General Lake, fays the Gazette, " embraced a refolution worthy of the troops he com-
" manded. He advanced under a heavy fire, with an order and
" intrepidity, for which no praife can be too high. After firing
" three or four rounds, they rufhed on with their bayonets,
" ftormed the redoubts, and drove the enemy through the village,
" who loft eleven pieces of cannon, two of which had been
" taken from the Dutch, and have not fince appeared in that
" quarter." In this action Colonel Bofville was killed, and fome hundreds of our brave troops killed and wounded. The fame Gazette informs us of the importance of this victory, for which fo much gallant blood was fpilt : " The works of Lin-
" celles have been deftroyed, and the poft left unoccupied."

Three weeks had now elapfed fince the capitulation of Valenciennes, when the Duke of York having at laft received intelligence, that the ammunition and ordnance that he had demanded, were at length permitted to be fhipped, began his march towards Weft Flanders on the 20th of the month. On the 23d, he fummoned the republican general O'Meara, to furrender the town of Dunkirk to his Britannic Majefty ; to which summons, on the next day, the republican general sent the following answer:

" General,
" Invested with the confidence of the French Republic, I
" have received your summons to surrender an important city.
" I answer by assuring you, that I shall defend it with the brave
" republicans, I have the honour to command.   O'MEARA."

Besides the heavy artillery for the siege, which had not as yet arrived, a grand flotilla of gun-boats was promised by our Cabinet to co-operate in the siege: the most solemn assurances were given to his Royal Highness, that, unless delayed by contrary winds, this flotilla should certainly be in the bay of Dunkirk on Saturday the 24th instant. The wind had been favourable for some time, yet the reinforcement did not sail from Woolwich till Monday the 26th, on which day Admiral Macbride, who was then in London, and who was to command that expedition, received his final orders. The public was, in the mean time, amused with the details of the bravery and intrepidity of our troops in skirmishing, and in repelling the sorties of the enemy; who, it was now found, were sixteen thousand strong. In one of these attacks, the Gazette of the 26th says, " The ardour of " the troops carried them further in the pursuit than was intended, " so that they came under the cannon, of the place by which means " considerable loss has been sustained." On this unfortunate occasion, the Austrian General Dalton, and Colonel Eld, of the Coldstream regiment of guards were killed. On the 27th, some heavy stores and artillery were landed off Nieuport; and three days after Major Huddleston arrived at Ostend, with a further supply of artillery, ammunition, and stores, for the reduction of Dunkirk. The French gun-boats greatly annoyed our troops during the whole of the time that our forces were within their reach. Admiral Macbride was therefore dispatched to London, where he arrived on the 31st, to enforce the necessity of sending immediately, a naval force of gun-boats, bomb-vessels, and other light craft, as well as more forces to co-operate with the besieging army.

CHAPTER XVIII.

SEPTEMBER, 1793.

CONTENTS.

The Duke of York had treated secretly with the Governor of Dunkirk for its Delivery—The plot detected—Naval support promised—Surprise and defeat of General Freytag, who, with Prince Adolphus, was taken prisoner—Effects of this general Defeat—The army rallies, upon learning the success of General Beaulieu near Ypres—The Dutch fly from Menin—The French fall upon Ghent and Bruges—Le Quesnoy surrenders at discretion—Toulon gained over by Lord Hood—He enters and takes possession of the Town, Harbour and Fleet, in the name of Louis XVII.—His Proclamations—Lord Hervey forces Tuscany out of its neutrality—Sir Gilbert Elliot Commissioner at Toulon.

BESIDES the general reliance which the Duke of York had in the intrepidity of his troops, and the full persuasion, that upon his arrival he should find the necessary artillery, in case he should be under the necessity of undertaking the siege; he had also an expectation of being admitted into the town by a golden key. He had kept up a secret correspondence with the former governor, General O'*Moran*, nor did he till his arrival know, that the plan had been discovered, and that General O'Moran was removed from his post (he has been since *executed* for the treachery). Although General O'Meara, who had at first succeeded his countryman, O'Moran, in the command of the garrison, answered the summons of the Duke of York, yet tho besieged had, at that time, actually removed O'Meara from the chief command, not choosing to repose so important a trust in a foreigner, and a countryman of the person who had so recently engaged to betray them.

On the 3d of the month, his Royal Highness received an express from England, that two fifty gun ships, some frigates and bomb ketches were under sailing orders for Dunkirk; and he began now to make fascines, gabions, and other necessary preparations for the siege. Since the siege of Dunkirk was the favourite measure of the British Cabinet, and had been resolved upon by them in the month of July, it is a matter of more than surprise to the public, that no naval force was ordered, nor artillery provided for the siege, till the month of September. Such gross delay and neglect cannot have existed, without the most criminal responsibility in some departments.

The nation is equally astonished, that there should have been such a total and unaccountable want of intelligence throughout the army, that the movements of General Houchard, with thirty-three thousand men, to raise the siege of Dunkirk, which was formally announced in the Convention on the 25th of the last month, should have been unknown or not provided against. The covering army of General Freytag was surprised and totally routed, before the Duke of York was even acquainted with the approach of the enemy. The first intelligence he received of it, was by a note written with a pencil. At the same moment a sortie from the garrison was announced, and a most precipitate retreat was the consequence. The loss of British troops in the confusion of such a surprise, was fortunately not very great; though his Royal Highness very narrowly escaped being surrounded and made a prisoner. All the ammunition and stores were either left to the enemy, or thrown into the canal: the fine train of artillery, which had moved so reluctantly from Woolwich-Warren, was only landed to become the prey of the enemy, or to be lost to us. Sixty-four of the heavy cannons were thrown into the canal; feven were buried in the earth, and forty-three left on the field. In the retreat of the Hanoverians, his Royal Highnefs Prince Adolphus and General Freytag were both wounded and taken prifoners. Nothing can more ftrongly befpeak the extreme confufion of the Hanoverian army, than the circumftance of their General and our Prince falling into the hands of the enemy. Our Gazette fays, that a patrole of cavalry " which ought to have been in the front, having taken " another road, they went into the village of Rexpoede, through " which one of the columns was to pafs, but which was then " occupied by the enemy." What a melancholy fituation for a commander in chief, upon whofe orders an army of eighteen thoufand men were to retreat, rally, or fight! himfelf difobeyed or abandoned by his patrole! ignorant of the fituation either of his own or the enemy's forces! a whole column of his army unwilling, or unable to obey his orders! the Gazette (if the meaning of its writer can, by any laboured conftruction, be extracted from his words) feems to admit this extremity of panic, diforder and confufion, by attributing the recapture of his Royal Highnefs and the Field Marfhal " to the *intrepidity and prefence* " *of mind of* General Walmoden, who, upon difcovering that " the enemy were in poffeffion of Rexpoede, had immediately " collected a body of troops, attacked it without hefitation, and " defeated them with great flaughter." The intelligent compiler of the Gazette informs us alfo, " that, in thefe repeated engage- " ments, nothing could exceed the fteadinefs and good behaviour " of the troops." If the flaughter made amongft them be the criterion of this fteadinefs, it is a ftrong, but a too melancholy proof of the fact. Above 3,500 Hanoverians were killed, befides very fevere loffes in every other corps that compofed this covering army.

Nothing could equal the general panic and confternation caufed by this unfortunate and difgraceful retreat at Oftend. General Ainflie, the commandant ordered an immediate embargo on all veffels, from the tranfports in the harbour, down to the smallest fishing-boats. The military chest was actually put on board, and it was a general expectation, and perhaps as general a wish, that the British troops should have returned to their native country. In great national misfortunes, like these, it is impossible to repress the sentiments of the public upon them. The disgrace and loss which this nation suffered from this fatal attempt upon Dunkirk, brought into the minds of every one, that the enterprise had been imposed by the British Cabinet upon the generals of the combined armies, who had decidedly and unanimously reprobated the plan; and that the dispatch, vigour, and resolution in the execution, had been counteracted and defeated by the very persons who had concerted and insisted upon the attempt. Not only humanity shudders at the loss of so many brave men, who fell upon this inglorious occasion, but Great Britain feels also a heavy loss in the fruitless waste of its treasures. Immense is the cost of so much ammunition, stores, and ordnance, transported at such a heavy expence. By our subsidiary treaties with Hanover and Hesse Cassel, the sum of thirty pounds is paid by the people of Great Britain for every subsidized soldier that falls in the war *: thus by the fall of 3,500 Hanoverians, on the 8th of this month, Great Britain became indebted to the Elector of Hanover, on one day, in the enormous sum of one hundred thousand guineas. A Landgrave of Hesse Cassel might not, on such an accumulation of wealth to his treasury, feel that poignancy of grief that rends the heart of our humane sovereign, upon the loss of so many of his beloved subjects. The flying army of the Duke of York, which had not been under cover for five nights, was at length rallied by the seasonable assurance, that the Austrian General Beaulieu had relieved Ypres, and totally defeated the French army in that quarter, which had in consequence fallen back to Bailleuil. Several days after this shameful defeat, Admiral Macbride arrived with his squadron

---

* It is a well known circumstance, that the subsidy dealers of Germany can procure a recruit for one ducat, when twenty guineas cannot purchase the service of one able-bodied man in England.

off Nieuport. His Royal Highnefs then took up his head quarters at Dixmude, from whence Sir James Murray, the Adjutant General, wrote to Mr. Dundas on the 14th, " that he took the " opportunity of Captain Robinfon, of the Brilliant frigate, fail- " ing to England, to inform him, that the Dutch pofts on the " Lys were forced by the enemy on the 12th. In confequence " of this, the troops of the Republic have abandoned Menin, " and have fallen upon Bruges and Ghent. His Royal Highnefs " meant on that day to march to Thouroute."

The effects of this flight of the Dutch troops, immediately after the general retreat of the Britifh army, added more vigour and energy to the enemy, than difmay or defpair to the confederates. The fucceffes of Beaulieu reanimated them in fome degree; and the furrender of Le Quefnoy at defcretion, happened about the fame time. Although our armies could not acquire the intelligence, till the Adjutant General wrote his famous Gazette Extraordinary of Sept. 11, that the enemy had, under General Houchard, *collected* " force for the relief of Dunkirk " from every quarter of the country, from the armies of the " Rhine and the Mozelle, and particularly that which had oc- " cupied the Camp de Cæfar." Yet they were not long ignorant of the admiffion of Lord Hood into Toulon, which was a circumftance, that did not fo nearly intereft them, as the collection and advance of Houchard's forces. This fatal furprife is the more unaccountable, when we reflect, that the general rendezvous of the enemy was on Mount Caffel, within view of, and not 15 miles diftant from Freytag's army. The French entered Furnes, and in two days, with the help of the inhabitants, removed from the town all the ftores which had been left there by the Britifh army.

Lord Hood, who commanded the Englifh fquadron in the Mediterranean, feems to have been fent out upon an uncertain, if not a forlorn hope, of making good any landing on the coaft of France; for he had not in his whole fleet, a land officer to take the command even of a fortrefs, when he entered Toulon, as ap-

pears by the appointment of Captain Elphinstone to such a command. He had been cruizing for some time off that port, and had dispatched a frigate, with a flag of truce, to Marseilles, which did not come within gun-shot of the town, but delivered a proclamation from Lord Hood, containing proposals for restoring Monarchy, and with it peace to France. It had not the desired effect upon the Marseillois; nothing, therefore, was further attempted upon that city. His Lordship sent a similar proclamation to Toulon, and the frigate was favourably received in the harbour. The proclamation was preceded by a preliminary declaration, which stated, that " if a candid and explicit decla-
" ration in favour of Monarchy should be made at Toulon and
" Marseilles, and the standard of Royalty hoisted, the ships in
" the harbour dismantled, and the port and forts provisionally
" at his disposition, so as to allow of the egress and regress with
" safety, the people of Provence should have all the assistance
" and support his Majesty's fleet could give; and when peace
" should take place, the port, ships, and stores should be restored
" to France." The Proclamation was addressed to the town and inhabitants of the South of France; it sets out with painting a very horrid picture of the present anarchy and tyranny of France: his Lordship tells them, " a situation so dreadful sensibly afflicts
" the coalesced powers, they see no other remedy but the re-
" establishment of the French Monarchy. *It is for this*, and
" the acts of aggression committed by the Executive Power of
" France, that we have armed, in conjunction with the coalesced
" powers." He then assures them, that he comes to offer them the force with which he was entrusted by his Sovereign, to crush, with promptitude, the factions, *to re-establish a regular Government in France*, &c. These declarations of our motives for the war, are not strictly consonant with those which Mr. Pitt avowed in the House of Commons. Our Ministers at home declare, that we enter into the war to defend our allies, and not to interfere with the internal government of France; they instruct our admirals at the head of our fleets, to pronounce to

Europe, that we have joined the confederacy to crush the present power in France, and restore its ancient monarchy.

The answer of the Inhabitants of Toulon was a declaration that they were tired of the present Constitution, and demanded that of 1789; they would accordingly proclaim Louis XVII. King according to that Constitution, and in every other particular agree to the proposals of Lord Hood; who thereupon published a second proclamation to this effect: " That whereas " the Sections of Toulon have, by their Commissioners to me, " made a solemn declaration in favour of Monarchy, have pro- " claimed Louis XVII. son of Louis XVI. their lawful King, " and have sworn to acknowledge him, and no longer suffer the " despotism of Tyrants, who at this time govern France, but " will do their utmost to establish Monarchy, as accepted by the " late Sovereign in 1789, and restore peace to their distracted " and ruinous country: I do hereby repeat, what I have already " declared to the people of the South of France, that I take " possession of Toulon, and hold it in trust only for Louis " XVII. until peace shall be re-established in France, which I " hope and trust will be soon."

As the people of this country pay and suffer so severely for the war, they are urgently called upon to look closely into the views and consequences of it. It is a matter of curious observation, that within the space of six weeks, during which no change in the principle of the war could have taken place, Valenciennes was surrendered to the Duke of York, in the name of the Emperor, his Royal Highness summoned Dunkirk in the name of his Britannic Majesty, and Lord Hood entered and seized upon Toulon, in the name of Louis XVII. Each of these three places equally belonged to the late King of France. An *uniform* system or principle in the confederated invasion of that kingdom, could not have given occasion to such variety of title or claim. What faith or consistency can be discovered in these acts of our Government? We countenance, and take into pay, the French emigrant nobility, who were prescribed by the Constitution of 1789, and we rear a standard in support of that very Constitution; our good ally the King of Prussia, keeps in prison La Fayette and Lameth, the most zealous supporters of that very constitution, which we proclaim at Toulon. How long will Great Britain join in a war of such separate and discordant interests? If the federacy be formed upon a common principle, the concealment of it from the nations which support it, is a strong suspicion, that it will not bear the fair light of day. Nations will not for ever suffer a night of darkness.

The advantages of the surrender of Toulon, though not taken possession of in the name of the King of England were turned to quick account by our Minister. So unusually numerous had been the late proselytes to his influence, that he was overwhelmed in despair at the *insufficiency of his means to satisfy the demands of ambition, and the hunger of faction*: for by these means alone we are taught by more than two thousand associations *instituted for supporting a due execution of the laws, can we arrive at the summit of wealth, honour, power, and dominion.* The reservoir of these means was actually dry, when the alarmed zeal of the Chancellor called upon his disinterested patriotism to accept of the Seals without any stipulation for a possible retreat. Inscrutable, as unexpected, are the ways of Providence in affording the means of preserving and forwarding the ends of its favourite institutions. That the re-possession of a French town by the French Monarch, should supply a British Minister with an increase of the *necessary* means of preserving the British Constitution at so critical a juncture, was a mystery disclosed only to the illuminated associators under Mr. Reeves, and to those, blest like himself, in fact or desire, with some consoling beams of ministerial influence. The first fruits of this seasonable harvest, were consecrated to soothe the alarms, and remunerate the convictions of the immaculate Baronet Sir Gilbert Elliot. He was appointed, by the King of Great Britain, to a splendid, honourable, and powerful situation in a French town, belonging to the French Monarch, with a salary of 7,500l. per annum, to be paid out of the British treasury; he was made commissioner to Toulon; an appointment unknown in English history. Admirable was the ingenuity of our constitutional Minister in fertilizing this new supply of means. The relative, as well as positive merits of the Chancellor were not to go unrewarded; his nephew, a barrister at law, was well entitled to share the profits of his uncle's prudent convictions of the necessity of this extensive and costly war. The overwhelming deluge of bankruptcies, one of its first effects at home, was a grateful shower of Danae to the Chancery. The office of purse-bearer was naturally confided to the fidelity of the nephew, and from the lamentable ruin of many, became to him worth 1500l. per annum. He was appointed Commissary General to Toulon, with a stipulation for forty shillings per diem of half-pay for life. Besides these a long list of subaltern well-wishing, and fairly promised proselytes, were largely gifted out of these trust estates of the infant *French Monarch*. The œconomical system of half-pay will, perhaps, secure the gratitude of the appointees during their lives, to their friendly benefactor. The trust, however, indemnify Great Britain for all the immediate advances made upon it. It may be not unfairly presumed, that the tardiness of Ministers to meet the Parliament in such national embarrassments, has been occasioned by their wishes and expectations to extend the means of that influence, *which is necessary to unite the members in a firm and solid majority, without which they can pursue no measures of public utility with steadiness or success*, by the capture of Dunkirk, St. Maloes, or some other parts of the French territories, so providentially favouring the increase of the *necessary influence* of the British Minister. This naturally accounts for the resolution of the British Cabinet after the capture of Valenciennes to divide the forces: here British blood, and British treasure were spent, to procure national advantages for a foreign people: *Austrian*, not *British* commissioners, were sent to Valenciennes.

How industriously have the docile pupils of Mr. Burke, laboured to verify the doctrines of their infallible master, that *the power of the King of England is more solid, real, and extensive, than what the King of France was possessed of before this miserable revolution.* They are resolved, that in future, no empty, vain title, shall disgrace the escutcheons of our Monarch. In future, the territorial possessions of the French Monarch, shall at least feed the prerogative of the King of Great Britain, *France,* and Ireland.

CHAPTER XIX.

OCTOBER, 1793.

CONTENTS.

Energy and activity in the French—Siege of Maubeuge raised—French army 170,000 strong—Nieuport defended by Major Matthews—Cowardice of the Dutch—The lines of Weissenbourg forced—Lord Howe in Torbay—Treaties with Sardinia and Naples—Fresh Treaty with Prussia—Negociation to bring Denmark into the confederacy—Genoa forced out of her neutrality—Tuscany forced by England to declare war against France—Manifesto of our King—The Emprunt Forcé—British property seized, and British subjects arrested—Death of the Queen—Mr. Burke's Reflections thereupon.

HOWEVER it may serve the views of certain persons at home, to keep up the irritation of the Nation against the French Republicans; and however largely the ministerial prints, and the association publications may, for this purpose, have indulged in invective and imprecation against that nation, and every measure adopted by it; yet is it a truth of too fatal consequence to this unfortunate country, that our anger has precipitated us into a labyrinth of ruin and disgrace. Such, in fact, was the infatuation of our deluded countrymen, that our failures of the preceding month had produced no other effect upon their minds, than the increase of a blind, and desperate abandonment of their cause to those, who were seeking to justify their error in engaging them in the war, by multiplying the difficulties of extracting them out of it. Those who disapproved of the commencement of the war, were more anxious than its advocates for its conclusion; but they saw no other road to honourable peace, than by carrying it on with vigour, when it was once begun. Though comparisons may be always odious, they are not always fruitless. Let the tardiness of co-operation from our Board of Ordnance and Admiralty, be contrasted with the spirit and energy of that Government, which has raised our pity, or excited our indignation: thousands of troops conveyed in waggons, drawn by post-horses, to the place of defence with unknown celerity, bespoke the *real* earnestness with which their Executive Council attended to the welfare of the Nation. Their victorious General Houchard was, with his whole Staff, put under arrest, for not having pursued with advantage, the discomfited enemy in their precipitate and disorderly retreat. Their success was punished, because it might have been more complete: here the causes of a failure, which could scarcely have been worse, were not even looked into. The contempt of the example which humbles us, is the extremity of folly. The Warren, and Dock-yard of Woolwich, are less distant from Dunkirk, than the Rhine, or the Moselle. Wurmser, and even Brunswick, are more terrible enemies to France, than the opposers of Mr. Reeves's Associations to Great Britain.

The expectation of the whole confederacy seemed to hang upon the fate of Maubeuge, which the Prince of Saxe Cobourg had, for some weeks, blockaded with an army of 70,000 men. He was attacked by the French, and though the Austrians behaved with their usual steadiness and bravery, they were forced to raise the siege, and cross the Sambre. After this defeat, the Prince became seriously apprehensive for the fate of Flanders, and applied for a reinforcement of 50,000 men. The French army of the North, now consisted of 170,000 men. They again entered Furnes, and laid siege to Nieuport: they were, however, fortunately checked by the steadiness and resolution of Major Matthews: he opened the sluices, though opposed by the Magistrates, and, with a handful of men, defended the town till reinforcements arrived. Such was the terror through all Flanders, of an invasion, that immense quantities of stores were destroyed, to prevent their falling into the hands of the enemy.

Such of the Dutch troops as were engaged before Maubeuge, disgraced themselves by the most infamous flight: whether it were from disinclination to the service, or from want of discipline or courage, these troops have never stood with the steadiness of soldiers: they appeared, nevertheless, to have been piqued at the reflections of the combined armies, upon their retreat from Menin: and, through the interest of their Hereditary Prince, they insisted upon General Beaulieu's being called to a court martial, for not having supported them, as it was pretended he might. The notoriety, however, of the good conduct of this veteran General, and of the dastardly behaviour of the fugitive Dutchmen was such, that they were prevailed upon prudently to drop the atttempt to disguise their own cowardice, by criminating the brave Beaulieu.

More favourable accounts were received from the army of the Rhine. General Wurmser, after an engagement of eleven hours, forced the lines of Weissenbourg, and took the French camp by assault; the Duke of Brunswick attacked them, at the same same time, in the rear. They took possession of Weissenbourg and Lauterbourg, and pursued the French to the gates of Strasbourg: the carnage was dreadful: full 15,000 fell in the course of the day.

The nation had not their usual consolation of repairing their misfortunes at land by their activity or success at sea. Lord Howe had spent the autumn, as he had the summer, in defending the entry of Torbay: he once was in sight of the French fleet for twenty-four hours; but the risk of engaging it was too great for his prudence to hazard in such a critical juncture. He was perhaps directed to avoid the infection of republicanism by coming into contact with any French vessel. This he seemed cautious of avoiding, and brought back his fleet, and the crews of every vessel, perfectly untainted to his old anchorage in Torbay. It was, indeed, said, that their superiority in sailing and running away prevented the British Admiral from coming to close quarters with the enemy: but the active spirit of the British seamen was with much difficulty formed to this new fyftem of nautical operations: *energy and action*, it might have been thought, too much refembled the ferocious republicans; and might, perhaps, have prevented the channel fleet from learning the new manœuvre of entering Breft Harbour, as the Mediterranean fquadron had that of Toulon.

Negociation was the general *panacea* for all our evils. It feemed to be the determination of our Cabinet, that if France could not be conquered, no nation of Europe fhould, at leaft, boaft of the advantage of having prudently avoided the rafh attempt. The miferies of fuch an undertaking fhould not be partial: the balance of power would not admit it; this *ultima ratio regum* fuperfeded the fovereign will of every independent ftate. All means were employed to draw other ftates into the confederacy; and the acceffion of every ally was a frefh knot to entangle Great Britain the more in this fyftem of ruinous perplexity. Threats, promifes, force, bribery, manifeftos, all means were employed, fo they had but the general object of crufhing the revolutionary Government of France. Sardinia demanded of us an annual fubfidy of 200,000l. and a conftant fleet on their coafts, to defend their country againft the aggreffions and invafions of the French Republic: it was granted: to laft as long as an inch of Savoy, or any of their territory, fhould be poffeffed by the French. The continuance of fuch a treaty, may, peradventure, be more earneftly wifhed for by Sardinia than the repoffeffion of their whole territory from the hands of their enemies. Our treaty with Naples is a guarantee to each other of their refpective States: an undertaking not to lay down arms till all places are reftored, which fhall be taken during the war; to act in concert in the Mediterranean; Naples fhall furnifh fix thoufand men, to be paid by England; England fhall keep a refpectable fleet in the Mediterranean; and Naples fhall provide four fhips of the line, four frigates, and four fmaller fhips of war.

Since the Parliament of Great Britain is not confulted in making treaties with foreign powers, but is only called upon to ratify, approve, and enforce the engagements, in which the Minifter fhall have thought proper to involve the Nation; the activity of the Cabinet was much more remarkable in negociating pretexts for continuing the war, than in haftening a peace by the vigour of our arms. Not fatisfied with the fubfifting treaty with Pruffia, that had firft involved us in the fatal confederacy, a new treaty was formally figned on the 14th of July laft, between their Britannic and Pruffian Majefties, not to lay down their arms but by common confent, and not until reftitution is obtained for any depredation which France may make upon either of the faid parties, or of their *friends or allies*. Here is a perpetuation of war to Britain, as long as France fhall be an enemy to any State that Pruffia may choofe to call a friend. Thus is the country under the direful neceffity of fupplying the exorbitant charges of a moft expenfive war, as long as any State of Europe fhall think proper to continue hoftile to France, either from public or private policy, to weaken and exhauft the refources of this kingdom, or to continue the advantages of our fubfidies to our lefs opulent allies. What a dreadful alternative for Great Britain, that it cannot withhold the fupplies for a ruinous war, without forfeiting the credit and faith of every Nation in Europe! Well, wifely, and virtuoufly did Mr. Fox urge the Parliament, to prevent his Majefty's Minifters, during the recefs, from entering into new engagements, which might render the conclufion of an honourable peace more remote and difficult. Many true patriots, like his Royal Highnefs of Clarence, were induced to vote for the war, becaufe the faith of our treaty with Holland called upon our concurrence in the defence of that Republic: the condition of the treaty having been complied with, the caufe of war had ceafed; and now juftice to ourfelves, obliged us to lay down the arms, which juftice to our allies had made us take up. As the Minifter had found one treaty fo efficient in prevailing upon the majority to commence the war, he naturally concluded, that a multiplicity of treaties would reconcile a ftill greater majority to its continuance.

Our Ambaſſador at Copenhagen entered into a correſpondence of argument with Count Bernſtorff, the miniſter of the Daniſh cabinet, upon the propriety and neceſſity of their entering into the armed confederacy againſt France. Hitherto, the prudent Dane has not been argued out of his neutrality; what other means may, hereafter, be attempted to induce or force him from it, time will diſcloſe.

The republic of Genoa, having large property in France, was induced to obſerve the ſtricteſt neutrality, to depart from which would be the ruin of the principal citizens of that State. The Government itſelf is ſaid to receive, upon loans to France, the annual ſum of 1,400,000 livres. Notwithſtanding this, Mr. Drake, the Britiſh Envoy to that State, peremptorily inſiſted upon an immediate and unqualified declaration of hoſtilities againſt France: no indemnification was, however, offered for the ſure loſs, in that caſe, of the property of their citizens or the State. This ſpirited, though ſmall republic was not to be bullied into deſtruction and ruin, and has declared, that if ſhe be to be forced from her neutrality, ſhe never can take part with thoſe who have threatened her with ſuch unprovoked injuſtice.

Our Envoy at Florence, Lord Hervey, undertook not only to intimidate the Grand Duke of Tuſcany out of his neutrality, by ſending off the French Ambaſſador, M. de la Flotte, in twenty-four hours, but to dictate to him the internal regulations concerning the French remaining within his territories, which the Britiſh Cabinet inſiſted upon. This was ſingular conduct in Great Britain towards the brother of the Emperor, who was the firſt engaged in the war againſt France, and who muſt have known the true intereſts, and had more influence over the conduct of his own brother, than any foreign power whatever. The Grand Duke, however, relinquiſhed the ſyſtem of neutrality, and declared war againſt the Republic on the 10th inſtant.

The ingenuity of our Miniſters was nearly exhauſted by the variety of meaſures they had adopted to augment and juſtify this armed confederacy. One only experiment remained to be tried;

this was, to commit the faith, credit, and juftice of the Nation to a public manifefto. Melancholy had been the precedents of their affociates in this line of operation. They had, however, the advantage of improving upon their attempts, correcting their faults, and avoiding their errors. The people of this country had a well-grounded right to expect precifion, firmnefs, and confiftency in fuch a declaration from the Throne. It was publifhed with immediate reference to the furrender of Toulon, but it is filent as to any approbation or confirmation of the proclamations and treaty of Lord Hood with the Toulonefe, the bafis of which was the acceptance of the Conftitution of 1789. It declares the objects of the war to have been, from the beginning, " to repel an unprovoked aggreffion, to contribute to the imme-" diate defence of his allies, to obtain for them and for himfelf, a " juft indemnification, and to provide, as far as circumftances " will allow, for the future fecurity of his own fubjects, and of " all other Nations of Europe." Hitherto there is nothing new in this avowal, but the *matter of indemnification* to ourfelves and our allies. This is certainly an artful, though very neceffary provifo, to be introduced into this declaration of our fyftem; and will, upon future explanation of the courts, in cafe of fuccefs, afford an uncontrovertible ground of equity, upon which the different claims upon the truft fund may be fettled and adjufted. In all trufts, the firft provifion fecured is for the payment and indemnification of the expences and charges of the truft. Well-advifed truftees never releafe their truft till this act of juftice be firft complied with. Neither Toulon nor any other part of France, feized and holden in truft for Louis XVII. can ever be difcharged of this indemnifying quality. A defign of making conquefts upon France has been repeatedly difavowed by all the combined powers. The truft of conquering France for Louis XVII. is undertaken at the rifk of thofe who have accepted of it, if the fund which fhall hereafter come into their hands fhall prove infufficient to anfwer their cofts and charges. Great indeed muft be the acceffion of French property to ourfelves and co-trustees, which will satisfy the claims of those, who have thus kindly and generously undertaken the management of the concerns of this infant Monarch.

The manifesto expresses, that his Majesty *wishes ardently to be able to treat for the re-establishment of the general tranquillity with a Government exercising a legal and permanent authority, animated with the wish for. general tranquillity, and possessing powers to enforce the observance of its engagements.* This general definition of a Government may be made pliant to every construction that a Minister shall choose to put upon it. It will equally exclude as admit of a negociation with the present Republic of France, and will justify a treaty upon any ground of popular prejudice or favour, that the supple Proteus will cringe to.

It speaks of the restoration of monarchy, but neither makes it the pretext for continuing the war, nor the condition of an honourable peace. A great part of this Proclamation deals in invective against the persons to whom it is addressed, and serves no end but that of provoking their irascibility, and driving them to fresh acts of violence, inhumanity, and vengeance.

No circumstances, since the commencement of the war, seem to have irritated the Convention more than, what they called *our treacherous* attempts upon Dunkirk, Marseilles, and Toulon. They converted all to their own purposes. Our negociations and treaties paved the way for further confiscations, not only of the men, whom they say we *corrupted*, but whomsoever they chose to connect with them. It was, therefore, a most improvident act to publish, in the Gazette, Lord Hood's unsuccesful treaty with the Marseillois. Scores were murdered upon suspicion of having treated with him. The unadvised seizure of Toulon made such an impression upon the mass of the people, that the new party of Danton, notwithstanding their enormities and cruelties, were now looked up to with love and confidence. By their *Emprunt forcé*, they brought into the Treasury all the hard cash in the kingdom: by this sweep, which was the boldest act of public robbery ever attempted, the Executive Government had, at once, possession of 41,666,666l. sterling, as a fund for the war, and a basis for an enlarged paper circulation. Soon after this, they passed a decree of confiscation of all British property in France, and put all British subjects under arrest.

The height of popular irritation, was the moment in which the inhuman Jacobins perpetrated their deeds of blood and horror. It was on one and the same day, that their army routed seventy thousand veteran troops, headed by the best generals of Europe, before Maubeuge, and their Convention butchered the respectful relict of their murdered Sovereign. If any thing could add to the inhuman and unjust treatment of this unfortunate and respectable Princess, it was the insulting mockery of a trial, and the bringing her own infants as witnesses against her, for crimes even out of physical possibility. The heroic and Christian fortitude, with which this venerable Queen underwent the long trial of humiliation and suffering, that preceded her execution, revives, in these days of infidelity, the animating examples of primitive Christianity, when the pride of the heathen was overcome, and the mild spirit of the gospel propagated in the blood of the humble and constant martyr. It is but justice to this much beloved, and much respected victim to licentious fury, to rescue her injured character from the impious aspersions of her pretended encomiast, Mr. Burke. Could that man, who tells us, that a * *true humility, the basis of the Christian system, is the low, but deep and firm foundation of all real virtue*, be so forgetful of his heroine and of himself, as to make her vanity survive all her virtues, and the heathenish vice of suicide extinguish, in her last moments, the grace of Christian consolation: † *in the last extremity, she will save herself from the last disgrace, and if she must fall, she will fall by no ignoble hand*. Could the man, who glories in the *Christian religion as his boast and comfort*, plant *the sharp antidote against disgrace concealed in the bosom* of a Christian Princess, *who added titles of veneration to those of*

* Letter to a Member, p. 93. † Reflections, p. 112.

enthufiaftic diftant and refpectful love? Claffical, fabulous, or heathenifh, as may be the occafional wanderings of this fublime writer, it was not tolerable in the awful view of our tranfit to the great tribunal, to fubftitute the falfe pride of an Ethnic matron, for the Chriftian dignity of fubmitting to a death of ignominy after the example of our divine Mafter. The only infult, at which his moft Chriftian Majefty and his royal confort felt indignant during their captivity, was the fufpicion of this very crime of *fuicide* * with which Mr. Burke, to his own fhame, and to the fcandal of the Chriftian caufe, has crowned the virtues of his *delightful vifion*.

* When Valazé, one of the Briffotine party, was condemned, he chofe to follow the recommendation of Mr. Burke, and ftabbed himfelf with a poniard; which circumftance produced an immediate decree of the Convention, that all perfons under accufation fhould be deprived of the means of preventing the juftice of their country by the crime of *fuicide*.

CHAPTER XX.

NOVEMBER, 1793.

CONTENTS.

The effect of the Manifesto upon the French—The Dutch answer it—State of Toulon—Disagreement between the Spanish and British Admirals—Unsuccessful expedition to Corsica—Violation of the Rights of Nations, in the Port of Genoa—Lord Howe chases a French fleet, which escapes him—Lord Moira's expedition resolved upon, with 10,000 British, and 6,000 Hessian troops, to penetrate by St. Maloes, into the interior parts of France—Brissot's party, and Egalité murdered—French successes on the Rhine.

THE manifesto, which is said to be the genuine, and a favourite production of Mr. Pitt, produced no other effect in France, than a contempt for the shuffling ambiguity of that part of it which declares a readiness to treat with any efficient Government, whilst we refuse to treat with their Executive Council; and of pity for the impotent arrogance of assuring them, that we will not insist upon the full price, but will abate considerably of what we might in justice demand of them for restoring their ancient monarchy. It produced, however, an immediate answer from the States General, which was a re-echoed avowal of all the reasons and motives for continuing the war, which are expressed in the declaration, excepting as to one of those motives, upon which they have very emphatically enlarged. The

British manifesto states, that one of the objects which his Majesty had in continuing the war was, *to obtain for his allies, and himself, a just indemnification*: which the Dutch improve upon, by saying, that their ultimate object was to obtain *a just indemnification for the enormous expenses occasioned to the Republic, by the violence of their common enemies.*

The situation, in the mean while, of our troops at Toulon, was very precarious: the Republican army daily increased, and constantly annoyed the town and the out-posts: reinforcements were frequently landed: upon this occasion five thousand Imperial troops were taken into our pay: the motly garrison composed of British, French, Spanish, Neapolitan, German, Sardinian, and Portuguese troops, exceeded *fourteen thousand men*. Very frequent accounts from Toulon were sent over and published in the Gazette, if it were but of a skirmish of two hundred men; and in order to prepossess the Nation with a favourable idea of this new acquisition, the health, spirits, and safety of the garrison, were regularly blazoned in all the pomp of official confidence. As our shrewd and trusty Admiral had succeeded so unexpectedly in negociating his entry into Toulon, he was too sanguine in his expectation of extending this new system of gaining ports, along the whole coast of France. He sent four ships of the line with private instructions to the different ports of France, two to Brest, one to L'Orient, and the other to Rochfort. In the multiplicity of tongues which were spoken by the different corps, frequent mistakes in the orders, produced no small confusion. Disagreements also arose to a considerable height between the Spanish and the English Admirals, concerning the disposition of the French ships: the Spanish claiming as nearest of kin to the infant Monarch, and in virtue of their old Family compact, the more immediate power and controul over the Trust Fund, which consisted of Bourbon property: the British Admiral urged the circumstances of acquisition and possession as the stronger claims to management and the prior right of indemnification, for the risks and charges of procuring the property.

Lord Hood finding that the inactivity of so many vessels in the harbour of Toulon would not much forward the general service, sent off a small squadron to extend his conquests into Corsica. General Paoli had promised to co-operate by land whenever the ships should appear off the coast. The expedition failed for two reasons, which the Gazette announces in more words than were absolutely necessary to inform us, that the Corsicans *would* do nothing, and the British squadron *could* do nothing, against the town of *Florenze*, which they were sent to take. Though the Gazette account be particularly diffuse in attempting to reconcile the failure of this expedition to the patient people of Great Britain, who are naturally fond of reading the successes of their fleets; the most efficient cause of the failure has been unfortunately forgotten by the compiler, which would have instantly soothed every disappointment. This was the fatal error of adopting the exploded system of *battering*, instead of *negociating* their entry into the town. Posterity, however, will be indebted to them for the discovery which they have made in this unsuccessful attempt upon the town of *Florenze:* viz. that a frigate may receive more damage than she can do against land batteries of superior weight of metal, elevated above her: and that the distances from the batteries to the ships, and from the ships to the batteries are reciprocal and equal. For we are informed, by this instructive Gazette, that *although a close and powerful cannonade had been kept up by the squadron, till a quarter before eight, no visible impression was made:* and yet that the ships of the squadron were *much damaged*; and therefore, upon the joint opinion of five British captains, that there was no prospect of success, the signal was made for discontinuing the attack. In the present regenerated spirit of the British Constitution, credulity on one side of the question, seems not to have been confined within this island. " *The Alcide is not materially damaged* " *in her masts or rigging, but the Ardent and Courageaux have suf-* " *fered very considerably in both, from being exposed to the raking* " *fire of the town of Florenze, though every information had assured* "*me, the distance of that place was too great for guns to have any* "*effect.*" Pity it was, that there were not some *friends of the* "*people* at Toulon, to have questioned the truth of this information, as they had that of an intended attack upon the Tower of London, in December 1792. The squadron had been lying in the gulf of Florenze from the 21st to the 30th of the month; during which time, it is presumed, by the ignorant, which is ever the greatest part of mankind, that the distances could have been ascertained, at which the fleet could either annoy the enemy, or be annoyed by them. The mighty force of artillery, which did so much damage to our fleet, consisted of two mortars, four twenty-four pounders, two eight pounders, and one four pounder, in the redoubt of Fornilli; and four mortars, and nine twenty-four pounders in the town of Florenze.

The powers of Lord Hood appear to have exceeded whatever had been before delegated to any British Admiral: every act of his, from this Proclamation to the Toulonese, to his sailing from their port, must be looked upon as the acts of those, from whom he received his orders. It was an improvement upon the old system of war, for a British squadron to enter a neutral port and capture their enemy's vessels, lying under the protection of a neutral power. Eight ships of the line, and six frigates from Toulon, entered the port of Genoa. The Scipio, of 74 guns, ranged along side the Modeste, a French frigate at anchor in the port, and summoned her to strike. The French answered with a broadside. The Scipio returned two broadsides, and boarded the frigate. Part of the crew were cut to pieces in attempting to defend her, the rest escaped by swimming to the shore. Two French cruizers shared the fate of the Modeste. In any former war, this would have been the most direct and flagrant violation of the laws of nations. It was a singular example set by that Government, which lately upbraided the French for having *exposed all their neighbouring nations to the repeated attacks of ferocious anarchy, the natural and public enemy of all public order.*

Providence seemed at length, to have afforded Lord Howe a

favourable opportunity of reviving the worn-down fpirits of his fleet, and regaining the declining confidence of his friends and patrons. An extract was fent up to the Admiralty, from the log-book of the Montague, the laft fhip come into port from Lord Howe's fleet; that on the 18th inft. in the morning, a French fquadron, confifting of feventeen fail, nine of the line, and the reft frigates, was feen bearing down on the Britifh fleet; that at ten o'clock they hauled their wind, on which Lord Howe made fignal for a general chafe. At fix in the evening, the Montague fprung her top-mafts, and was obliged to bring to, being then, according to computation, three leagues a-ftern of the French fquadron, and five miles a-head of Lord Howe's fleet. Incredible was the exultation of the nation at the receipt of this news: the failures at Dunkirk, Maubeuge, and Corfica were forgotten; every paft misfortune, every pending hazard, were fwallowed up in the anticipated furety of annihilating, by by this capture, the remaining maritime force of France. Lord Howe, after three weeks abfence, emerged from the mift that had enveloped both fleets, and brought back all his own fhips fafe into port. He received the well-earned laurels for having prevented any of them from falling into the hands of the ferocious republicans. The Britifh fleet was confoled in the affurance, that the French were ftill quicker in running away, than we could be in purfuing them.

The year was drawing towards a conclufion, and the Minifter was not a little anxious to improve the balance of the yearly accounts, which he muft foon lay before Parliament. No very large profits had arifen out of any of his ventures: immenfe fums had been advanced, and loft in Flanders: the whole equipment for the Channel fervice had returned no gain: the profits of the Mediterranean treaty were ftill doubtful, and ftill coftly: the advances made in foreign engagements could not yet make any return: confidence and credit began to decline, and the approaching hour of accounting to the Nation, made him refolve upon hazarding, what he had been long preffed and urged in vain to attempt. The Earl of Moira, had, in the courfe of the month of June, expreffed his opinion, that the only effectual meafure for reftoring monarchy and peace to France, would be to give fubftantial fuccour to the Royalifts within the kingdom. Innumerable applications and offers upon this fubject had been made to the Minifter in the courfe of the year. The original objection againft this plan muft have been, that it did not exactly fall in with our *lately avowed* fyftem of indemification. Cities that might fall into the hands of the Royalifts, even with our affiftance, could not be taken and holden either in the name of the Emperor, as Valenciennes; nor in that of the King of Great Britain, as Dunkirk was fummoned; nor in truft for Louis XVII. like Toulon. The Earl of Moira, not being initiated in all the political fecrets and private alliances of the Minifter, had expreffed the opinion of a judicious and brave officer, and of an upright and fincere patriot; and he then expreffed his readinefs to attempt the execution of the plan, which his judgment directed him to propofe for the good and honour of his country. His fervices were then accepted; and were to be called for, when the better judgment of the Minifter fhould point out the favourable moment of fuccefs. Difpatch in execution favoured too much of republican energy; cautious progreffion was the true mode of enfuring effect to prudent meafures: the Fabian fyftem could alone counteract that of anarchy and confufion. *Unus homo nobis cunctando reftituit rem.* However, after much confultation, infinite reluctance, and fome preparation, it was publicly refolved upon, to fend out an expedition, under Lord Moira, to the interior of France, by the avenue of St. Maloes, which was to be immediately attacked and *tak n*; he was to have with him 10,000 Britifh, and 6000 Heffian troops.

The accounts which were in this month publifhed by the National Convention, were very unfavourable to the caufe of the Royalifts. But as no credit was to be given to this horde of liars and affaffins, it might have been an additional inducement to their enemies, to act upon the contrary suppofition of their fuccefs. Although fome of their accounts have certainly been exaggerated, yet, unfortunately for this country, too much truth of our fufferings and difgraces and of their own fuccefs, has been firft announced from their Affembly. From hence we learnt the condemnation, by the Revolutionary Tribunal, and the execution of Briffot and his whole party, in thirty-feven minutes, which fufficed to ftrike of the heads of thefe criminals, and to dig a grave for *federalifm*; this was the crime for which they were condemned; and that the infamous monfter of bafenefs and iniquity, Egalité, fuffered fome days after for the fame caufe; that the Republicans had difcovered and defeated a plot for delivering up Strafburg to the combined forces; and that, after having executed feveral hundreds for being concerned in it, they had raifed the fiege of Landau, and gained very fignal advantages over the combined armies of the Rhine.

CHAPTER XXI.

DECEMBER, 1793.

CONTENTS.

Mr. Muir and Mr. Palmer sentenced to be transported for seditious practices, in attempting to bring about a Reform in Parliament—Accusation and acquittal of Mr. Hamilton Rowan—Trial and acquittal of the Proprietors of the Morning Chronicle—Convention at Edinburgh—Heads of them arrested—Part of St. Domingo surrendered by the Royalists, in the name of Louis XVII. *—Plot of Strasburg discovered—Attempt to entangle Switzerland in the general Confederacy—America preserves her neutrality—Turkish Ambassador in London—Enumeration of National Misfortunes.*

NOTWITHSTANDING the many and important occasions which called upon the attention of Government in the several theatres of war, in which we are unfortunately engaged, the most unrelenting spirit of prosecuting every exertion at home to procure a Parliamentary Reform, was kept up and enforced by examples of unprecedented rigour. This favourite object seems to have been lately pursued with more regularity and perseverence by its advocates in Scotland, than in any other part of the British Empire. Mr. Muir was the first person found guilty of sedition, for the part he had taken at different meetings, convened for the purpose of bringing about this reform: he was sentenced by the Court *to be transported beyond the seas, to such place as his Majesty, with the advice of his Privy Council, should judge proper, for the space of fourteen years.* Mr. Palmer was also condemned to be transported for seven years, for a similar offence. The severity of these sentences, which, it is to be presumed, were intended to deter people from pursuing the same object, did not produce the effect which was intended or expected. Mr. Muir was conveyed in the dead of the night on board a King's ship in Leith Roads. Most of the societies in that part of the Kingdom immediately published declarations of their resolutions to persevere in their peaceable endeavours to procure a reform of the abuses of which they complained. The amiable qualities of the individuals who were condemned, excited a general sympathy for their sufferings; and the general predilection for the opinions upon Parliamentary Reform, to which they were looked upon as martyrs, provoked discussions upon the very question. Messrs. Muir and Palmer have been some time confined in chains, with the common felons, on board the hulks at Woolwich.

An attempt was made, in a most extraordinary manner, to draw Mr. Hamilton Rowan, of Ireland, into a like sentence: he had scarcely arrived at Edinburgh when he was apprehended as a seditious person, and taken before the Sheriff, where he underwent a very minute and inquisitorial examination. The petition of the Procurator Fiscal to the Sheriff for the warrant to arrest him, set forth, that meetings had been called and holden in that country for the avowed purpose of overturning the Constitution, and that Mr. H. Rowan, being Secretary of the United Irishmen in Dublin, had sent over an address from them to the persons styling themselves the Convention of the Friends of the People in Scotland, and this with a wicked and malevolent intention of forwarding the most seditious purposes. Nothing seditious being proved against Mr. H. Rowan, he was dismissed upon giving bail to the amount of 3,000 merks.

The acquittal of Mr. H. Rowan put a stop, for some short

time, to the frequency of accufations and informations in Scotland againſt perſons, for being friends and well-wiſhers to a Parliamentary Reform. In England, however, the fpirit of information and profecution, which had been blown into fuch an unconftitutional flame by * Mr. Reeves's aſſociators, received a moſt powerful and timely check in the good fenfe, uprightneſs, and firmneſs of an Engliſh Jury. The Attorney General had filed an information againſt Mr. Lambert and others, for printing and publiſhing a feditious libel in the Morning Chronicle, which confiſted of a bare infertion, without any comment, of the proceedings and refolutions of a fociety for political information, holden at Derby in July, 1792. After a trial of many hours, the Jury, at feven o'clock in the evening, went to Lord Kenyon's houfe with a fpecial verdict *Guilty of publiſhing, but with no malicious intent.* His Lordſhip telling them that he could not record this verdict, the Jury withdrew, and, at five o'clock in the morning, returned with a general verdict, *Not guilty*. It is faid, that Mr. Reeves, the aſſociator, was a very anxious attendant upon this trial, and was heard in court to have declared, that no defeat of the combined armies, no lofs of fleets could be fo prejudicial to the fyftem of this aſſociation, as the acquittal of the *defendants*. This was the firſt profecution ever brought againſt the propietors of this inſtructive, learned, and truly conſtitutional newfpaper fince its firſt inſtitution.

A very numerous aſſociation met at Edinburgh, who ſtyled themfelves a Convention of Delegates for obtaining Univerfal Suffrage and Annual Parliaments: many perfons of great refpectability belonged to it: after feveral meetings, in different places in that city, Meſſrs. Gerald, Margarot, Sinclair, Calander, Rofs Sen. and Jun. Skirving, and Brown, Members of this

---

* It is impoſſible to fpeak in too flattering terms of the fenfible, eloquent, and conſtitutional fpeech, which Mr. Erſkine made on the 22d of laſt January, at the Meeting of the Friends to the Liberty of the Prefs, when they met to proteſt againſt Mr. Reeves's and fuch Aſſociations for the general purpofe of information and profecution.

Convention from different focieties in England and Scotland, for obtaining a reform of the reprefentation in Parliament, were taken into cuftody, by order of the Sheriff, and carried before him to be examined. This was the firft fociety that had declared its principle of the fpecific mode of reform which they aimed at: they rather difpleafed fome well-wifhers to the general caufe of reform, by affecting an imitation of the French Convention in their title, and in their mode of addreffing each other in their meetings, by the appellation of *citizen*. Thefe circumftances, though trivial in themfelves, and not infringing any laws of the land, might, perhaps, with more prudence and policy have been omitted. They appear to have been adopted by men in the moment of irritation, at being foiled in a variety of legal attempts to bring their grievances under the confideration of Parliament; in order to attract attention by circumftances altogether new, though in themfelves innocent and legal. It befpeaks, particularly in the cool and wary character of the Scotch, a firm and unshaken determination, to perfevere, againft every poffible prejudice, in their legal and conftitutional efforts, to procure a reform in the reprefentation of the people in Parliament.

In the long dearth of joyful tidings, the feelings of the good people of the metropolis were gratified, by the unaccuftomed found of the Park and Tower guns, to announce to them, not the defeat of the French army, nor the capture of their fleet, nor the fuccefs of Lord Moira's expedition, but the landing of fome hundred men on the now defolated Ifland of St. Domingo. The fort of St. Nicholai, which was poffeffed by the Royalift party, who were too weak to keep it, had furrendered it up in the name of Louis XVII. to a detachment of Britifh troops from Jamaica. Jeremie, which was called the key of the Ifland, had followed the example.

The doctrine of Trufts, was not equally underftood by the Germans as by us: our late avowal, that *indemnification* was an object for continuing the war (it could not have been our object in commencing it) throws indeed fome light upon the fubject; for the sure means of indemnification are to possess the property out of which the reimbursement is to arise. The city of Strasburg offered to submit in this manner, to General Wurmser; but he not understanding the finesse of the system, foolishly declined entering upon this condition, and gave the citizens six days, to propose other conditions: in this interval 45,000 republican troops arrived, the plot was discovered, and avenged in the best blood of Alsace.

Our negociating Minister was indefatigable in his efforts to strengthen the confederacy against the enemy, which had hitherto baffled every effort and exertion against them. Lord Robert Fitzgerald was directed to persuade, or intimidate the Swiss Cantons out of their neutrality; but hitherto the attempt has proved unsuccessful. The prudence and firmness of the American States, have hitherto kept them from entering into an alliance with France, as well as induced them to resist the attempts of our Cabinet to draw them out of their neutrality. To complete, in short, the system of a general confederacy of all the powers of Europe, we are gratified by the new and unprecedented sight of a Turkish Ambassador in London. This preference of the Divan to our court, we hope is grounded in some treaty beneficial to the commercial interests of the country: but as every fresh confederate, in this fatal combination against France, is an additional winding to the labyrinth, no well wisher to his country, can hope to see the crusade embellished by the Ottoman Crescent.

The first year of this disastrous and calamitous warfare is now closed. The enormous price of the dearly bought experience is the least of the evils we have to lament. The soul sickens at every view that presents itself. Never did a system of measures pronounce so harsh, so lamentable a condemnation of the advisers. Well, indeed, may Britain weep at the catastrophe.

The defenceless and abandoned Royalists, every where vanquished and butchered: mowed down at Lyons, from one hundred and forty, to twenty-five thousand souls: unable to gain the sea-shore, either to be succoured or transported: fresh accounts of unarmed multitudes of twenty thousand, butchered in cold blood: Earl Moira's expedition dropt, from conviction of the improbability of its succeeding against the activity and energy of the enemy. Toulon disgracefully abandoned, before witnesses from every nation in Europe, with the piteous boast of having left the arsenals and ships in flames, and the unmanly regret of our impotence to extend the devastation. The armies of the Rhine driven back with unheard of slaughter, traversing, with giant strides, the ground which by inches they had gained, and drenched with the blood of melancholy victory. An enraged enemy glutting their insatiable vengeance in the blood of their *royal* countrymen, immolated to the menacing pride and cruelties of an inefficient federacy of crowned heads in the cause of Royalty. At home credit on the wane; bankruptcies innumerable; manufactures at a stand; the poor out of work; the middle classes staggering under the pressure of existing, and threatened with an accumulation of fresh taxes; the rich soured at the enormity of their present payments to the State, and forced, by the sympathy of human nature, to the daily increasing contributions to their own poor, as well as the numerous distressed emigrants from France, whose exile we have hitherto softened, but whose return we have rendered desperate. No prospect of success; no advantage seen in it, if obtained. The prosperity of the nation vanished, its happiness destroyed, its welfare endangered. Some frighted into discontent and dismay, by the boundless prospect of existing miseries; others soured and irritated at the calumny of sedition and treason: many fearing the propagation and prevalence of French principles: more dreading the energy of French arms, and the seducing examples of French successes: all bewailing past losses and misfortunes: none catching a ray of future conquest: all groaning under the throbbing pangs of national distresses and calamities: except those, who, by their *seasonable convictions*, have secured to themselves honours, preferments, and wealth, from the continuance and extension of their country's wretchedness.

CHAPTER XXII.

CONCLUSION.

THOUGH such be the gloomy situation of public affairs, we must not encourage the despondency which it is too likely to excite. We have faithfully detailed the events which have led to it, and we think it is impossible to overlook the principle to which those events are ascribable. The character of the public mind may, in general, be collected from public measures: if it be tainted with prejudice, it will be found favourable to measures unsound in their principle, and ruinous in their tendency. When the powerful convictions of the public judgment are made to yield to the influence of an insidious eloquence, or rendered subservient to the projects of a Machiavelian system, it becomes incompetent to the duty of watching over the public interests, it is neither disposed nor capable of suggesting the measures of sound policy, and is often too deeply interested in the success of the worst of measures to restrain their adoption, or to avert their consequences. The vice of the principle is suddenly felt in the calamities, with which it is attended. In vain can we hope relief from the evils we now feel, or security from their increase, but by calmly and dispassionately investigating the causes which have led to them. Let us individually endeavour to eradicate from our minds, those opinions which we may have allowed to acquire a growth, that over-shadows the dictates of unbiassed truth and justice. Let us, each individually consider, whether we have not allowed our immediate and particular interests to influence our public conduct, and, with a view to a temporary advantage to ourselves, given our sanction to meafures, which, unlefs timely checked, may put in hazard thofe blefsings, which a Conftitution founded like the Conftitution of England, not on the vifions of a heated or diftempered imagination, but on principles, which unchecked in their operation by the arm of violence or mifreprefentations of calumny muft neceffarily produce. Let us, fpurning the feditious opinions of a Paine, and regardlefs of the brilliant eloquence of a Burke, look at our Conftitution as we received it from our anceftors. Let us, with minds ftrongly impreffed with the hiftory of thofe times, which gave to our country the illuftrious family which now graces the throne, decide whether the prerogatives allotted our Monarch by the Conftitution do or do not exceed thofe of the ancient monarchy of France? Let us, from the hiftory of thofe days, which defined the rights and duties of a Houfe of Commons, collect, whether independence of character and integrity of principle be an effential, or a departure from its original inftitution; and when we fhall have traced in the wifdom which directed, and in the firmnefs which effected the Revolution, that line of demarcation which feparates prerogative from privilege, let us endeavour to afcertain the motives which could induce, and the nature of the policy which could encourage doctrines, that traduce the character, and betray the real interefts of our Conftitution. Viewed in its genuine form, it ftrikes by its majefty, and charms with its fimplicity. It bears not the terror of indefinite prerogative, nor alarms by the indulgence of unreftrained privilege. The knowledge of its principles are the feeds of public order and tranquillity. It is but from the traduction of its genius and pirit, that danger can be apprehended. True to its principles, internal diffenfion could never difturb us, external violence might in vain affail us. Whether this monument, the work of ages, has not of late been defaced by the opinions of perfons in fituations too commanding of attention not to give force and extent to their fentiments, is a point of enquiry in which every individual is deeply concerned. Whether thofe opinions were the refult of a malignant intent, or the effects of an imperfect knowledge of the subject, however the difference of motive may weigh in the scale of morality, it has not, I am afraid, in any degree varied the political consequences. Affirming, that the Constitution of England has prescribed boundaries to the prerogative, we reject as aspersion, if not as sedition, the doctrine which asserts that those boundaries have been passed. Affirming, that an independent House of Commons does make a part of the British Constitution, we reject, as calumny, the opinions which maintain the contrary. But when we reject such doctrines as unconstitutional, we cannot feel ourselves wholly indifferent to any mark of public attention conferred on those who have maintained or favoured them; for in the consequences of that attention we trace the principle of no small portion of the existing discontent. To dispel the gloom which obscures the public judgment, the strongest lights of truth and reason are necessary. Such lights are not to be expected from those who have wilfully favoured the delusion. Under these circumstances, it were a want of gratitude to the individual, it were a want of regard for the public interest, to overlook that manly intrepidity, which in the hour of the most formidable and accumulated prejudice stood between the country and the agitation and alarm under which it acted. When the language of personal invective was substituted for fair discussion, when the strongest personal provocation might have drawn the individual from the vindication of the Constitution to the vindication of his own character and conduct, we found Mr. Fox disregarding every danger, but that which might affect the Constitution of his Country, stating, illustrating, and vindicating its principles, with a force of eloquence, which nothing but a genuine sense of its value could have inspired. When malice would paint him hostile to the Government of his country, his defence were instructions for rendering that Government impervious to all assaults. Disdaining the advantage which he might have derived from the ruin of a rival statesman, we found him anxious to avert that very mischief which would alone insure it. Charged with enmity to our Constitution, he vindicated its perfections: charged with the ambitious views of displacing his rival, he instructed him in those lessons which could alone render him worthy to retain his situation. Conversant with the various resources of his country, and its general attachment to the Constitution, he execrated the policy which gave ground to our enemies to consider us a divided people, and reprobated the measures which tended to divide us. A steady adherence to the Rights of Nations is, at all times, something more than a duty; it is the soundest policy; it gives lustre to success, and dignity to adversity. He strenuously opposed that policy, which renders justice pliant to the indefinite variety of human events. His pursuits in life had not led him to study our Penal Code in its minute detail; his mind, however, was too curious in its general researches to have overlooked its principles, which involved the lives and liberties of his fellow-subjects. On a question of widening the Criminal Code, we found him illustrating the policy of our ancestors in simplifying the law of treason, with a power which the most learned and acute of his opponents found irresistible. His opposition to a war for procuring objects which were attainable by negociation is well known; and we now severely feel the consequences of rejecting, as the language of faction, the dictates of sound judgment and pure patriotism. In vain was the necessity aggravated in description; in vain did eloquence attempt to mislead his judgment, by fastening on his passions; no art could conceal from him the real interests of his country: he saw them distinctly through the hazy mist of prejudice and passion; and he stated prophetically the effects of departing from that system of neutrality, which would at once have secured and improved them. Whilst *passions instructed reason*, he was unable to bear up against the tide of opinion: though lamenting the event of the contest, we found him anxious to avert the accomplishment of his predictions. With the voice of patriotism, he exhorted those who had the conduct of the war, to display the greatness and energy of their country, in the wisdom and vigour of conducting it. Here we will pause. Though few may consider themselves competent to decide upon the necessity of

BOOKS,
PUBLISHED BY M. CAREY, No. 118, MARKET-STREET.

AN IMPARTIAL HISTORY
OF THE
FRENCH REVOLUTION;
From its Commencement to the
EXECUTION OF THE QUEEN, AND THE DEPUTIES OF THE GIRONDE PARTY.

EXTRACT FROM THE PREFACE.

" The authors have prefumed to affix to their title, the epithet Impartial; and the reafon is, becaufe they cannot charge themfelves with feeling the fmalleft bias to any party, but that of truth and liberty; and they flatter themfelves, that their readers will find not only every circumftance fairly reprefented, but every cenfurable action, whoever were the authors or actors, marked in its proper colours. If it was neceffary to make a declaration of their own principles, they would fay, they are neither tory nor republican—They love liberty as Englifh whigs, and execrates every criminal act, by which fo noble a caufe is endangered and difgraced.

" In the prefent ferment of the public mind, they cannot flatter themfelves with the hopes of feeing this claim univerfally acknowledged. On the contrary, *they are well affured that thefe pages will not be acceptable to the zealots of either party*. But when time fhall have diffipated the clouds of political deception, and appeafed the tumult of the paffions, they will, with fome confidence, expect that verdict from public opinion, which candour and moderation feldom fail to receive."

Extract from the Critical Review, January 1794, 12th Page.

" We have certainly derived much pleafure, and acquired much information from the perufal of thefe volumes; and we think them, both for matter and ftyle, worthy the attention of all who intereft themfelves in events, which have fo juftly excited the curiofity and aftonifhment of mankind."

(Price a Quarter Dollar.)
SHORT ACCOUNT OF ALGIERS.

Containing—A defcription of that country—of the manners and cuftoms of the inhabitants—and of their feveral wars againft Spain, France, England, Holland, Venice and other powers of Europe—from the ufurpation of Barbaroffa and the invafion of the Emperor Charles V. to the prefent time—with a concife view of the origin of the war between Algiers and the United States.

Embellifhed with a map of Barbary, comprehending Morocco, Fez, Algiers, Tunis, and Tripoli.

SHORT ACCOUNT OF THE MALIGNANT FEVER,

Lately prevalent in Philadelphia, with a ftatement of the proceedings that took place on the fubject in different parts of the United States. To which are added, accounts of the plague in London and Marfeilles, and a lift of the dead in Philadelphia, from Auguft, to the middle of December, 1793.

BY MATHEW CAREY.

(Price Half a Dollar in blue paper—Three Quarters of a Dollar bound.)

BOOKS PUBLISHED BY M. CAREY.

(Price Nineteen Dollars and one-fifth.)
AMERICAN MUSEUM,

From its commencement in January, 1787, to its termination in December 1792. Twelve volumes 8vo.

"The American Museum is not only eminently calculated to disseminate political, agricultural, philosophical, and other valuable information—but it has been uniformly conducted with taste, attention, and propriety. If, to these important objects be superadded the more immediate design, of rescuing public documents from oblivion, I will venture to pronounce, as my sentiment, that a more useful literary plan has never been undertaken in America, nor one more deserving of public encouragement."

GEN. WASHINGTON.

(Price One Dollar Thirty-three Cents.)
YOUNG MISSES' MAGAZINE.

Containing—Dialogues between a Governess and several Young Ladies of Quality her scholars. In which each Lady is made to speak according to her particular genius, temper, and inclination—Their several faults are pointed out, and the easy way to amend them, as well as to think, and speak, and act properly; no less care being taken to form their hearts to goodness, than to enlighten their understandings with useful knowledge. A short and clear abridgment is also given of sacred and prophane History, and some lessons in Geography. The useful is blended throughout with the agreeable, the whole being interspersed with proper reflexions and moral Tales.

Translated from the French of
MADEM. LE PRINCE DE BEAUMONT.
In Four Volumes.

Extract from the Critical Review, August 1737, p. 177.

"When it is remembered how much the happiness of society depends upon the education of its individuals, we shall be pardoned for taking notice of one of the best works that has been written to that end; since, however trifling it may at first appear, it is certainly important in the main. The intention of these dialogues is to give a just way of thinking, speaking, and acting to young people, according to their different stations of life; and they every where contribute to enlighten the understanding, and to form the heart to goodness. Here we find the useful and agreeable happily blendid, a short and clear abridgment of sacred and prophane history, and some lessons in geography."

(Price 62 1-2 Cents.)
CHARLOTTE—A TALE OF TRUTH.

A Novel—By Mrs. ROWSON, of the New Theatre, Philadelphia; Author of Victoria, the Inquisitor, Fille de Chambre, &c.

Extract from the Critical Review, April 1791, p. 468.

"IT may be a Tale of Truth, for it is not unnatural, and it is a tale of real distress—Charlotte, by the artifice of a teacher, recommended to a school, from humanity rather than a conviction of her integrity, or the regularity of her former conduct, is enticed from her governess, and accompanies a young officer to America. The marriage ceremony, if not forgotten, is postponed, and Charlotte dies a martyr to the inconstancy of her lover, and the treachery of his friend. The situations are artless and affecting.—the descriptions natural and pathetic; we should feel for Charlotte if such a person ever existed, who for one error, scarcely, perhaps, deserved so severe a punishment. If it is a fiction, poetic justice is not, we think, properly distributed."

www.ingramcontent.com/pod-product-compliance
Lightning Source LLC
Chambersburg PA
CBHW021357230426
43666CB00006B/553